Tremors of Violence

TREMORS OF VIOLENCE
Muslim Survivors of Ethnic Strife in Western India

Rowena Robinson

SAGE Publications
New Delhi/Thousand Oaks/London

First published in 2005 by

Sage Publications India Pvt Ltd
B-42, Panchsheel Enclave
New Delhi 110017
www.indiasage.com

Sage Publications Inc
2455 Teller Road
Thousand Oaks, California 91320

Sage Publications Ltd
1 Oliver's Yard, 55 City Road
London EC1Y 1SP

Published by Tejeshwar Singh for Sage Publications India Pvt Ltd, photo-typeset in 10/12 pt Sanskrit-Palatino by Star Compugraphics Private Limited, Delhi and printed at Chaman Enterprises, New Delhi.

Library of Congress Cataloging-in-Publication Data

Robinson, Rowena, 1967–
    Tremors of violence: Muslim survivors of ethnic strife in western India/Rowena Robinson.
       p. cm.
    Includes bibliographical references and index.
    1. Victims of violent crimes—India—Gujarat. 2. Victims of violent crimes—India—Bombay. 3. Muslims—Violence against—India—Gujarat. 4. Muslims—Violence against—India—Bombay. 5. Ethnic conflict—India—Gujarat. 6. Ethnic conflict—India—Bombay. I. Title.

HV6250.3.I42G857   303.6'088'2970954—dc22   2005021040

ISBN: 0–7619–3408–1 (pb)

Sage Production Team: Deepa Dharmadhikari, Mathew P.J. and Santosh Rawat

To My Teachers at D. School

CONTENTS

CONTENTS

ACKNOWLEDGEMENTS

This is partly the product of work done at the Oxford Centre for Islamic Studies, Oxford, where I spent several months in 2003 and 2004 on a Ford Foundation Fellowship. The Bodleian library was the source of innumerable books and materials and the Centre itself a conducive place for reading and writing.

Some of the chapters of this book were presented at seminars in Oxford, Cambridge and New Delhi and I received very valuable suggestions as a result. My thanks to all those who participated.

I am deeply grateful to the men and women who shape the stories of this book; some names have been altered in the text but those who shared their experiences and allowed me entry into their worlds have changed my life in a real and unforgettable way.

I thank Valentine Gandhi for his help in preparing the maps. The editors at Sage have always been a pleasure to work with and I thank them for their unfailing courtesy and efficiency.

Mumbai
July 2005

*A society which does not defend all,
defends none*

chapter one

inaugurating responsibility

Implicit in the summons to 'feel with me in my suffering' is the postulate
that the cause of my suffering can be the cause of yours
(Agnes Heller 1984: 10).

'You know, Tuton, we are only what we remember, nothing more...
all we have is the memory of what we have done or not done;
whom we might have touched, even for a moment...'
(Romesh Gunesekera, *Reef*, p. 190).

In the north Indian plains, it is common to hear a man going to the toilet—that impure *sandas* often outside or behind the home—refer to his visit as 'going to Pakistan'. In the brutal communal discourses we have been made to countenance, more so over the last decades, the Indian Muslim *is* a Pakistani, a scorned being who should 'go to Pakistan'. Indeed, as the social geography of Indian cities manifests, the Muslim in fact *lives* in Pakistan, *many* Pakistans, *mini* Pakistans. This introduction may be deemed then as a deliberate invitation to the reader to enter into these Pakistans, to walk the spaces and cross the thresholds of homes in an effort to comprehend the ordinary worlds and tragically extraordinary experiences of Muslim survivors of communal violence in contemporary urban India. While the ethnographic sites of this book are specific, of course, its arguments assume greater generality. We will address the specifics in due course; first, we need negotiate the academics.

In a lecture delivered in South Africa during the 1990s, Gayatri Chakravorty Spivak makes an elegant assertion of the economy of responsibility inherent in the practice, in fact, in the 'thinking' of academic freedom.

It seems to me more and more that, when we think of academic freedom in/or post post-colonial freedom, we must be able to think freedom this way—freedom to acknowledge insertion into responsibility rather than freedom to choose responsibility; whereas it may be that to be human is to be always already in an *impersonal economy* of responsibility (Spivak 1992: 7) [emphasis added].

By the last phrase, Spivak is declaring the intrinsic impossibility of choosing not to be responsible. She acknowledges that not everyone may readily admit that responsibility taking, interestingly, as an illustration (1992: 24):

...a group of young Asian migrant women in London, who had entered and emerged out of the secondary school system, [who] showed no concern for the oppression of homeworkers in their own community...

The immediate doubt that might be raised by the aforementioned example is of course swiftly removed, for Spivak does not appear to be arguing for *more or less* responsibility based on any notion of common ethnic, national or community origin. (Is this itself questionable?). To return, at once Spivak queries herself (1992: 25–26):

Why must the women of the developing world behave with a responsibility imposed from above when women in the developed world claim rights?...What can one learn or unlearn by this unreal contact between the subject of rights in the North and the subject of insertion into responsibility in the South? That something must be lost in order that something be gained? That the subject above contradicts what the best believe that the subject below should be taught about freedom as a right and therefore an end? Our only concern is that such questions be made accessible to as many students as possible, in the interest of academic freedom as the absolute means to acknowledge that insertion.

While primordial or ethnic links are given no privilege over the impersonal economy in the assertion of responsibility by Spivak, I would like to suggest the possibility of another frame of responsibility, one which is based neither on the commonality of ethnic origin or nationality per se nor on impersonality. Impersonal responsibility it appears to me is an act of distance; it is available for those outside the frame. Muslim survivors of violence with whom I have been working placed me in the representation as Christian, as belonging to a fellow minority group, whose co-members have been under attack in different parts of the country. Was I not part of a shared economy of pain? My engagement was not akin to that of just any researcher; there were skeins that drew me further inside. In a paper on Ricardo Falla, the Guatemalan anthropologist and Jesuit priest, who worked with Mayan peasants even as they formed themselves into communities of resistance against the military might of the authorities, Beatriz Manz records her conversations with him (1995). What did it mean to pursue an anthropology *comprometida*? The anthropologist in the first world, regardless of her national or ethnic background, does not necessarily lack critical reflection or empathy or even responsibility; what she is divested of, crucially, is insecurity.[1] Manz acknowledges this in her questions to Falla. As she says:

> The inconsistency between the experience of a researcher in the field and life in the academy, the disconnection as far as security—not just personal safety but material security—is so great for so many anthropologists, especially those of us involved in disenfranchised, military oppressed communities.

Does the impersonal economy of responsibility only underscore the inequalities of threat? Firdaus, Haji Abdul Rehman, Ashraf and others who speak later understood me to be part of a situation of shared distress in which 'Christians had also been targeted and killed'. Indeed, they were acutely aware that those who chose not to define themselves by religion were *also* not immune from risk, if they stood with or spoke with Muslims. In the sphere of equal intimacy, the intimacy of love or of friendship, responsibility may be a privilege more than an obligation; one is permitted responsibility, one does not merely assume it. In the shared economy of risk and camaraderie, survivor, activist and friend Ashraf expressed pleasure that I was writing this and pressed that I should write well. I did not hide my fears and weakness from him; writing about Muslim sufferers of violence could produce unpleasant consequences. 'Do not worry; we are there', Ashraf reassured me; the abider sustaining the anthropologist.

inserting rationale

Every story of communal conflict leads back to stories of past conflicts, past violence.

My tangible brush with ethnic conflict in India came about in 1984, when over three unholy days Delhi's Sikhs were being massacred in the wake of Indira Gandhi's assassination. Day One of the riots dawned uneasily in Nizamuddin, where we lived. Fires were burning in nearly Jangpura and Bhogal market. A car was set aflame at the boundaries of the 'colony', as a neighbourhood is, without irony, called in Delhi. Few Sikh neighbours remained, many had fled in the night, mercifully warned by a hazy network of informers. When the men uncertainly grouped on the street, the Sikhs were told: 'Don't leave; we are there'. But one said: 'You say this now; when the mobs come you will leave us to our fate'. As my puzzled father told my mother later, he spoke earlier than his Hindu neighbours: 'I give you my word. We will not go'. Thus was set in motion a system of neighbourhood watch that may well have been the envy of other Delhi colonies. The neighbourhood, though tragically not the city, remained unscarred.

Why this book? Why Muslims? Elsewhere (Robinson 2003) I have recorded my inability to speak, despite urging from others, during a period not long ago when Christians were being systematically attacked in different places across the country.[2] I am now able perhaps to avail of the words of Waqar Khan, a protagonist in one of the many stories told here: 'Why should Christians alone stand up for Christians? Muslims like me should do it.'

In words resoundingly similar in a book in which she, as a Christian, bears witness to the truths and possibilities of the Hindu faith, Diana Eck asks (*Encountering God*, 1993: 220):

Why should it be the burden of Jews alone to speak out if a Roman Catholic convent is built right on the border of Auschwitz or if the Nation of Islam publishes an accusatory tract on Jewish complicity in black oppression? Why should Muslims have to be the first to speak out if a mosque is threatened or attacked with arson or if a newspaper publishes an article portraying Muslims as fanatical? Why should we think it is primarily the Hindu community that is hurt if a temple is desecrated or its divine images broken?

For Eck, keeping the image of another is a sacred trust and it is inextricably linked with guarding one another's rights and speaking out when another is attacked or targeted hatefully. She is recalled here for she articulates an alternative basis for the expression of responsibility to that expressed by Spivak. Here too responsibility is not an option, but it is one embedded in the parity of belongingness and mutuality; in other words, it is *co-responsibility*. Each is hazarding something here because each is dependent on the others for her image of herself.

The notion of responsibility tentatively introduced here surrenders the impersonal economy in favour of the co-responsibility of individuals or communities, though not necessarily defined by religion. Muslim friends have been kind enough to include me in an understanding of unity that extends beyond notions of ethnic or religious identity per se to those of friendship and shared struggles. Responsibility is rarely an option, though for those who occupy the same political sphere, with all its growing intolerance and constraint, it could involve its own knots. And, while it is a duty, it may not be a right: certainly, the closer our shared worlds are, the more we need to ensure that we do not assume speech without assent.

The moral economy of responsibility does not in any way close off critique. As their voices in the text indicate, Muslims are not only victims of violence; however, the evidence recorded here as elsewhere underscores the inequitable enormity of loss they have borne in the years following Partition and, especially, in recent decades (see, for instance, Desai 1984; Gupta 2000). More significantly, there are lines of strife within the community and inequities that need redress. It is useful to return to Eck for her understanding here for it offers a perspective for us to take whether as anthropologists, religious studies scholars or even just believers. On the one hand, each community needs to benefit from the 'internal dynamic of self-criticism' for no tradition has 'only one view and one voice' (Eck 1993: 223). On the other, self-reflective critical examination of another's criteria of values is also not unimaginable.

The urgency of responsibility is cast as well by the obviously related fact or act: the making of India, as idea and polity. This is now for us a work, a labour in which, as scholars and writers, we have a crucial and critical involvement. Again, we may not permit ourselves Spivak's effortless but unstoppable theorization. That 'India' is an artificial construct (Spivak 1990: 39) or even that identity is rarely a 'thing' that one can speak of in the singular are arguments that are just a little too jaded. We surely may not rely on them if they would lead us to deny the contemporary struggles India's (or *Indias'*) peoples are engaged in to reconstruct its politics and shape its future. The argument goes on that India: '... isn't a place that we Indians can think of as anything, unless we are trying to present a reactive front, against another kind of argument.'

Surely not; that luxury is not ours and Spivak must be speaking of other beings. We may discursively locate India differently on the world map: remove it from a position of binary opposition to the West by relating it instead with South and South East Asia, for instance. This will underscore its presence, not eliminate it. We live and work in an India (perhaps even in many Indias) but India (or Bharat or Hindustan) is also *work* for us. It is not a thing accomplished but it is also not nothingness; as state, as polity, as society and even as idea it engages us—as citizens, as members of communities and as participants in battles, material or ideological—in its (re)construction. India may not be a fact, but for the Muslims we speak with and for me, it is definitely a process—in which we all have a part, however minor, to play.

tracing roots

I have an enduring interest in questions and themes related to the anthropology and sociology of religion in contemporary India, in particular minority religions. At various junctures, Christianity and conversion have been the focus of my attention; always the relationships across religious boundaries and those between religion and the state have been at the fulcrum. In this work these themes re-emerge, against the background of and the discourse on inter-community violence.

The literature on the implications of violence for the making and the marking of identity, collective and individual, is increasing (see, for example, Bloch 1986; Das and Nandy 1986; Durkheim 1965 [1912]; Girard 1977; and Scarry 1985 for an early exposition). While it is clearly recognized that the use of violence and pain for the explicit purpose of demarcating 'Self' and/or 'Other' can be minimal and in most modern societies, often benignly symbolic, the possibilities of a sacred or secular 'excess' of violence are all too potent. The growing awareness of the critical and traumatic effect of genocide, pogroms of violence, riots and conflict in the institution of memory, the carving up of the social world and the defining of group and individual subjectivities is reflected in research now increasingly available (Das et al. 2000, 2001; Fridman 2000; Kleinman 1997; Rothberg 2000; Wiedmer 1999; Young 2000).

In the south Asian context too, anthropologists, historians and sociologists have begun to mark and to understand the brutal and tragic re-organizations of self, community, the material world, social and physical space that are the outcome of 'communal' riots and other forms of violent group engagements (see, for instance, Das 1990; Mayaram 1997; Mehta and Chatterji 2001; Srinivasan 1990). Mehta and Chatterji (2001) address questions of language and discuss how violent events restructure people's language and the way in which they speak about places or about others. The realm of the discursive is reshaped by acts of violence, but the memories of violence impinge themselves also on practice, on the organization of events, on the management of roles and relationships, on the use of space, on dress codes and on mobility of women and men, on Muslim enactment as well as thought.

There is some space for remarking on the projects of violence in communal riots and genocidal pogroms. Kakar (1995: 25) and other scholars speak of the 'vocabulary' of violence ritualized in the humiliating attacks on body, property, place of worship, even monument. It is worth re-looking at such accounts for the formidable agony reveals not only a frightening repetition of particular kinds of violent acts but also, sometimes, peculiarly precise gradations in the texture of torture. Kakar quotes his cousin's description of violence in Partition Lahore (1995: 35):

> We did try to retaliate, at least the younger Sangh [Rashtriya Swayamsevak Sangh] members like me. And of course the Sikhs. A police inspector told me of going to a Sikh village where there was reported massacre of the Muslims. As the police entered the village they passed under a kind of welcoming arch which was a rope strung out between the poles. To this rope, attached with short pieces of string, were the circumcised penises of all the Muslim men who had lived in the village, hanging there if they were small eels drying in the sun.

Such accounts may be compared (and contrasted with) the 'semiotics of terror' Tanika Sarkar records for Gujarat violence in 2002 (2002: 2874):

> VHP [Vishwa Hindu Parishad] leaflets, openly circulating in Gujarat today, signed by the state general secretary, Chinubhai Patel, promise: 'We will cut them and their blood will flow like rivers. 'We will kill Muslims the way we destroyed Babri mosque'. This is followed by a poem
> 'The volcano which was inactive...has erupted. It has burnt the arse of *miyas* and made them dance nude. We have untied the penises that were tied till now. We have widened the tight vaginas of the *bibis*...'

Attention should be paid to the ways in which embodied markers of Muslim identity (such as circumcised penises or the wearing of a prayer cap or *henna*-died beard) are jerked into the glare of ridicule and made violently noticeable. The practice of Muslim communal prayer at the mosque again renders them visible and alarmingly easy to target. Muslim women who don the *purdah* and do not bear *bindis* are readily identifiable. The process of identifying and targeting specific groups and persons through the use of survey and census data has become a sophisticated task over the last decades through the sustained efforts of Hindu communal organizations. Nevertheless, every riot equally searches for and swoops down on the marks of difference (and those who bear them) rendered the more glaring by the excess of violent images associated with them in the spreading communal propaganda.

Several examples of the morbid manipulation of bodies in the battle to sacrilege every aspect of difference are available. Sarkar goes on to write in the context of the recent violence against Muslims in Gujarat, for instance (2002: 2875–76), and it is worth quoting at length what she has to say:

> But why, then, the deliberate and large-scale killing of children, of babies, most often in the presence of their parents? For generations, anxieties had been whipped up about Muslim fertility rates, of their uncontrolled breeding and imminent outnumbering of the Hindu majority.... Fed on such self-invented self-doubt, Hindu mobs swooped down upon Muslim women and children.... First, to possess and dishonour them and their men, second to taste what is denied to them and what, according to their understanding, explains Muslim virility. Third, to physically destroy the vagina and the womb, and, thereby, to symbolically destroy the sources of pleasure, reproduction and nurture for Muslim men, and for Muslim children. Then, by beatings, to punish the fertile female body. Then, by physically destroying the children,...by cutting up the foetus and burning it, to achieve a symbolic destruction of future generations, of the very future of Muslims themselves. The burning of men, women and children...: it was to destroy evidence, it was to make Muslims vanish, it was also to desecrate Muslim deaths by denying them an Islamic burial, and forcing a Hindu cremation upon them; a kind of a macabre post-mortem forced conversion.

The ruthless parody of Muslim sacred symbols, rituals and images and the terrible violation of their ways of life, experience and being are vividly brought out here. Death, and that by violence, is not enough. Torture is ritualized; it parodies key symbols of Muslim identity and practice at the moment of annihilation and severance. Mosques and monuments are treated to the same kinds of symbolic and real violence.

In the past, the spread of communal ideologies had a more intermittent and sporadic quality; riots erupted and ebbed. The packaging of ideology through modern systems of communication technology (audio cassettes, video cassettes, compact discs) and their more continuous spread through television and the media; through public celebrations and speeches has altered its reach exponentially. The work of communal organizations has spread and become more continuous and sustained; fed often by funds from particular communities of Non-Resident Indian (NRI) Hindus (see, for instance, Robinson 2001). The role of the state and police at the time of violence has become increasingly suspect. Against this, and the kinds of violence we saw happening in Gujarat and other places in recent years, this book wishes to enquire into how Muslim victims and survivors reconstruct their modes of being brutalized by actual and symbolic violence. The kinds of questions the book will be exploring include: When individuals and households have suffered the trauma of communal violence, sometimes more than once or in more than one generation, how does the process of 'recovery' reshape the way in which they look at themselves, their place in their own 'community' and their relations with others?

How do Muslims construct their identity under such conditions? Do they suppress the elements of their identity that are the targets of such hatred? Do they re-stress them and re-draw their boundaries even more rigidly? Do they come under the influence of movements aimed at the rigid defining of the faith? Or are there fractured attempts at reform within the community? How does the experience of violence reshape the organization of relations not just between neighbours and communities but with the state? Savagely 'othered' and perceived as alien within Hindu communal discourses, how do Muslims perceive themselves in relation to other Indians? How do the memories of violence restructure the organization of events or the use of space? How do they affect, *differently*, men and women: re-fashioning dress codes, norms of public and interactive behaviour and mobility? How do Muslims of different sectarian traditions work out the implications for identity and practice that the experience of violence and stereotyping perhaps force them to consider?

A paper by Mehta and Chatterji (2001: 202) based on a study of Dharavi in Mumbai seeks to understand that period in the lives of riot victims between 'the end of the riots and the resumption of everyday life'. How do people 'establish links between collective disorder and rehabilitation work'? This study seeks to go beyond this endeavour—to explore the worlds of everyday life not just in the periods immediately following a riot situation (or *repeated* riot situations) but even after, to trace varying trajectories out of violence, attempts to shape different relationships, structure new worlds or retrieve lost ones. More urgently, this book seeks to just create the space to talk about Muslims and, what is of greater significance, to listen to them: their speech and their silences, imperatives and equivocations. Categorized as 'Other', taunted as Pakistani if not vilified as terrorist, the Muslim in India today is an anonymous and frightening figure. Fear and anonymity are, of course, crucial to the maintenance of cultures of hostility and violence.[3]

The effort here is to demystify Muslims by entering those Indian urban spaces designated 'Pakistan', meeting with those who have experienced violence and brutality in the raw and who have a painful perception of themselves being recollected with suspicion, indeed with despisement, and reliving with them in their words their experiences of trauma and hurt, and attempts at retrieval and repair. The nuance of individual voices affirms subjectivity: shadowy facelessness recedes to reveal context, complexity and character. There is further an urgency to make an effort to articulate the outline of a theory of Muslim position (and positionality) exclusive of the usual recourse to vacillation that has typically tended to accompany such efforts in the past. The violence, described as genocidal by many, against Muslims in Gujarat (2002) wrung many of us inside out, our own indifference to religious identity receiving a severe jerk and our familial traditions steeped in benign pluralism thoroughly troubled. The time and the moment to speak was now; for if we did not we might find that our reticence had cost us our world.

violent pasts

Every time someone speaks in the pages ahead, there is a reference to a certain past experience of violence. Mumbai 1993, Gujarat 2002: for Muslims, for us, these are signposts of a nation out of hand. They represent without any doubt two of the most horrendous attacks on Muslims in the post-Independence period. While the violence of Partition always lurks in the shadows of any discussion on communal riots, no experience may ever be wholly erased. Ahmedabad 1969, Gujarat 1985, Mumbai 1974, Jogeshwari 1991, Baroda 1982, Bhiwandi 1984: the spectres of the past mercilessly haunt the present. This section attempts a brief overview of the increasing communalization of Indian society and polity from the late 1980s onwards, which impression obviously forms the crucible out of which the words we are listening to have been forged. It is generally agreed (see for instance Basu 1996; Desai 1984; Gupta 2000; Rajgopal 1987; Tambiah 1997; Varshney 2002) that the curve of communal violence took an undoubted upward turn from the late 1970s onwards. Each spell of collective violence only appeared to confirm the greater degree of organization and planning that went into its creation and management.

It was the 1980s and 1990s, however, during which Hindu–Muslim hostility and communal violence began to seriously take political centre-stage. Against the backdrop of the growing forces of Hindu nationalism focused particularly around the Babri Masjid–Ramjanmabhoomi issue, attacks on Muslims increased in ferocity and scale of execution. While the role of organizations such as the Jan Sangh, the Shiv Sena and, importantly, the Rashtriya Swayamsevak Sangh (RSS) as well as Muslim outfits such as the Majlis-e-Ittehadul-Muslimeen in provoking violence had at various point of time been cited, the last two decades saw a magnification on an unprecedented level. There has always been doubt cast as well on the role of the police and para-military forces in assessing and containing violence; their active connivance or passive concurrence with Hindu rioters has begun to assume proportions devastating to the Indian state.

Since the emergence of the Ayodhya dispute, organizations such as the Vishwa Hindu Parishad (VHP) and the Bajrang Dal have put it at the centre of their socio-political campaign. The Bharatiya Janata Party (BJP) with which such organizations as well as the RSS are aligned has the building of a temple to Ram in Ayodhya at the very spot where the Babri Masjid stood before it was destroyed in 1992 at the crux of its party agenda. The Ayodhya issue as well as the general failure of the Indian National Congress to quell internal dissidence, resolve the issue of its leadership following the death of Rajiv Gandhi and put forward a viable national vision for the future, led to favourable conditions for the political ascendancy of the BJP. Indeed, the Congress cannot be said to have had an enviable record of containing communal discord during its reign at the Centre or in various states. In 1984 the BJP had two seats in the Lok Sabha; in 1989 it had 85 and two years later it was the main opposition party with 120 seats. By 1996, the BJP could come to power as a minority government, if only for a few days. In 1998, it came to power again with over 180 seats, but could not sustain the minority government beyond some months. It finally emerged as the lead-party in the government after the next elections, at the head of an alliance of parties termed the National Democratic Alliance.

This highly compressed version of events is obviously partial and incomplete. It may be worthwhile referring to Tambiah (1997: 247–48) here who gives a highly composite summary of the 1990s' ethnic and political strife in India in which he visualizes the 'Ayodhya dispute' as an extremely condensed symbol of a range of criticisms and complaints held against the Congress by those out of power or in the opposition. The temple issue is for him the main dispute in the 1990s but it is also 'an immense umbrella' which covers many other matters. Among others, these include the charge of favouring the minorities, especially the Muslims, on the grounds of the government's decision in the wake of the 1984 Shah Bano case. Also included are:

....the recommendation by the Mandal Commission of affirmative action in favor of the backward classes, which higher-caste Hindus found threatening; the violence in the Punjab and the threatened secession by the Sikhs; the violence likewise in Kashmir, exacerbating Hindu–Muslim animosities; the need for a uniform civil code for all Indian citizens; the 'pseudo-secularism' of the nation-state fathered by Nehru and perpetuated by the Congress (I); the rejuvenation of the nation by making Hindu culture a bulwark against Western secularism, consumerism, and sexual eroticism; the continued corruption of the Congress (I) regime and the train of scandals it has spawned.

The soaring violence of the 1980s and 1990s has had particular features. These have largely been carefully executed attacks against Muslims that took place across different states and they have involved increasingly heavier losses to Muslim life and property.

Lists of Muslim homes and properties owned by them have typically been used by those perpetrating the violence to identify their targets. The violence has typically been preceded or sustained by vicious propaganda communicated through public speeches, audio and videotapes, pamphlets, leaflets and graffiti. The *rath yatras* to 'free' the birthplace of Ram during this period left in their wake a bloody trail of communal violence.

In recent times the worst riots have suspiciously begun to take on the dimensions of pogroms. In Mumbai, after the demolition of the Babri Masjid on 6 December 1992, there were several attacks by Muslims on Hindu temples and shrines in the city. Apart from other sporadic incidents of violence, in early January six Hindus were killed in a slum in Jogeshwari called Radhabai Chawl. This became the justification for the terrible violence wreaked on Muslims all over Mumbai in the days that followed, with the active involvement of the Shiv Sena and the undoubted collusion, at many places, of the authorities. In 2002, on 27 February, more than 50 persons, most if not all Hindus, aboard a train at Godhra in Gujarat were burnt to death. While evidence subsequently gathered has thrown some of the related theories in doubt, suspicion fell on some Muslims in Godhra for their involvement in the crime. The felony, horrendous as it was, was used to legitimize the killing, rape and looting of thousands of Muslims across a large part of the state. Again, the connivance of those charged with protection of citizens under the law has been shown up. In a recent judgement in the infamous Best Bakery Case of Gujarat, the Supreme Court went so far as to indict the Gujarat government in the following words:

When the investigating agency helps the accused, the witnesses are threatened to depose falsely and prosecutor acts in a manner as if he was defending the accused, and the Court was acting merely as an onlooker and there is no fair trail at all, justice becomes the victim.... The modern day 'Neros' were looking elsewhere when Best Bakery and innocent children and women were burning, and were probably deliberating how the perpetrators of the crime can be saved or protected.

One of the factors that most disturbs many of the Muslims who speak in these pages is the vitiation of the public sphere over the past several years by the increasing expression of hate speech. They often point to the way in which many Hindu right-wing leaders have been allowed to speak publicly of Muslims in language that is abrasive and offensive in the extreme. It is their understanding (and mine) that this escalation in aggressive speech and its growing permissibility is one of the crucial factors setting apart the last two decades—and especially the last few years—from the earlier period.[4]

Consider for a moment the kinds of pamphlets available in Gujarat prior to and during the course of the 2002 violence. Several pamphlets asked Hindus to save the country by boycotting Muslims economically and socially. A VHP pamphlet, after issuing a warning, well-calculated to induce fear, about Muslims coming in truckloads to kill Hindus in their own houses, says:

> Those who talk of Hindu–Muslim unity are only maligning their own religion. There can be no equality between Hindus and Muslims. They do not consider Bharat as their mother-land. Hindu–Muslim unity is a farce. Communal harmony and brotherhood is all a drama. The day their (the Muslim) population becomes 25 or 30 per cent, that day Hindus will be in danger. They will then divide the country into many Pakistans and raise Islam's green flag on Delhi's Red Fort. That is their final dream.[5]

The Justice Srikrishna Commission report on the Mumbai violence stated that large-scale rioting commenced from 6 January 1993 (Srikrishna n.d.: 22). This violence against Muslims was essentially provoked by communal propaganda circulated by Hindu communal organizations and by writings in newspapers such as *Saamna* and *Navakal*. Further, the propaganda was taken over

> ...by Shiv Sena and its leaders who continued to whip up communal frenzy by their statements and acts and writings and directives issued by the Shiv Sena Pramukh Bal Thackeray. The attitude of Shiv Sena as reflected in the 'TIME' interview given by Bal Thackeray and its doctrine of 'retaliation', as expounded by Shri Sarpotdar and Shri Manohar Joshi, together with the thinking of Shiv Sainiks that 'Shiv Sena's

terror was the true guarantee of the safety of citizens', were responsible for the vigilantism of Shiv Sainiks. Because some criminal Muslims killed innocent Hindus in one corner of the city [Jogeshwari], the Shiv Sainiks 'retaliated' against several innocent Muslims in other corners of the city.

There should be no attempt to read here any suggestion that communal propaganda is a thing Hindus of a particular ideology indulge in and not Muslims or others. Quite simply, however, we need to understand that the last decade or more has seen the growing ghettoization and vulnerability of Muslims everywhere resulting in the increasing futility of anything they might attempt to counter or pre-empt the onslaught they face. Even in Mumbai in 1992–93, while Muslims were indicted for indulging in attacks, looting, arson and rioting, there was *no* evidence found that Muslim organizations of the type of the Shiv Sena, for instance, had been involved in managing or provoking violence. One would have to admit the dispersed and random character of Muslim communal violence at the present juncture.

Muslims, even more now than in the past, suffer both at the hands of rioters and the police: indeed, in Mumbai's terrible violence of 1992–93, the most deaths occurred due to police firing and incidents of stabbing. In Gujarat in 2002, the action of mobs can be clearly identified as the biggest culprit. Various reports have spoken of mobs of thousands, reaching up to 10,000 and more in some cases. This shows the extent to which neither fear of the police or other authorities nor a need for furtiveness seems to have been felt by the killers and marauders. At the same time as the increasing scale and intensity of violence, the marginalization of Muslims, both cultural and material, has been of major concern to them. The anticipation of violence must clearly have a role of some significance to play in fixing Muslim expectations at a low level and in sustaining a sub-dued or defensive cultural profile. These are themes that shall certainly re-emerge at various moments in the text.

It is true that globally Muslims and Islam have come in for some rough treatment over the last decade or so with the growth of ter-rorist activity, often attributed to militant outfits in the Middle East. While the Palestinian struggle against Israel feeds some of these images of a militant Islam, it has also been sustained, among other factors, by Iraqi aggression, Afghanistan's troubled contemporary history and, to an extent, extremist activity in Kashmir. Of course, the September 11, 2001 attacks on the World Trade Centre in New York compacted and intensified beyond all recognition this antipathy to the religionists of Prophet Mohammad. Muslims in India were already 'Other', somehow bearing the burden of responsibility for Partition and of being heir to a violent tradition of Islam on the subcontinent associated with a long trail of temple destruction and 'forced' conversions.[6] Even so, they have felt acutely the heat of the current climate, which has been further exacerbated by terrorist strikes in Mumbai and, recently, Gujarat and, of course, the whole issue of the Babri Masjid.

The Babri Masjid issue written according to a script in which the Muslim ruler Babar plays the villain using power and force to destroy the temple and birthplace of the innocent child Ram, reduces all Muslims (through a logic too complex or confused to comprehend) to the sons of the alien raider Babar, traitors at once to the country and its ancient heritage. The power that this insidious call to save 'Ram' and 'Bharat' in a single gesture has to isolate, indeed excise, Muslims from the social fabric and the body politic is captured by a recent slogan, one of many used in this long battle, plastered on walls in many cities as part of the continuing exercise to build the temple in Ayodhya.

Babar ne toda tha Ram ka dham
Aapka kaun hai—Babar ya Ram [?]
[Babar destroyed Ram's dwelling
Who is yours—Babar or Ram?]

The hostility and threat can be further extended: Ayodhya was not safe, what about other sacred places? On the footpaths of Mumbai, for instance, a year or so ago, I found being sold a large poster of Shivaji with the following words printed on it:

Kashi ki kala jaati (The art of Kashi would vanish)
Mathura mein masjid basti (In Mathura there would be a masjid)
Agar Shivaji na hote (If Shivaji had not been there)
To sunnat sabki hoti (All of us would be circumcised)

With all this, not without surprise, Muslims find themselves at the receiving end of an intolerable degree of suspicion and mistrust.[7] All the Muslims who speak here have encountered closely if not always personally the savagery of inter-community strife in post-Independence India. So many have been forced to migrate—within the same city, to other places, to other states sometimes—as a direct result of such violence. We should not underestimate the extent to which dislocation—indeed, having to take into account the possibility of relocation due to *conflict*—might structure and inhibit, if not in fact distort, the social and economic trajectories of individual families. We would not be perverse to begin to wonder about the cumulative effect of multiple dislocations on the community as a whole. For all this, there can be little doubt of the attachment to *watan*. In Yusufbhai's words:

> *Ye hamara watan hai. Vo musalman nahi jo watan se gaddari kare.*
> [This is our *watan* [homeland]. He is not a Muslim, who is a traitor to his homeland.]

ethnographic locations

This study hopes to address some of the questions raised in an earlier section through qualitative ethnographic methods, in Mumbai and also in two cities in Gujarat, using in particular life-histories and narratives of Muslim men and women as modes of exploration. Based on narratives and interviews of Muslim men and women, it tries to understand the world and the worldviews of those who have seen and lived through one or, sometimes, several violent confrontations and episodes in their lives. The work seeks to explore difficult and troubling questions: what are the ways in which the memories of violence bring about shifts in everyday practices of living, in ideas of space and time, in the understanding of what it means to be Muslim in India today? How do people, who have experienced violence, sometimes repeatedly, against themselves or their families, live with the memories of those events? How do they perceive their neighbours, their land, themselves and their practices so terribly travestied during times of violence?

Beginning the summer of 2003, I began collecting data and meeting with survivors of collective violence and those who live and work with them. Many became friends; certainly, my world has been greatly enlarged and enhanced. The work began in Mumbai where I reside and am employed; after Gujarat 2002, it seemed to me as well as others critical that voices from there be listened to. Certainly, it seemed crucial also to endeavour to imagine the worlds of those who have lived so closely and for so long under the shadow of continual violence. Over three separate visits between July 2003 and April 2004, I worked there intensively: in Baroda, more briefly, and in Ahmedabad, for a longer period. While immersion to the extent perhaps achievable in Mumbai was not possible, for obvious reasons, the efforts have been extremely engaging as well as eminently, if painfully, instructive.

It was not difficult to locate the families and individuals with whom these conversations took place; the help of local Muslim youth groups was very helpful in this connection. Most of the exchanges took over an hour and often much longer, and in Ahmedabad and Mumbai I was able to visit some of the families more than once. The interview mode was reworked to make it as open and flexible as possible to elicit narratives rather than answers. I asked a few questions—about survival strategies, compensation struggles and forms of dislocation (geographical, economic and so on) suffered as a consequence of communal conflict. This usually led to long tales, moving backwards and forwards in time, which touched on so many aspects of the personal experiences of ethnic violence that have been recorded in these pages. A great deal was uncovered about violence itself 'as it happened', even when no question was directly raised in this regard. It was not always easy to filter out family or kin when speaking with one person; I did try to ensure that children were mostly out of earshot for it was not desirable for them to hear again these stories of pain, betrayal and loss. For adults too forgetting has a value, though many understood clearly that society as a whole must never be allowed to forget and the project of writing fed that aim.

With social workers, activists and members of religious organizations, these issues were somewhat less troubling. Acutely sensitive to the bad press received in general by Muslims in recent times, they are disposed to lend voice to any effort that tried to form rather than fracture bridges of understanding. Through questions regarding the location and identity of the Muslim community particularly against the backdrop of savage violence and the community efforts at rehabilitation and reform, personal experiences of conflict and trajectories of belief also emerged. All manner of divisions and distinctions tumbled forth and the collectivity or 'community'—though never missing—proved much harder to pin down and far more multi-layered than previously imagined.

The fact of my being a woman and, particularly, Christian constructed in particular ways my access to Muslims as well as their perception (and reception) of me. I do not mean to suggest that Muslims would close themselves off from Hindus. Surely not, for some of the most prominent persons struggling on their behalf are Hindus. It is not simple though for an ordinary person to obtain the kind of admittance I was privileged to gain. If Muslims have to bear the suspicion of outsiders, they are themselves at this juncture wary of them—particularly when questions of a very sensitive nature are being posed. While I wore my normal *salwar-kameez* or sari, I usually removed my *bindi*, in deference to the fact that I was moving around in largely Muslim areas. It would not have been possible to achieve the level of ease or confidence with many of the women here, if I were not a woman myself. Even though I do not primarily define myself by faith, my religious affiliation unambiguously made me part of the predicament that so closely concerned us all.

It was apparent to me from the outset that there was no easy or conscionable way for me to enter these shattered and painfully mended worlds without some purpose—however limited—defining itself that was not consumed wholly by academic output but incorporated benefit in social terms. I was interested in some of the painstaking efforts in education being made at the grass-roots level in different places. Slowly, I began to meet some of the persons engaged in trying to improve educational standards in the slums for Muslims and non-Muslims through financial assistance as well as the provision of extra tuition to help the weaker students. There are also labours underway to get young people, dropouts, back into the educational system. While contributing my mite to some of these efforts, I also attempt wherever necessary to spread the information to families in need about the availability of these and other resources and how to access them. The proceeds of this book are pledged towards such efforts in improving access to modern education for Muslims as well as for others in some of the areas where I worked.

outline

While I began working with some ideas and questions in mind, it was clear to me that listening to the stories might change these. The chapters construct themselves around the narratives or some of their focal themes. Every chapter has in turn been informed by my reading of theoretical literature surrounding each theme. The result is probably stories within stories, their depth barely scoured in the course of a single slim volume. One chapter has its location elsewhere—in the apparently dreary territory of figures—though the tie of the sad tale it has to tell with the text as a whole is unfortunately all too transparent.

We first enter the worlds of violence remembered and the images along which these recollections are borne. The experience of trauma marks understandings of space and time, transforming them, in fact deforming them with the imprint of suffering. Beard, *burqa* or bearing: a savage excess is made to overlay the visible markers of Muslim identity. The break of time and the warp of space agitate routine, inserting fresh wariness into the where and when of what is possible. The chapter cannot contain the countless consequences, it merely seeks to trace some of the patterns and discuss some of the dimensions of the experience of traumatic violence that emerge from survivors' living and reliving those memories.

There is a broader setting of cumulative deprivation and dependency within which violence is experienced that quite possibly permits if it does not produce greater susceptibility to it. The next chapter organizes itself around this subject, elucidating with as much carefulness as possible, given the serious constraint of the inadequacy of data available (this itself perhaps a part of the problem), the facets of disprivilege and marginality characterizing the majority of the Muslim community. Further connections are pondered regarding the ethnic homogeneity of security forces and their capacity for impartiality when called to play a role during periods of inter-community conflict. The questions these issues could raise for the makers of policy are discussed at a later point in the text.

One of the more privileging and deeply humbling aspects of this work has been the opportunity it has given me to know and listen to so many Muslim women. Their utterances locate the experience of extraordinary violence within individual and familial worlds. Though we do not seek at any point to minimize the horror of collective brutality, it is undoubted that women's recollections defy presumption for they quiver with the traces of violences more incessant even when less excessive. The structures of narration call attention to the social situations of distress, in ways which if not altogether predictable certainly have some implications for our understanding of the complex and difficult relationships between community suffering in its enormity and its social recognition and recompense.

While women's narratives continually shift the locus of violence, in the utterances of men violence is more swiftly situated in the exterior. The margins of the 'us' sway uneasily back and forth as political and (inter-)national scripts enable, or more importantly, obstruct particular formations. There are deep fractures and significant struggles: various ideological positions grapple each other. This and the chapter after it simmer with the discord, while also taking seriously the individuality of responses and circumstance and revealing the futility of any expectation of homogeneity. The voices of male survivors invoke the image of a community injured and attacked by others and by the State; the affirmation of endurance is rendered no less real for its chafing against the ineffectuality of comeback.

While one of the paths may proceed towards a greater isolation and separation often along the lines of strictly-defined faith, out of the ashes of destruction sometimes arises a stronger determination to participate in the making of conditions which might prevent its occurrence. These efforts do not of course always take similar form and there are disagreements of various kinds. Most of the labours charted at this point in the book are shaped tangibly by context; what has been focused on are some of the individuals and the life-experiences and trajectories through which they reach the positions they occupy. What is of interest as well is the different ways in which Muslims who consider themselves 'reformist' or 'secular', work with religious leaders and the questions raised through these engagements.

It may be going very much against the tide to do so, but there appears to be some urgency for us to articulate a theory for the backwardness of Muslims. The data from chapter three as well as suggestions from the rest of the book demonstrate that for the most part they are not much better off than the Scheduled Castes or Scheduled Tribes according to most indices of development or standard of living. In the final chapter, an attempt is made to review the position of Muslims in Indian society and polity through the work on political theory of Iris Marion Young. Violence is both part and product of the complex of factors that contribute to Muslim deprivation. If we are to plan for an India of the future, we need to consider seriously the relationship of security and equal opportunity with social stability. Experiences of some South-East Asian countries demonstrate the crucial links.[8]

notes

1. Spivak has been asked this question earlier in India (1990: 68). Her answer: 'I...[am]...really therefore most interested in your notion of the "freedom" involved with being an NRI [Non-Resident Indian]. One never quite understands this "freedom"'. Later, in the course of the same interview (1990: 70), she suggests that an Indian woman academic would share with her the incapacity to speak too quickly about subaltern women with whom she has 'not learnt to make...[herself]...acceptable other than as a concerned benevolent person who is free to come and go'. Further, she argues that she finds this 'to be a much more difficult problem to work at than all of the differences between living abroad and living at home'. One needs to acknowledge the questions Spivak wishes to bring to the discussion on involvement here. Indeed, in the contemporary socio-political climate, even the foreign scholar is not immune to certain constraints: witness, for instance, the fate of the work on Shivaji by James Laine. Therefore, given the complexity of circumstances involved, I do not wish to overstate the case. Suffice to say, there are differences of degree as well as of kind, perhaps, implicated. The Indian woman academic does have to negotiate ways to 'make herself acceptable' with those alongside whom she wishes to speak and while it may be a difficult problem for anyone to work at, it is particularly *crucial* to her for there are critical limits to her freedom 'to come and go' without being touched in very real ways by what she seeks to know.

2. I refer in particular to the years 1997–1999. There is no attempt to suggest that the attacks have ceased completely since then; activists aver otherwise. However, that was a period of particularly intense and sustained assaults, a period which many Indian Christians spoke of as their 'darkest days'.

3. Recall Constantine Cavafy's (1864–1933) words: 'And now, what's going to happen to us without barbarians? They were, those people, a kind of solution'.

4. There has, however, been a recent Supreme Court judgement upholding the right of the authorities in Karnataka to ban Praveen Togadia of the VHP from

addressing the public. The judgement states in no uncertain terms (*Communalism Combat*, April–May 2004, pp. 71–79):

No person, however big he may assume or claim to be, should be allowed, irrespective of the position he may assume or claim to hold in public life, to either act in a manner or make speeches which would destroy secularism recognised by the Constitution of India, 1950 (in short the 'Constitution'). Secularism is not to be confused with communal or religious concepts of an individual or a group of persons. It means that (the) State should have no religion of its own and no one could proclaim to make the State have one such, or endeavour to create a theocratic State.

Persons belonging to different religions live throughout the length and breadth of the country. Each person, whatever be his religion, must get an assurance from the State that he has the protection of law freely to profess, practice and propagate his religion and freedom of conscience. Otherwise, the rule of law will be replaced by individual perceptions of one's own presumptuous good social order.

Therefore, whenever the concerned authorities in charge of law and order find that a person's speeches or actions are likely to trigger communal antagonism and hatred resulting in fissiparous tendencies gaining foothold, undermining and affecting communal harmony, prohibitory orders need necessarily to be passed, to effectively avert such untoward happenings.

Communal harmony should not be made to suffer and be made dependent upon (the) will of an individual or a group of individuals, whatever be their religion, be it of minority or that of the majority. Persons belonging to different religions must feel assured that they can live in peace with persons belonging to other religions.

While permitting holding of a meeting organised by groups or an individual, which is likely to disturb public peace, tranquillity and orderliness, irrespective of the name, cover and methodology it may assume and adopt, the administration has a duty to find out who are the speakers and participants and also take into account previous instances and the antecedents involving or concerning those persons. If they feel that the presence or participation of any person in the meeting or congregation would be objectionable, for some patent or latent reasons, as well as past track record of such happenings in other places involving such participants, necessary prohibitory orders can be passed.

Quick decisions and swift as well as effective action necessitated in such cases may not justify or permit the authorities to give prior opportunity or consideration at length of the pros and cons. The imminent need to intervene instantly having regard to the sensitivity and perniciously perilous consequences it may result in, if not prevented forthwith, cannot be lost sight of.

5. Janyala Sreenivas, 'Communal Harmony is Drama: VHP Pamphlet', *The Indian Express*, 12 April 2002, pp. 1–2.

6. The efforts of a large body of scholarship (see, for instance, Dale 2003; Eaton 1997; Ernst 1992; Zaidi 1989) to contest and thoroughly complicate this entrenched and highly simplistic popular view appears to have had little success, at least with right-wing Hindu ideologues.

7. The basis of this suspicion of the disloyalty of Muslims requires thorough cross-examination. If addressed, as one significant instance, in terms of the place and role of Muslims in the Indian security forces, the data challenges the assumptions. As Khalidi (2003: 23–24) unfortunately has to record, a recent poll by a well known marketing research company revealed that a large number of Hindus believe that Muslims should not be allowed in the Armed Forces. Yet, it is undoubted that Muslims have proven their loyalty in three wars with Pakistan (four if the Kargil battle is included). Culling from a variety of data, he shows that there have been only three known cases of Muslims in the Army charged with spying for Pakistan; many more Hindus have been charged for the same. He has to note, perhaps even more regrettably, that none other than George Fernandes voiced in 1985 the opinion that: 'The Muslim is not wanted in the Armed Forces because he is always suspect— whether we want to admit it or not, most Indians consider Muslims a fifth column for Pakistan' (Khalidi 2003: 23).

8. I deliberately do not turn to the 'West' here, for we need examples from countries in or close to our own region, which also have long traditions of ethnic and religious diversity and which like us grapple with the modern notions of democracy, equality before law and secularism. See, for instance, Joanna Pfaff-Czarnecka, Darini Rajasingham-Senanayake, Ashis Nandy and Edmund Terence Gomez, *Ethnic futures: The state and identity politics in Asia* (1999), which compares India with Sri Lanka, Malaysia and Nepal.

chapter two

space, time and the stigma of identity

Teri galiyon mein ne rakhenge kadam
Aaj ke baad...
(Words from a song from film *Hawas*,
lyrics Sawan Kumar).

Alighting at Sion station prior to walking down to Dharavi's famous '90 Foot Road' I unobtrusively move my hand across my forehead and remove my *bindi*. I am entering Social Nagar, Muslim space on the social map of Mumbai.

While riding to Juhapura on the back of a friend's two-wheeler, she urges me to pull my *dupatta* over my head. We are about to enter Ahmedabad's 'Pakistan'.

On 13 March 2003, a day before Muharram, a bomb left in a local train went off just as the train entered Mulund station in north Mumbai. The blast left a trail of bloodshed: more than 10 persons were killed and nearly fifty injured. A friend, living in Mulund, took the train the next morning. Clearly, nothing else could be spoken of. There was a sustainable belief that one of several radical Muslim groups could be responsible for the blast, but little else was till then known. One of the passengers casually remarked to her companion: 'They must have got on at VT [Victoria Terminus, now renamed Chhatrapati Shivaji Terminus], planted the bomb and got off at Kurla' [Kurla is one of the stations before Mulund on the Central Line, another space unmistakably Muslim, unmistakably 'Other'].

Perhaps no newspaper mentioned Muharram at all; perhaps we were among the few to notice the association. And why?

Muharram, after all, was much more significant ritually to the minority Shias, rather than the majority Sunnis, though *tazias* [ritual processions] were taken out in various cities including Mumbai. Had the self been so programmed to be ever alert to the ways in which larger religious or political calendars and configurations could so deeply curve and confound our little realms? Enter our world: one structured by images of temporality that scrape again and again deep historical wounds, whose healing only ever appears to recede.

There are two kind of stories I want to relate in this chapter. The first regards the physical re-organization of urban spaces that has altered Mumbai in the years after 1992–93 and that is slowly working itself out in other cities such as Baroda and Ahmedabad— sites in 2002, of orchestrated attacks on Muslims.[1] The second is the remembrance and recollection of spaces and the ways in which time is recorded in the memories of survivors of violence. These are intertwining stories, of course, as we shall see in the course of this chapter.

At the outset I must specify two things. There will be obvious differences in the ways people remember both individually and in terms of the two contexts, separated by a considerable temporal lapse. The implications of this difference is a theme that is explored more deeply in the intimacy of women's stories related later in the text. What we seek to recall here are the kinds of spatial categorizations working themselves out in urban spaces fractured by possible conflicts and the memories of past violence.

Second, since my main focus was never 'the violence' but always the 'after violence', at no point did I ever enquire of anyone I spoke with about the details of what happened to them. This was all the more pertinent in Mumbai, because of the years that had passed since the actual experience of extraordinary violence. Nevertheless, everywhere people's narratives, sometimes continuous, sometimes spasmodic, engaged with their ideas of the 'what happened' in several different registers.

Bodies, space, time are all inscribed and altered by violence. In the aftermath, occupying the same social spaces may or may not be possible. Even where people attempt to reoccupy the zones of hurt, theirs is a beleaguered 'normalcy' that has to be slowly and painfully wrung out of the quotidian, now rendered grotesquely unfamiliar.

This process is aided by several factors including, importantly, the instating in the wake of extraordinary violence, a space for the public acknowledgement of suffering and for the setting into action of appropriate modes of redress (see Das and Kleinman 2001: 19).

Speaking of the need to confront trauma, which she considers central to the process of healing, Herman (1994: 9) argues that:

> To hold traumatic reality in consciousness requires a social context that affirms and protects the victim and that joins victim and witness in a common alliance. For the individual victim, this social context is created by relationships with friends, lovers, and family. For the larger society, the social context is created by political movements that give voice to the disempowered.

In democratic societies everywhere, as well as for reasons going deep into the reality of south Asian understandings of politics and justice, redress is never sufficient if it is not state-led or state-legitimized. Indeed, the agony of the Gujarat victims of violence was rendered the more acute for their believing that the State had abandoned them to the more diluted forms of attention made available by community activists or non-sectarian, non-governmental organizations. Hurt was magnified when the government first announced a difference in the compensation to be paid to families of those who died in the Godhra train crash and those who died in the violence that followed it. This notification was later withdrawn.

Herman, however, believes that for the individual survivor of trauma, the pursuit of a 'fantasy of compensation' may be counter-productive, for it 'ties the patient's fate to that of the perpetrator' (1994: 190). At a social and political level, however, the need for compensation, both material as well as symbolic—an acknowledgement of harm or holding accountable the perpetrators—must be reinforced. Indeed, the absence of any manner of justice in the case of enormous social crimes in India is itself feeding the cycles of illegal and distorted forms of terrorist vengeance inserting greater vulnerability into our urban spaces, especially in Mumbai.

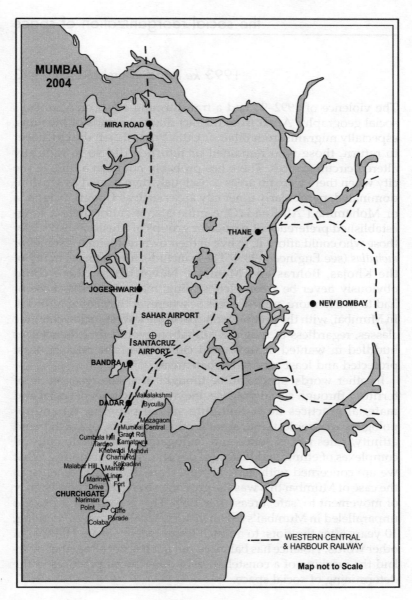

Map 2.1: Mumbai

the social reorganization of space

1993 *ke baad*: Mumbai after 1993

The violence of 1992–93 had a transforming effect on Mumbai's social geography. Apart from the fact that thousands of Muslims, especially migrants from Bihar or Uttar Pradesh, left the city never to return, those who remained or returned did so in radically altered circumstances. There has probably not been a time in the city when there were no areas consciously demarcated as Muslim-dominated, particularly inner city areas such as Dongri, Nagpada or Mohammad Ali Road. One must also mention here a long-established preference of particular groups of Muslims, especially those who could afford it, to live in their own residential colonies or *mohallas* (see Engineer 1989). These include, for instance, many of the Khojas, Bohras and Memons. Nevertheless, there could obviously never be a complete sealing; many Muslims chose or had to live in more 'mixed' areas or wherever they could afford it. In Mumbai, with the premium on space, the lowest socio-economic classes, regardless of religious affiliation, would find themselves huddled in wanted or unwanted closeness in the poorest, least protected and least serviced urban areas.

In other words, space can be thought of as the recognition of territory through social practice. Inevitably, a clutch of social and material practices must configure spatial patterns. As anthropologists we would think, among other elements, of kinship and affinity, rules of residence and endogamy, or intricate cultural complexes of ethnic and historical devotions and memories. What we are concerned with here, however, are defining moments; in the case of Mumbai this was the growing strength and consistency of movement to 'safe' areas after 1993. This is certainly a process unparalleled in Mumbai's urban history. Muslims are *still* moving, 10 years after the riots; to a much lesser extent, so are Hindus. In other words, violence has balanced out if it has not altogether over-laid the working of a constellation of other social practices in the determining of social space.

Mumtaz lives in Borivli (East), a place known as Kajupada. The people here are mostly involved in work such as tailoring, building and the like. In this area of small tenements, not too many lives were lost in the violence, for people, forewarned, had fled. They returned to houses broken into and looted. Mumtaz's own family had moved to the relatively safe, because it was Muslim-dominated, area of Jogeshwari (West). On 25 January, they went to her maternal uncle's house in Surat. Her father's family is from Jalgaon. People had come from outside in trucks and looted the houses, their neighbours said to them. Mumtaz feels the neighbours were unable to stop the marauders. When they returned to their house, two or three months after the violence, they too felt: 'We cannot stay here'. However, as Mumtaz said, in the absence of money, they did not have the option to move. It has now been twelve years and things are 'as normal'. Other people moved; there are people moving even now. Several have gone to Mira Road. People move as and when they can 'adjust' she says. 'To adjust', in the way that Mumtaz used the term, means to be able to acquire the means to move.

Muslims have moved not so much into 'new' areas, but into those where there were already fair numbers of their own. The movement of Muslims has taken at least three directions. Some areas in Central Mumbai have seen the greater concentration. These include places mentioned earlier such as Nagpada, Madanpura, Bhendi Bazar or Mohammad Ali Road. Some parts of Wadala, such as Kidwai Nagar, or Byculla are considered strong and, therefore, relatively 'safe' Muslim areas.

Moving further outwards, Jogeshwari (West) saw considerable in-movement of Muslims after the violence. Other places to which people moved were Kurla and Govandi. Millat Nagar, a large complex of apartments with its own shopping complex, off Lokhandwala in Andheri (West) is a sanctuary for the middle-class Muslim. Indeed, many non-Muslim tenants left their flats in Millat Nagar after 1993 as hostility to their presence began to subtly grow. Finally, Mira Road, a distant suburb in north-west Mumbai and Mumbra, one in north-east Mumbai, have become the two other distinct and noticeable areas of Muslim concentration over the last ten years.

At all times, when we speak of these larger movements we need to understand that there has so far been no official documentation of them to which we can take recourse for actual numbers. Further, as anthropologists, we also need at each moment to record individual trajectories of movement and to separate these from any discussion of the total complex of dislocation and relocation. Not always do the stories of individuals fit our grand patterns; the minutiae of people's decisions in the work of re-composing piece by piece their everyday lives reveal complex motivations, difficult and different understandings of their altered worlds. I will be accenting those subjective stories by and by.

To return to the account, if partial, of partitions that have worked themselves out on the metropolitan map of Mumbai. Dharavi reveals a particularly infamous instance. Down one of the alleys off the 90 Foot Road is a complex of neighbourhoods. A settlement of Tamil Hindus leads on to a predominantly Muslim neighbourhood—Nawab Nagar. During the violence, the Tamils constructed a wall blocking their *chawl* from the Muslim one, a wall which effectively cut off easy access of Muslims to their own homes, except through a small opening. It was several months after the riots that Muslims managed to prevail upon the municipal authorities to break the wall down as it obstructed their entry and exit from Nawab Nagar. The Tamils worked out another option: relocation. Over half the residences in their area now house Muslims.

Baroda and Ahmedabad in Gujarat: new patterns emerging

A great deal has now been documented about the complex environment that has set in place following the worst of the violence of 2002. What is recorded here develops both from the written sources and my engagements with Muslims and social activists in these two cities of Gujarat.

Mumbai's violence took place in two bouts: one in December 1992 and a second one in January 1993. Muslims stayed in relief camps for some months and were persuaded slowly to return to their houses. These returns were complicated and difficult and in some cases not achievable. The city was a place of tension for Muslims. One man in Mumbai's Kidwai Nagar, who took to keeping a beard after the 1984 Bhiwandi–Mumbai riots, recorded that in the weeks following the January violence, people with (*daadi*) beards, especially if alone, and assumed to be Muslim, sometimes found themselves under attack. In his own family, if some work had to be done in a public place or at a distance, the family sent one of the brothers or cousins who did not sport a beard. However, most survivors agreed that in Mumbai the situation of overt and anonymous hostility towards anyone perceived as Muslim came to an abrupt and artificial end when the bomb blasts rent the city two months later. As individuals record, though, in the micro-situations of small neighbourhoods and *chawls*, the stories were agonizingly other.

In no way, though, can Mumbai and Gujarat's cities, with which I achieved a small degree of familiarity, be considered to have taken similar trajectories out of the madness of the most recent episodes of horrific violence. 'Nothing is normal' says Cedric Prakash, a Jesuit and deeply committed activist, from Ahmedabad. While this is a statement true wherever we talk of profound violence, in each case the histories tend to differ to some extent. In Mumbai, the active participation of the police and State authorities, *after* the violence, took the form of redressal and an effort to involve civilians in the prevention of future violence through the formation of the now famous *mohalla* committees (Barve 2003). As Waqar Khan from Dharavi put it:

> *Police ki vardi pe jo khun ka daag laga tha, unko use mitana tha. Is liye mohalla committees shuru kiye gaye. Communal harmony ke prayas kiye gaye.* [The police needed to remove the stain of blood that had tainted their uniforms in the violence. Hence, they set up the *mohalla* committees and made efforts to build communal harmony].

The efforts to get monetary compensation were long drawn and arduous; they were, though, set in place. The Srikrishna Commission, investigating the violence and the bomb blasts, had a troubled regime: its report remains one on which the State refuses to act. However, it provided a public, legitimate space for the articulation of suffering. To recall again Das and Kleinman on the movement from chaos to quotidian in the context of great social crimes (2001: 19):

> ...in the life of a community, justice is neither everything nor nothing.... [T]he very setting-into-process of public

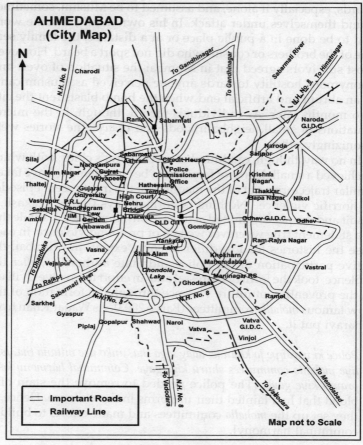

Map 2.2: Ahmedabad

acknowledgement of hurt can allow new opportunities to be created for resumption of everyday life.

Survivors from Gujarat tell a different tale. For one, people could not go back to their houses for months. In many cases, the return has been made, to shattered homes, *more than a year* after the violence. Almost everywhere, social workers or community leaders continue to provide support and encouragement to the residents by staying among them. Indeed, the violence itself has continued

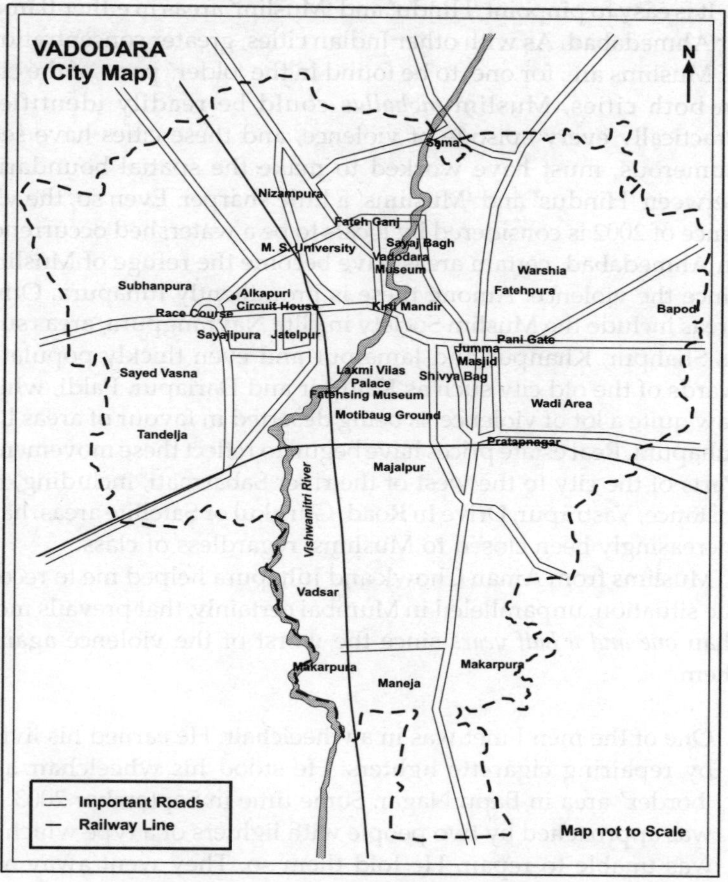

Map 2.3: Baroda

for many months, rather than remaining conflict which peaked and died soon after. Violence continues to plague the state: every few days or weeks smaller incidents take place; every now and then tension is reinforced by the declaration of *bandhs* or by aggressive demonstrations or public celebrations of festivals. As one among other activists in Ahmedabad was to say, the level of prevailing insecurity even two years after the worst of the violence prevents the setting-in-motion of any stable forms of neighbourhood peace negotiation and conflict settlement.

It is easy to pinpoint 'Hindu' and 'Muslim' areas in either Baroda or Ahmedabad. As with other Indian cities, greater concentrations of Muslims are, for one, to be found in the 'older' parts of the city. In both cities, Muslim *mohallas* could be readily identified. Practically every episode of violence, and these cities have seen numerous, must have worked to make the spatial boundaries between 'Hindus' and 'Muslims' a little sharper. Even so, the violence of 2002 is considered by locals to be a watershed occurrence. In Ahmedabad, certain areas have become the refuge of Muslims since the violence. Among these is prominently Juhapura. Other areas include the Muslim Society in elite Navrangpura, areas such as Shahpur, Khanpur and Jamalpur and even thickly populated wards of the old city such as Kalupur and Dariapur. Paldi, which saw quite a lot of violence, is being deserted in favour of areas like Juhapura. Real estate prices have begun to reflect these movements. Parts of the city to the west of the river Sabarmati, including, for instance, Vastrapur, Drive In Road, Gurukul or Satellite areas, have increasingly been closed to Muslims, regardless of class.

Muslims from Aman Chowk and Juhapura helped me to record the situation, unparalleled in Mumbai certainly, that prevails more than *one and a half years* since the worst of the violence against them.

One of the men I met was in a wheelchair. He earned his living by repairing cigarette lighters. He stood his wheelchair at a 'border' area in Bapu Nagar. Some time in September 2003, he was approached by two people with lighters of a type which he was unable to repair. He told them so. They went away and returned a while later with three others. They surrounded his wheelchair and asked him his name and where he came from. When he told them, they said: *'Miyan log yahan nahin dikhne chahiye'* [Muslims should not be seen here]. Though he went to lodge a complaint with the police, he asserted, they would not register an FIR. He claimed that he was told that if Muslims went to Hindu areas, this would occur. Since then, he has not ventured out of his neighbourhood.

Autorickshaw drivers said they were facing considerable difficulties. The Sabarmati has become the symbolic divide for areas designated 'Muslim' or 'Hindu'. An autorickshaw driver who had recently taken a passenger to the Gurukul area, was asked, by the man, his name and which part of the city he came from. When he set the man down, he was paid, but the man said to him in parting: *'Abhi Musalmaan ka pul ke is paar koi kaam nahi hai'* [Now Muslims do not have any excuse to be on this (western) side of the Sabarmati].

Juhapura's women had a quite different take on the notion of 'safe areas'. As Aminaben spoke about the trouble on the borders of Juhapura, I commented: 'But you are safe here, is it not?' She burst out:

> Yes, we are safe here. But how is this? They [Hindus] close off all our options to move out from here. We are confined here, but within two or three months of the riots, they started coming here. They bring their carts and park them here, and bring their goods into our area to sell. But our people are not allowed to go out and cannot venture into their areas.

While we have become familiar with accounts of rural victims of violence in Gujarat not being allowed, in some cases, to return to their villages, Aminaben's voice, as those of the others here, articulates the quandary of not wanting to stay in, but *not being allowed to leave* the ghetto.

While a few areas in Baroda, such as Fatehgunj, continue to struggle to retain their pluralistic identity, the long years of conflict have ensured that ethnic demarcations here are as patent as elsewhere in Gujarat. Indeed, there is definite indication that the violence inclined towards 'purifying' particular neighbourhoods by driving the few Muslims out,[2] and certain areas, such as Pratap Nagar, Raopura, Mandvi or Tandalja, the last located suitably far from the city centre, are the recourse of displaced Muslims. While many people have moved back to rebuild shops or shelter in shattered homes, the battle lines are fiercely drawn and well recognized by all.

As Feldman (2000: 53) has written in the context of Protestant-Catholic strife in Belfast, ghettoization in Northern Ireland worked as a mechanism of geographical control to limit and manage the social, bodily and perceptual contact between the estranged confessional groups. In the city of Belfast itself, in the life of the everyday, a person's visual experience was very closely linked to attempting to maintain ethnic contact avoidance. This was, indeed, the typical bodily stance in the urban context. Residential separation of Catholics and Protestants provided an immediate environmental support for enabling such prompt visual studies of ethnic identity.

The dilemma of those who do not wish to partake of these polarities is brought out by what a highly committed social activist, who continues to determinedly live and work in a Muslim-dominated area, said while talking of a protest march organized against the current political regime:

> We put up a protest in their area. Right near Hanuman Tekri[3].... People say: 'You went there?' We said: 'Yes, why not? Have they got a *theka* on this place?' Let them be frightened by our presence.... Let them worry that we have come with the people [protesters] right up to them. Otherwise, they will take up whole places, we will cut ourselves off and find ourselves pushed to the margins. Why should that be? If we don't sleep at nights, let them also keep awake one night. Otherwise, soon we will find that we are forced to remain inside our houses. Not able to go out at all. We have to confront them in those very spaces.

There is something else more visible and yet more insidious that connects the spaces occupied by Muslims: their overwhelming decay and the notable lack of civic services in most such areas. From Mumbra to Madanpura, from Kurla to Wadala, in the inner areas of Baroda and Ahmedabad, in Tandalja or Juhapura, roads are poor and badly maintained. Tarring is sporadic and even tarred roads are full of potholes and rarely touched up. In many areas, rubbish piles high and is not cleared for weeks if not months. While these are the characteristics of all slum areas and Muslims share in this deprivation with Dalits and the mass of the urban poor, in comparison with other *religious* communities, they are the worst off in terms of conditions of living and access to various kinds of resources (Shariff 1995, 1999; Razzack and Gumber 2002). What emerges, further, is the relative lack of political clout of Muslims, their inability to make demands on collective resources that will merit attention.[4] Moreover, such conditions feed continuously into popular images of Muslims as 'dirty' and 'unhygienic' and, in more ways than one, therefore, dispensable.

These images of themselves as well as the obvious lack of facilities in Muslim-dominated areas have clearly begun to work on the consciousness of Muslims themselves, not just reinforcing a complex of persecution but spurring on groups and individuals to take the fight for better facilities forward to the State and make it responsible for improving conditions.[5] A Muslim activist from Ahmedabad argued:

Urban facilities have not found their way into Muslim areas. There are no parks, no widened roads, no recreation facilities, no modern education facilities, no old age facilities. These are implicitly denied to Muslims because they are located elsewhere, though on the face of it they are created for everyone. I hold the State responsible for this denial.

characteristics of space during and after violence

Every city in India that has seen major conflicts between Hindus and Muslims has acquired a history of spaces that mimic international boundaries. While India and Pakistan have their borders and border disputes, every city has its 'Pakistan' and within each neighbourhood, boundaries innocuous or otherwise, designate 'India' from 'Pakistan'. These boundaries are reinforced during the times of violence; most violence occurs in what people designate as 'border' areas, places where Hindus and Muslims 'takkar pe aate hain' [clash together]. This pattern is itself, of course, a product of the segregation of living spaces. In other words, the separation of communal grounds of social spaces by no means averts violence. It must be thought of, on the other hand, as a mechanism for the containment and management of violence, by restricting it as far as possible to these crossing points or border areas. Each bout of violence can yield a further uprooting and re-organization of the boundary lines. This can have deeply problematic implications.

In a brilliant study conducted by YUVA in Jogeshwari (East) in 1996, the authors showed that Muslims have been systematically

pushed, over the last two decades, into a smaller and smaller settlement area at the peak of a hill, surrounded by Hindu settlements
all around and having almost no access routes out of their pocket
except through these Hindu areas. In the 1970s, Muslims and
Hindus were interspersed throughout the area as a whole, though
there were larger and smaller religion-based pockets here and
there. Each riot has, however, led to the further concentration of
Muslims. As Muslims tried to move inwards from the boundary
line with each bout of violence, the boundary itself shifted further
towards the interior, thereby reducing considerably the space
available for habitation. Today Muslims are largely ghettoized in
Prem Nagar which is, of course, East Jogeshwari's 'Pakistan' and
the road that divides it from the Hindu area is, ironically enough,
Gandhi Market road.

When Sajjid showed me around the area, he pointed out the
road, saying: 'This is an international border'. With my new-found
knowledge I said: 'Yes, I know. India–Pakistan'. He was grave when
he replied, out of the deep hurt of constantly coming up against
the label 'anti-national': 'No. Both sides are India, but they are
now divided'. Everywhere one goes one encounters the same military language of borders and divisions, 'mini-Indias' and 'mini-
Pakistans' with their own histories of violent battles, marking their
spaces in particular ways and calling on the memories of another
Partition to legitimise the sundered lines. Not always are Muslims
sensitive to the derogatory implications of living in 'Pakistan'.
Sometimes, they adopt the term themselves, proudly. For Muslims
in Bandra Plot, the fact that their area is called 'Pakistan' seems to
signify its potency and strength in the eyes of potential attackers,
who are thereby frightened of 'trying anything' there. One recalls
here Goffman's analysis of the flaunting of their traits by the
'militant' stigmatized (1973: 138).

In several areas in these cities I was shown the logistics of the
use of space in riots and conflict: the alleys and back-ways through
which attacks are surreptitiously and somewhat stealthily initiated
as well as, more problematically, the sites selected for open, hector-
ing demonstrations of identity.[6] While Muslim and Hindu religious
processions have commonly been the cause of conflict for routing
their way through each other's areas, Muslims in Mumbai tried to
make a distinction between the accepted celebrations of the annual
calendar and the deliberately instituted *maha aartis*, which are now

recognized to have contributed a great deal to the exacerbation of violence against them, especially in 1993 (Srikrishna n.d.).

As one Jogeshwari survivor asserted:

If you go from here to the station, near the station on the main road there is a small temple. There are other temples in that area. However, they will not do the *maha aarti* in those temples. They will do it in this one, on the main road. Now it is the main road, there is the station. In the inner area, they will not do, but near the station. Now, there is the main road. The station is there. You will find Muslims there, Hindus will also be there. They will do it there and any Muslim who is passing by will be targeted, abused.

I digress a moment to point out a particularity of the speech used here. Everywhere in this survivor's speech as well as in other narratives in this chapter we find the reduced, impersonal and anonymous reference to the 'Other', the enemy, referred to simply in the third person plural. This mode of reference emerges particularly, as Mehta and Chatterji (2001: 234–35) point out in their study of Dharavi conducted in 1994 and 1995, when people are talking of the violence itself, its provocations or its outcomes. It is much rarer when people speak of the specifics of surviving and rebuilding their lives. The longer duration under review here, however, allows us to notice deeper ambivalence and to reckon with the impossibility of positing such neat dichotomies. While Muslims like to emphasise that most Hindus are not 'bad' people, 'they' holds its own as a malevolent spirit over their speech. It emerges sometimes as the attackers of the past, but oftener as the police and administration or particular political parties of the *very* present, against whom the Muslims perceive their struggle to be far from finished.

To return to our theme, space takes on peculiar qualities in periods of violence, which sometimes remain well after the worst of the conflict is over. In particular, is the aspect of its congealing, its contraction. In Baroda, a Muslim woman who returned to her home with its blackened walls, 18 months after the February violence, was pointing out which neighbours were involved with the attackers. 'Our area is okay', she said. 'This street is fine. It is there, behind from where people attacked', she said. She made it sound at a considerable distance, but when she took me and pointed out the area, she was talking about people from houses just two narrow lanes away.

What about the neighbours next door? She laughed uncertainly. 'My neighbour just came out to call me', she said, 'to give me home-made pickle. I talk to the children across our terraces. There is still *aana-jaana* [visiting back and forth] among us. But now there is very little trust'. The space of safety, the moral zone of trust is fissured and has contracted sharply.

The contraction of space emerges in a different way, when people speak about the detailed management of the violence. It lends a disturbing dimension to the visually available marks of destruction. Farhan's house in Baroda's Behrampura area was looted for seven long hours by rioters, after which the house was burnt using gas cylinders. One room at the rear of the large house was, however, left untouched. This room shares a wall with the house of his neighbour, a BJP party member. The boundaries between the hurt and the unhurt are almost unbearably slim. In Mandvi as in other commercial areas, shops belonging to Muslims, which were a little isolated, were selectively burnt. Those shops which were too close to shops belonging to Hindus were looted but were not burnt. In many areas, Muslim homes housing Hindu tenants remained untouched.

Space (and time) is marked by the location of new police *chowkis* and *thanas*. Every riot sees the creation, restoration or relocation of police beat posts and police stations. Muslims must be one of the most highly policed sections of the urban population in most Indian cities. A high concentration of Muslims is almost syn-onymous (or synchronous) with heavy (and also perhaps high-handed) policing. This is, of course, compounded by the fact that most Muslims live in congested, low-income areas, which are plagued with (and Muslims are not necessarily on the periphery of these activities) crime, petty thefts, smuggling and prostitution (see Chandavarkar 1998; Hansen 2003). Indeed, the reorganization of urban space in the wake of such horrifying riots could permit more effortlessly the production and maintenance of inequitable procedures for containing violence by the state.

People remember riots by recalling when and where police *chowkis* came up. Police are as much the 'Other' for Muslims as

Hindus are. For Muslims, the *chowkis* invariably represent control over them; the keepers of the *chowki* vanish when violence occurs and Muslims are attacked.

Sultana recalled that the police *chowki* near her house in inner Baroda had come up after the 1982 riots. But its presence did not help them in 2002. The police stated to the Muslims that they had not been told to protect them. They told the Muslims that they must not counterattack if stones are thrown. Only if a mob comes into the colony could they do something in reaction. A Muslim policeman attached to the *chowki* had fired in the air when a mob had come earlier on. He was transferred by afternoon that very day.

The coming up of new police *chowkis* only feeds popular perceptions and official definitions of particular areas as 'trouble spots', 'communally sensitive' or 'volatile'. The continuous presence of the police force at the threshold, as it were, the constant patrolling of such areas, the frequent 'combing operations' or house raids in the event of acts defined by the state as acts of terror, combined with the detainment, usually of males, for 'questioning' in such cases—all these inherently *produce* instability for the outside observer even as they apparently control it. On the other hand, those *within* view such mechanisms as displays of state power generating constraint, while bypassing the standard routes of gathering evidence or prosecuting through the courts.[7]

Each riot brings the police closer to the heart of the slums and shanty towns where the *chowkis* are set up; police *chowkis* often mark the Hindu–Muslim 'borders' in these localities.

People in the area recalled that prior to 1984, Govandi in Mumbai came under the control of the Trombay police station. Riots in 1984 led to the setting up of the Deonar police *thana*. In 1992–93, Govandi was badly affected by violence. After this, the Shivaji Nagar police station was set up. Cases of 1992–93 still come under the Deonar police station.

The last 10 years have deeply divided Mumbai's social space. Flags, green and saffron, are now used increasingly to demarcate 'Muslim' and 'Hindu' residential spaces, not just religious ones. Perhaps these also protect in a situation of violence, by allowing those who are running for shelter to recognize and avoid 'enemy' spaces. Tridents are these days displayed on vehicles. '10 or 12 years ago', said a retired police officer to me, 'police intelligence recognized illegal activities by these flags'. A saffron flag was often a sign for a place selling local liquor clandestinely. A green flag more often than not marked a place selling illegal cannabis-based drugs such as *charas* and *ganja*. 'Today these flags have assumed a totally different meaning'.

Many public spaces in Mumbai became, in effect, Hindu spaces in the immediate aftermath of the violence. In some cases, this demarcation persists long years after. In Tulsiwadi, the neighbourhood park in which both Hindu and Muslim children used to play, is now rarely frequented by the latter. Muslims perceive themselves to be denied access to public space, while Hindus hegemonize it and use their domination of space physically and vocally to terrorize Muslims. A prominent elderly social activist from Mumbai said:

> Muslims are not allowed to pray outside the mosques, on the road. They do not do this on purpose: the mosques are too small. All kinds of limitations are placed on their processions. However, if Ganpati *pandals* are allowed a certain amount of space, no action is taken even if they exceed this limit. In their processions, they shout all kinds of illegal slogans against Muslims. *'Is mulk mein rehna hai, to Hindu ho kar rehna hoga. Is mulk ka raj Hindu raj hai'* [If you want to live in this country, you will have to live as a Hindu. The government of this country is a Hindu government].[8]

An important part of the movement towards healing for Muslims, as many non-governmental organizations working with them have realized, is the process of recovery of rights to use urban public spaces—for entertainment, for work or even for protest.

When Ariel Sharon was due to visit Mumbai in 2003, a number of Muslims of varying political affiliation got together with non-sectarian groups to protest against the visit at the city's popular zone for such protests: Hutatma Chowk in south Mumbai. Sharon had left the country by then, but the number of police personnel surrounding the area was larger than the number of the protestors. One of the participants said to me: 'This is the usual case. When

Muslims come out to protest, they are hedged in like this. We have to constantly fight for the right to be here'. One recalls the words of the social activist from Baroda: 'We have to confront them in those very spaces'.

In Ahmedabad, Muslims venturing to the Law Garden, a well-maintained municipal park, have had threats issued to them or taunts thrown at them. From a different perspective, in Baroda, in August 2003, a family of Muslims who had only recently returned to their shattered houses after the violence of 2002, told of their fears for their safety the next day, a day on which the Congress had planned a *bandh* against the government's policies. We had little with which to reassure them: each *bandh* in the past year had brought uncertainty and tension for the Muslims in particular. My companion, a Gujarati Hindu and social worker, told them:

> I cannot say what will happen. Probably there will be no vio-lence since it is a *bandh* organized by the Opposition. But if you feel unsafe, go back to where you were staying earlier. If you cannot go there, go anywhere. If nothing else, go to Kamati Baug [Maharaja Sayajirao Public Garden] and sit there. Let's see what they will do. Don't stay at home if you are frightened. Don't take any risk at all.

The defiance of asserting 'citizenship' lies in trying to enforce the neutrality and safety of highly visible public places, trying to see how far a government, already under heavy scrutiny following the violence, will dare to go. It also speaks, of course, of the extent to which norms had been shattered in the past months, when no space, public or private, could guarantee safety.

I turn briefly to a consideration of the fate of sacred spaces as a result of violence. The terrible difference of the 2002 violence of Gujarat from any earlier violence has been underlined by the *subsequent* treatment of places of worship. Places of worship have been attacked and destroyed in all inter-community conflicts. Rebuilding these by local state authorities together with the people has been part of the typical mechanisms of peace-building followed over the decades. The first major place of worship to be destroyed and *not* rebuilt is, of course, the Babri Masjid. It is not surprising that after the demolition, the then Prime Minister, P.V. Narasimha Rao, had committed himself quite unequivocally, perhaps even

automatically, to the reconstruction of the *masjid*; the assurance
later vanished from the rhetoric of the Congress.

Rebuilding *masjids*, *dargarhs* and temples after violence has
been part of Gujarati state practice. It is a practice on which people
repeatedly commented, because of its striking absence following
the 2002 carnage. At this time, hundreds of small sacred places
were razed to the ground; debris was removed and the areas tarred
over. Where this did not occur, the authorities have manifestly
refused to accept the obligation to rebuild Muslim sacred sites. In
other words, standard administrative procedures for 'riot' management, however problematic these may occasionally be, were not
followed in the wake of the violence of 2002 in Gujarat.

I began this chapter by speaking of the ease with which the map
of terrorism can be located on the map of the physical isolation of
Muslims. Newspaper headlines routinely speak this language:
'Mira Road is a haven for terrorists', for example (*The Times of India*,
16 September 2003, p. 3). When these conjunctions are so readily
made, Muslims have to struggle constantly against the implicit
judgements of anti-nationality and criminality. The presence
of Muslims in any positive effort against terrorism, for peace or
relief work is highlighted by well-intentioned media persons. For
Muslims, though, the subtle implication is that 'normally' they
would not be involved. As actor Farooque Shaikh said in the context of the August 2003 blasts in Mumbai (*The Times of India*,
2 September 2003, p. 14):

> This time too, headlines were made out of the fact that Muslims
> had helped victims and donated blood, as if this was an extra-
> ordinary happening. The whole thing should've been reported
> without singling out any particular community.

There can be other implications of the isolation of community:
security, especially for women. A Muslim woman with a small
child and holding a large bag got on a local train at Kurla. As she
told another passenger, whom she recognized as a Muslim: I'm
going for a wedding. The bag holds clothes and jewellery. Normally
I would not go alone. But my husband put me on the train and he
said: 'There will be no problem. You will just get off at Mumbra
and your brothers will be there'.

displacement and subjectivity

When we look at spatial displacement due to the riots, we find that individual trajectories of movement both gel with the larger patterns and reveal their singularity. Why did people move? Simply out of a sense of fear of their neighbours? Many families stayed behind: they had no choice. Families moved when resources and circumstances made it possible for them to do so. While several families moved permanently, *many more* moved temporarily, living in relief camps or with kin in 'safe' areas until their homes were rebuilt and minimal safety ensured. Displacement was sometimes the result of a combination of circumstances. In Kausar's case, movement resulted from the fact of her parents' divorce, which took place under the shadow of the Mumbai riots. Her mother moved with the two children not to a Muslim-dominated area, but a 'neutral' one, a place, far from central Mumbai, which had not seen riots in the past and, more importantly, one where she could afford a small home. Saira returned to her locality after the violence, but moved back, for a long period, to her natal home; her husband had taken the opportunity of the chaos created by the riots to abandon her and her six-month-old child.

Obviously kin ties and available and accessible networks of support apart from affordability and simple 'safety' work together to determine where people think of moving. Security in a Muslim-dominated area may nonetheless be bought at a price. For some, the price is greater social control. Hazira Ali, who moved to Kurla (East), when the taunts of her Hindu neighbours made it difficult for her to continue living in her earlier neighbourhood, was now closer to her married daughter. Surrounded by well-meaning Muslims, she could leave her children at home without fear, when she went out to work or shop. However, she had to deal with constant surveillance and veiled comment from her own people about her other daughter, who despite having passed her teens was not yet married off. Hazira continually fights off pressure to defend her daughter's right to study and pursue a career, in an environment just barely conducive for education for girls.

Displacement can take other forms: when people could not move, they sometimes sent their wives or children away. This has led to the long-term dispersal of families which once lived together, and their scattering, sometimes over vast distances (see also Kanapathipillai 1990: 321–44). Nevertheless, the option is often taken, by families keen to secure their young from further violence. Haji Abdul Rehman sent his youngest son to live with his brothers in the Uttar Pradesh village from which he came. This enabled the defraying of costs as well as provided security for at least one son in the event of future riots. Firdaus' wife lives in the village, several hundred miles from Mumbai. He travels to visit her and his children on the weekends. Several people from Naroda–Patia and Shah Alam took advantage of a Mumbai philanthropist's offer to pay for the board and schooling of their remaining children as well as the orphaned children of their areas in her school in Raigarh district of Maharashtra.

Always, movement implicates radical changes in the nature of one's interactions. Sometimes, these irretrievable shifts in social worlds have been embraced for positive and creative outcomes. I will tell just one story here briefly, that of Feroz Ashraf, a middle-class Muslim, who was compelled to move from Malad to Jogeshwari (West) after the Mumbai violence. As he told me: 'My son almost dragged me here. He told me we must move'. The housing society in which he lived was divided: some advised him to leave, others said they would look after his family. In the end, it became obvious that protection could not be taken for granted in the event of an attack. The family moved to a relief camp in Millat Nagar and later sold their flat. In moving, he lost the 'secular ethos' he was used to and was propelled back into the circle of community, with which, not being a practising Muslim, he had little in common. He lost 'Holi and Diwali', which he used to celebrate with verve. As he said, 'When we came to Jogeshwari, it was the first time in my life that I was staying in a "Muslim area"'. For a while, Ashraf resisted getting intimate with his neighbours. However, his growing awareness of their poor conditions of life spurred interest. He began to visit the mosque to establish firmer links with the community and to get involved thoroughly with welfare and education activities among the deprived Muslims in his neighbourhood.

riot in the time of memory

Everywhere in this chapter, we must remember that the idea of time is not as an empty vehicle carrying history, so to speak. Time is very much a product of subjectivity and the action of human beings. It is something dynamic. In other words, the sense of time being employed here derives from Koselleck (1985) who argues that time is not merely a medium in which histories occur. Rather, histories occur *through* time not simply *in* it. The following paragraphs, hence, will attempt to trace what happens to time, indeed to History with the capital 'H', in the memories of witnesses of great social violence. Memories of riot invariably lead to stories of other riots, other violence. Communities and individuals typically extend the margins of violence 'backwards and forwards' (Das and Kleinman 2001: 26) creating narratives whose temporality breaks through the artificial world of the conventional 'anthropological present'. In other words, the time of memory of a riot is always longer than any one particular span of violence. In several of the narratives I often perceived violence linking itself with life trajectories. In many ways, a riot is marked as a disruptive event by authoritative, official voices (see Pandey 1990) and, today, the voice of the media. Riots are graded and hierarchized: major and minor, widespread or localized. Mumbai 1993 was a major riot: it was recognized as such by all, even those who quite innocently believed that Mumbai had *never* seen riots before. Nevertheless, at the level of individual experience the scale of a riot may be meaningless. For a family that loses its only son in a tiny skirmish, it little matters that the violence was not officially demarcated as 'major'.[9]

Or does it? It might in two important respects. The first is practical: compensation may often be available only for killings and injuries in collective violence officially designated as 'riot', as apart from some minor local skirmish. Second, large-scale violence is often taken to be impersonal and not preventable. It comes like a storm and overwhelms people: there is no escape. There is always the hidden query about lesser violence: could one have prevented it? Such logic allows people to come to terms with death by attributing it to an anonymous outside force, rather than any internal lack. However, these are differences of degree. Even in large-scale violence, particular areas or persons may be less or differently affected than others, not allowing survivors the cushion of such response.

Das (1990) records the case of a woman who, in the 1984 riots against Sikhs in Delhi, was one of the few to lose all her sons. Unable to experience her loss in terms of the collectively shared grief, she could not return to everyday life and, finally, committed suicide. In my own fieldwork, several cases arose of persons who could not fully place their losses within the framework of the overall violence that engulfed their city. Tabassum Appa, for instance, who lost her only son in the violence lamented that he had gone out to purchase milk, against her advice; otherwise, he would still be alive. Few people had been killed in the area: only those who ventured outside the Muslim-dominated *basti*. Yusufbhai and his wife who lost their son said, wrongly but without irony: 'There have never been riots in Bombay. Just this once and... this happened'.

Sometimes the stories of riots go right back to the time of Partition; sometimes they extend themselves even further into the past. There are attempts to both tie past and present as well as to foreground the present against the past. Some of these stories are for community consumption, narrated usually by men. When one listens to them carefully over a period of time, one hears fragments which repeat themselves and which are also to be found in the ideological tracts or speeches of members of Muslim religious organizations or Ulema, though there may continue to be fluidity about the way such ideologies are assembled by the individual imagination. Consider the voice of Haji Abdul Rehman from Dharavi:

Muslims have been targeted for 1,400 years. The Jews have been after them for all these years. America supports the Jewish cause. India has only been following in the footsteps of America and doing the work of the Jews for them. Islam has been suppressed and injustices have continued to be done against those who believe in it.

In this interpretation, violence against Muslims in India is only a mimesis of violence done to Muslims in other parts of the world. Hindus and the particularity of Indian history are worked out of this narrative; the agency rests only with the Jews. The idea that riots are part of a history of Muslim suffering repeats itself again and again. A member of the Raza Academy of Mumbai, reintroduced further on in the text, had exactly the same words to use:

> The biggest enemies of Islam are the Jews. And this enmity is not recent. It began 1,400 years ago. Indian policy has been with Palestine; we [our organization] are against friendship with Israel. What Israel has done to Palestine, they [the attackers] are trying to now do with Muslims in Bombay and Gujarat.

As Alauddin from Ahmedabad had to say: 'If you suppress Islam, it will leap up again'. The idea of Muslim suffering and eternal revival re-emerged in the voice of a member of the Jamaat-i-Ulema e-Hind:

> Though Muslims sacrificed a great deal for freedom, they have never experienced the happiness of freedom. They have seen only killing and violence. This is their illness and their destiny. They are suffering it, bearing it. If Muslims are uprooted a hundred times, they will come back a hundred times.

Such understandings of riot located in Islamic sacred history and the *longue durée* of Muslim past on the subcontinent only rarely emerged in survivor's narratives. Other readings, folding larger historical events into personal and familial histories, were more usual, especially among women. In Baroda and Ahmedabad, where women were still locked in the images of the violence, tales tended to be fragmented and to trail off. Memories were often in the present tense and returned again and again to the scenes of violence. Mumbai's women told very different stories, where the violence of riot had been woven into tales of life; middle-aged and older women looked back at their lives, domesticating 'riot' by placing it within an overall framework of coping. These differences are further discussed in another chapter.

Here, let us consider these voices. Men in Baroda spoke of the difference between earlier riots and the violence of 2002. As Farhan said:

> In earlier riots we had only the gate burnt or stones thrown from outside. We would go out and face it and attack back and things would be over. This time it was: *'Ghar jale to ban mein; ban mein lage aag'* [We ran from the burning house to the forest and the forest caught fire].

Women also spoke of the shift but in different tones. Sultana spoke of riots in 1969 and those which she saw in 1982.

> Earlier, the houses used to be attacked from the back or the gate was burnt. People might go away, but at least one old person would stay behind. The gate or the outside would be attacked. The attackers would harrass and go away. If you did not go outside, it was safe. Not this time.

In both men's and women's speech, time is told from riot to riot, though there emerges a shift from continuity to discontinuity. In both, the twist of time is partly imagined through the re-orientation of spaces, which is itself a troubling signal of an altered world. In Farhan's speech the shift emerges as one from equivalence or the competitive balance of power, a feud-like situation, to one of being dispelled from the space of the social altogether. The political continuity of Muslims has been de-recognized; they are no longer legitimate competitors in the once orchestrated time of ritual violence.[10] Muslims have been announced as *per se* 'abnormal', their anomalousness jutting out into 'normal' time. Women do not speak the language of retaliation at all. Sultana motions more towards ostracism manifest through the intrusion of private, domestic space, the space of women, which had, according to her, once re-mained inviolate. The exterior was always prey to trespass; now interiority has been transgressed. She does not mention but implicitly hints at what other women spoke of more: the violation of women, which was rampant in 2002, a violation which in the manner of its enactment sought to annul Muslim sexuality and regeneration and signal a close to a Muslim future.[11]

To turn to other ways in which riot engaged memory. In Mumbai, some women could only compare the violence of 1993 to that of Partition and, often, that was not a Partition they themselves had been witness to. Stories of violence have filtered down inter-generationally through grandparents and parents. Saira's father lived in that part of Punjab that went to Pakistan at Partition. Being poor and not having much land, the multiple displacements of Partition brought him ultimately to Mumbai, where he started driving a taxi. As Saira said: 'We had never seen such violence as in 1993, only heard about it from our parents'. Sultana in Baroda talked of the violence of 1969, about which her mother and grand-father had spoken to her during her childhood. She herself, as a young girl, saw communal violence in 1982, 'when this police *chowki* came up' she said, pointing to the one right across her front door. While violence extends itself back in time in these narratives of women, it is particularized, not generalized. It relates to the specific displacement or damage said to have been suffered by members of the family, rather than to transcendent notions of an unaltered past of Islamic agony.

Traumatic memory imprints itself on time in other ways. When I first tried to meet Tabassum Appa in Mumbai, it was Ganesh Chaturthi. She refused, saying it was not safe even for me to come out on that day. This was a little surprising, for Mumbai's greatest violence was not associated with festive time. Unmistakably, though, the knowledge that festivals have long been possible occasions for communal conflict has seeped into imagination and practice. The 'affliction of memory', in Allen Young's words (2000: 258), cruelly and inexorably, holds in its grasp the life-world of the sufferer. Fridays, days of community prayer for Muslims, have become marked in Baroda and Ahmedabad. Often protests and *bandhs* have been timed for that day of the week, and in the many months of 2002 these were repeatedly accompanied by violence.

One of the most intriguing characteristics, especially of women's remembrances, was their typical elision of a framing narrative within which they located their losses. For most women in Mumbai who suffered extreme losses particularly in January 1993, the early phase of the violence (in December 1992) is hardly mentioned at all. Some women do not mention 1992 at all. Some, at the most, acknowledge that at that time '*jhagda suru ho gaya tha* [the clashes had started]'. While it may be mentioned when specific discussion is taking place of contemporary politics, in these narratives of loss there is almost *uniformly* no mention of the Babri Masjid at all. This is despite the fact that performed acknowledgement is profound: Mumbai's Muslims remain still, afraid and alert every 6 December.[12]

In such accounts, 'riot' begins with or just before the specific loss of the speaker. Najma Bibi's account begins 'It was the 13th [of January]'. It was the day she lost her son. Hazira Ali acknowledged that they had heard violence was going on in the city, but had not expected anything to happen in their area. Then, on the 10th, the mobs came to her house. She lost her husband and son. There are many more such examples. In fact, people rarely even mention that they are talking about January 1993 rather than December 1992; they assume that the listener must understand this.[13]

Of course, the erasure may have several reasons behind it. For one, the passage of time since the violence itself may have dimmed the relevance of chronology, leaving only the sense of personal hurt as a reality. Women in Baroda and Ahmedabad, for whom violence was still a relatively fresh memory, were not able to similarly remove *Godhrakaand* [the Godhra episode] from their narratives, though the extremely close conjuncture of events in this case makes this understandable.[14] Women may also have got accustomed to telling their stories in the way that had presumably been demanded so many times of them by the media, committees of enquiry and bureaucracy: as accounts of loss suffered, no frills attached. Muslims reacted with violence in December; in January they were the targets of sustained attacks.

All these reasons do not fully explain why men did not usually leave out mention of Ayodhya and Babri Masjid when they spoke of the 1993 violence. For certainly, brevity was not imposed on the women when they spoke with me. Even so, it was men who more typically felt the need to locate their words in political and national frames; women did not. Their words were connected by the frame of life-history, struggles with kin and family, with children and, indeed, with men. The postures adopted by men could sometimes be related to the influence over them of religious organizations. Certainly, they could be read within the logic of the 'community honour' men and elders held themselves responsible for, honour that was savaged by the breaking of the Babri Masjid. It is not that women were incapable of thinking politically or working their localized and personal narratives into the unfolding of larger, national events. The work of rebuilding life by mediating fragile kin links, fractured neighbourhood relations and recalcitrant bureaucracies often brought these women in conflict with men, even of their own community. A stress on 'community honour' typically has restricting implications for women. It is not surprising if they should attempt to hold themselves at somewhat of a remove from it.

symbol as stigma

One of the troubled questions feeding this study was regarding the ways in which ritual and embodied markers of Muslim identity are brought under the glare of ridicule and made violently conspicuous at moments of terrible strife. Muslim women who wear some form of the *purdah* and do not bear *bindis* are easily identifiable. Given the practice of collective community worship, Muslims are also rendered very visible at the mosque and hence easy to target. The process of identifying and homing in on specific groups and persons through the use of census data and surveys has become alarmingly routine over the last decades through the persistent labours of Hindu communal organizations. Even so, every riot equally hunts for and swoops down on the identifiers (and those who bear them) of difference turned that much more obtrusive because of the excess of violent imagery associated with them through the reach of communal propaganda.

Goffman's incomparable treatment of stigma defines it as an 'undesired differentness' which turns 'normals' away or calls forth negative attention from them. Blemishes of body or character or contaminations of 'race, nation, and religion' can equally be stigmatized (1973: 14–15). Identity is locked into alienating attribute by stigma; symbol reduced to slighting stereotype. Various scholars have analysed aspects of Muslim identity through this lens. This is the way in which Mehta (2000: 92–93) looks at how the symbol of circumcision (*khatna* or *musalmani*) among Muslim males, multi-valent in meaning is stigmatized as *katua* especially at moments of conflict between Hindus and Muslims. While *khatna* implicates masculinity in a particular way, it is the sign of community marked on the body. The links with spirituality and the removal of bodily impurity are never far behind.

For Hindus, though, circumcision marks the Muslim as irreversibly different. The circumcised become, with violent disparagement, the *katua*, the 'cut' and, the use of the term perhaps, indicates the attempt to finish off the Muslims through castration. Another slur more commonly used, especially in Mumbai, to indicate the circumcised Muslim is *landiya*. Mobs have been commonly known to come shouting slogans such as '*Kamar pe lungi muhn men pan, bhago landiya Pakistan*' [You who wear *lungis* and chew betel leaves, you circumcised ones leave for Pakistan] (Engineer 1995a: 162), '*Landiya ko pakdo*' [catch the circumcised], '*kaat do uski*' [cut it off] and the like.

Tendulkar[15] recollects how he heard for the first time, in the days following the fury and violence of the Partition, the word being employed to refer to Muslims.

> The word was *Laandya*. It literally meant 'an animal whose tail has been cut', generally a dog. When I heard it for the first time in a new context to suggest a Muslim, I could not catch its meaning. Then I was enlightened on the subject by my Hindu friends. Muslims were circumcised after their birth. I, too, tried to use this word in my speech... and felt very self-conscious, embarrassed and thrilled at the same time. That word became a household word during those days among the boys of my age. They would always refer to a Muslim as *Laandya*. The bias which had been intentionally and unintentionally sown in our minds when we were children now grew into confirmed opinion. Muslims were an aggressive, rowdy, savage, rabid minority... dogs with a cut tail.

Female Muslim identity is similarly signaled, for attackers, by the use of the *burqa* and the significant absence of the *bindi*. The *burqa* and *purdah* practices of Muslim women along with their presumed 'higher fertility', apparently indicated by increasing Muslim birth rates, coalesce to produce a vision of the inaccessible, elusive female 'Other', threatening the Hindu community through her excessive fecundity. For Sarkar (2002), the violent, punishing possession of the Muslim woman's sexuality emasculates and dishonours the Muslim male. The killing of her children signals the beginning of the end of Muslim perpetuity. Not for nothing does the victorious slogan circulating in Gujarat claim (Sarkar 2002: 2876):

The volcano which was inactive has erupted
It has burnt the arse of *miyas* and made them dance nude
We have untied the penises that were tied till now
We have widened the tight vaginas of the *bibis*.

My interest in this section lies in interrogating the effortlessness of identification of the 'Other' apparently assumed in such a thesis. For as Malkki (1995) has pointed out in her analysis of the butchery of Hutus by Tutsis, while the killers employed a repetoire of racial and physical signs to aid victim selection including height, colour or style of walking, doubts were always possible. All Hutus were not short and stocky, nor all Tutsis tall and graceful. In their insightful work on political violence in Northern Ireland, Feldman (1991; 2000) and Burton (1978; 1979) write about 'telling': the habituated practice of discerning Protestant from Catholic in order to avoid or to attack. As Burton (1979: 62) defines it:

Telling... takes the form of a series of semiological systems whose signs (name, face, demeanor, dress, phonetic or linguistic variations, color, icons, and territory...) are connected to confessionally signified groups....

While the segregation of social spaces provides a particular *certainty* of identity in some cases, it is not always sufficient. According to Feldman, 'telling is more frequently and forcefully applied to potentially out-of-place bodies and to ethnically plural spaces, such as the mass transport system or the downtown commercial centre' (2000: 53). How did it work? In the case of Belfast it strove to establish *certainty* by assembling a complex of images. Thus, 'telling' brought together a cluster of imaginary and projected images of body politics and of ethnicity made flesh, as it were. Such visual imaginaries transcribed themselves onto the dress, deportment and physical features of the ethnic 'Other', wherever encountered, and played a critical role in the construction of identity in urban everyday life.

As with the literature, victims in Gujarat seem to concur in the apparent assurance of identity thus provided. As an autorickshaw *wallah* in Ahmedabad said: 'If they cannot tell from looking at us, they make us take off our pants. Then they know'. The *burqa*'s and *ridha*'s high visibility was equally troubling: 'If two or three women are out in *burqas*, they become easy targets for attack'. One might here choose to record Bharucha's (2003: 4238) conversation with his publisher in the wake of the Babri Masjid riots:

> The publisher looked at my beard, sniggered, and then remarked, somewhat derisively: 'You must be an intellectual'. I didn't quite know how to respond to his sarcasm, so I said the first thing that came to my mind: 'Actually I've been mistaken for a terrorist'. To which the publisher responded without batting an eyelid: 'It's a good thing you haven't been mistaken for a Muslim'.

The menace is unmistakable, but the doubts linger. Is identification so easy? Feldman himself, more tentatively, tends to argue (2000: 53):

> Victim selection in sectarian violence frequently fuses social space, the body, and ethnicity in a visual diagnostic for homicide, and this can directly result in the killing of someone from one's own group in space classified as Other—a consequence that reveals the discrepancy between the visual-spatial imaginary and the real.

Or even the dress or physiognomy classified categorically as 'Other' may belie. In our ethnography, everywhere we come across fluttering images of the lack of certitude as, for instance, the retired police officer who said:

> On 7 January [1993] between Nagpada and Grant Road there were 16 dead bodies. Seven of these were Muslim, and the killers were also Muslim. How did they die? They happened

to have come to the area in a tempo with the slogan 'Jai Sri Ram' imprinted on it. The same thing happened with Hindus as well. When they set out to attack, they did not think that even Madrasis and Bengalis wear *lungis*. They forgot that even Shivaji wore a *dadi* [beard] when they caught those with *dadis* and killed them. Sometimes, those killed were Hindus.

Who the attacker is remains critical. In Gujarat, in the face of huge attacking mobs, some women did escape to safer areas by donning saris and *bindis* and putting that mark of 'safety' on their daughters' foreheads as well. Women sometimes used Hindu names; one notable activist even made an identity card in an assumed Hindu name in order to be able to move around with a degree of safety during the period of violence. When attackers are expected to emerge from the same social world as the victims, however, such identifiers are ambiguous, even irrelevant. As one Muslim woman in Mumbai said:

> During the 1992–93 riots, my daughter was in college. Her friends, out of love, said to her: 'Shaheen, put on a *bindi*'. I told her not to do it. I said it did not make her safe. 'You are, anyway, safe from those who do not know you. With those who know you, even putting on a *bindi* will not save you'.

With the *burqa* and *ridha*, it was not always transparent whether the distress was with its easy identification or the fact that its use also always implicated mobility restrictions for Muslim women, which meant that, in times of conflict, they were unable to run to safety or *even to know in which direction danger lay*. In Baroda and Ahmedabad, this anxiety was echoed by several women and men. A long-time resident of Mumbai, Feroz Ashraf said:

> During my childhood I had heard of large scale communal violence in Bihar in 1946–47. Since women in most families followed strict *purdah* and did not even know the lanes in the area they could not escape. Huge mobs of rioters came and many women were raped and killed. After that in many parts of Bihar, including in my family, the *purdah* system was discontinued. We wanted our women to be able to protect

themselves in such an eventuality. They should know their way around and not have to depend on someone else during a crisis.

The case of the *ridha* is specially, and tragically, ironic. The garment, worn by Bohra women, with its pastel shades, lively prints and embroidered edges, is distinctly different from the black swathes of the *burqa*. It is so different, in fact, that the religious head of the Bohras, the Syedna, had in the past specifically ordered the women of the community to don it as he directed the men to wear the golden caps specific to this community. This was a measure meant to ensure that Bohras were never confused with (other) *Muslims* and so protected from targeting by Hindus in the event of a communal conflagration. How the logic so viciously backfired in 2002, when Bohras were, in so many areas, made specific targets of attack is a story that is now sadly well-known.

And is circumcision itself—that indelible mark so painfully inscribed on the body—so incontrovertibly incriminating? Perhaps one should recall Mukul Kesavan's jewel of a novel *Looking Through Glass* set against the backdrop of Partition in which the Hindu narrator needs to undergo circumcision for medical reasons. For several terrifying minutes, the reader accompanies the narrator as he flees from what are likely to be Hindu mobs in Delhi's streets, until he reaches the safety of a relief camp, harbouring mainly Muslims. What would the mob have done to him, if they had pulled down his trousers? Would his pleas of being Hindu have mattered? We are left to imagine.[16]

In a recent paper, Appadurai (1998) is centrally concerned with looking at a range of situations of violent ethnic conflict triggered, according to him, by the uncertainties of globalization, though the link is not clearly explored. The emphasis is on analyzing how the body is the site and target, in macabre and degrading but not necessarily arbitrary or unpredictable ways, of graphic forms of violence and violation. While Appadurai approaches his theme with the same query as many other scholars—the indeterminacy and instability of 'body maps' carried by different sides in a situation of ethnic conflict—his conclusions reach completely elsewhere. He is apparently keen to alter established theory by arguing that rather than producing 'abstract tokens of ethnicity out of the bodies of real persons' (1998: 920), ethnic violence produces 'real persons' out of bodies and deceptive labels.[17] This surprising thesis receives little substantiation and is, in fact, somewhat essentialist, even 'primordialist' (Bharucha 2003: 4247) for it appears to suggest that 'person' can be located in some way on the body of a victim in the act of ritual killing. Apart from other difficulties, for all its reliance on it, the paper leaves startlingly unexplained the way in which it defines the concept of person.

It remains difficult for me to follow Appadurai's trail and, acknowledging debt to Feldman's classic mode of analysis here, I stress the question of the ambiguity of identification, for reason that many survivors have noted the *accenting* of signs of Muslim identity in the period *after* the riots. Thus, attributed differences are duly actualized; real ambiguities turn into reified certainties ('dead certainties', as Bharucha [2003: 4248], would say but not in Appadurai's original sense of 'real persons'). It is occasionally possible, at the micro-level, to perceive these changes instating themselves in particular families or individuals. As a Mumbai Muslim who lost a close relation in the 1992–93 violence said:

Many Muslims began to grow beards after the violence. They felt that if they are being attacked even without a beard, why not wear one and be Muslim properly at least. We are proud of being Muslim and are not afraid of dying.

Another Muslim woman argued:

The *burqa* is a refuge. If I am a Muslim and there is no one to save me, if the government does not save me, why shouldn't I be a good Muslim so that my God will save me.

Apart from such shifts captured in the practices of specific families, other elements of change are discernible: in particular, the growing influence of certain Muslim religious organizations and an orientation, among some at least, towards faith more rigidly defined. Out of the same constellation of circumstances, there may also arise rejection, as we have seen, of some of the visible symbols of Muslim identity. Though the possibilities of conflict are rife everywhere, it does not always emerge. We explore, elsewhere, the tensions.

notes

1. A very important aspect of Mumbai's violence in 1993 is the simultaneous terrorist bomb attacks at 12 different sites that took place in March leaving hundreds dead and wounded. This is now recognized as an act of 'revenge' for the violence done to Muslims in 1992 and especially in the early months of 1993, and was probably managed by certain Muslim underworld elements. This too has, no doubt, contributed to some of the urban unease characteristic of today's Mumbai, though Mumbai-ites are now being said to take these things in their stride.

2. A friend mentioned how it was being said proudly of the posh Sama area in the wake of the violence: 'It has been cleaned up'.

3. A BJP stronghold and the site of a terrible massacre of Muslims in the violence in Gujarat in 2002.

4. There has been some important documentation of 'gerrymandering' in Indian urban areas and more detailed work needs to be done in this area. To give one example, prior to 1973, Jogeshwari (East) comprised one political ward. At that time, facilities came to the entire ward and serious political attempts were made to unite communities. In 1973, the area was bifurcated into two wards. Ward 99 came to comprise mainly Muslims. By 1992, five wards had been created, reflecting further the demographic shifts in the area, recorded briefly in our text. One of these wards, 129, comprises Jogeshwari's Muslim pocket. Thus, the construction of ward boundaries has legitimized the segregation and political isolation of Muslims (Punwani 1991; YUVA 1996).

5. When I was doing fieldwork in Muslim areas, I also understood with something of a shock what role sheer differences in elevation can play in times of violence. So many of these low slum areas occupied by Muslims are surrounded or bordered by tall buildings of 'Hindu' apartments. These buildings became the vantage points, the positions of strategic advantage, from which attacks could so easily be launched on the congested areas below.

6. In 2002, however, in Gujarat, mobs roamed freely during the violence. One of the indicators of the strength of organization of the riots emerges from the sheer size of the 'mobs' that came to loot and kill, particularly in the cities. The various reports have spoken of mobs of thousands, reaching up to 10,000 and more in some cases (Human Rights Watch 2002). Mobs of such size cannot consist only of the social rejects, the 'criminal classes' often charged with indulging in communal violence nor can they be mobilized or organized into killing squads without a degree of involvement on the part of those in authority. While in the Mumbai riots of 1992–93, the largest number of people died in police firing or in incidents of stabbing, in Gujarat the action of the mobs can be clearly identified as the biggest culprit. This shows the extent to which neither fear nor a need for furtiveness seems to have been felt by the killers and marauders.

7. One day last year when I visited Dongri, the person I was supposed to meet was in a tizzy. The brother of a friend of hers had been suddenly picked up by

the police for 'questioning'. On phoning the police station it was discovered that he was stopped because he was found chatting with someone who was apparently an acquaintance of somebody whom the police were on the look-out for. As my friend said to me:

> They just have to enquire with some of the responsible people here. In such a congested area, where everyone knows everybody else, all are fully aware of who are the people likely to create trouble. And people do want to avoid trouble. So they will help. Why do they pick up innocent people?

One is constrained to wonder if the police are so wholly innocent of the knowledge that they could enquire and get correct information before picking people arbitrarily off the streets. Was this really a data-collection exercise or one which sought to control through instilling fear by seemingly random acts of state power?

The State Minorities Commission comes across numerous cases daily that seem to suggest the abuse of state authority. In an apparent search for members of the banned Students' Islamic Movement of India (SIMI), Kurla was cordoned off at 2 am one morning, while police woke up people and went through houses and huts in the poorest areas, questioning over a 100 young men on the footpaths. There are several such cases that may be evidenced.

8. While my informant was asserting that such slogans are routine, the Srikrishna Commission report as well as other enquiry reports on the Mumbai riots of 1992–93, pointed to the role of *maha aartis* in precipitating violence. After the performance of these *aartis*, mobs shouting slogans fanned out in attack of Muslims.

9. Scholars have earlier spoken of 'riot' as a break in time, a period almost carnival-like in the way in which reversals of norm reign and in the ways in which mobs perform the torture of inversion not available to them individually or in 'normal' time (see Sarkar 2002; Mehta 2000). What is discussed here is more survivors' location of riot in the trajectories of their lives but also the ways in which their understanding of hurt often recedes from the larger framing narratives in which it is sought to be enclosed either by community leaders, government officials or even academics.

10. Ritual in the sense of the remembered specificity and the patterned nature of each attack and its reprisal (see Appadurai 1998).

11. I quote extensively from Sarkar (2002: 2872–76): '... Hindu mobs swooped down upon Muslim women and children with multiple but related aims. First, to possess and dishonour them and their men. Second to taste what is denied to them and what, according to their understanding, explains Muslim virility. Third, to physically destroy the vagina and the womb, and, thereby, to symbolically destroy the sources of pleasure, reproduction and nurture for Muslim men, and for Muslim children. Then, by beatings, to punish the fertile female body. Then, by physically destroying the children, to signify an end to Muslim growth. Then, by cutting up the foetus and burning it, to achieve a symbolic destruction of future generations, of the very future of

Muslims themselves'. See also Rakesh Shukla, 'Basal Instincts: Repressed Sexuality as a Trigger for Violence', *The Times of India*, 16 April 2005, p. 12.

12. The fear relates to the possibility of violence from the 'Other' (Hindus). It also relates, increasingly, to the possibility of terror strikes by Muslim radical groups or individuals for which they may have to face reprisal.

13. In their analysis of Dharavi, Mehta and Chatterji (2001: 212) argue with a considerable degree of emphasis that narratives of violence are made possible by the event of the Babri mosque and the violence in Dharavi itself. The material here shows that, for women at least, that assertion must be challenged.

14. Violence against Muslims in Gujarat broke out the very day after the burning of the train at Godhra. In 1992, the initial violence was more by Muslims especially against places of worship, though there were some incidents of stabbing. It appears that these were largely the work of criminal elements. The Srikrishna report (nd.: 22) states that: 'As far as the December 1992 phase of the rioting by the Muslims is concerned, there is no material to show that it was anything other than a spontaneous reaction of leaderless and incensed Muslim mobs, which commenced as peaceful protest, but soon degenerated into riots. The Hindus must share a part of the blame in provoking the Muslims by their celebration rallies, inciting slogans and *rasta rokos* which were all organised mostly by Shiv Sainiks, and to a marginal extent by BJP activists....

   Turning to the events of January 1993, the commission's view is that though several incidents of violence took place during the period from 15 December 1992 to 5 January 1993, large-scale rioting and violence commenced from 6 January 1993 by Hindus brought to fever pitch by communally inciting propaganda unleashed by Hindu communal organizations and writings in newspapers like *Saamna* and *Navaakal*. It was taken over by the Shiv Sena and its leaders who continued to whip up communal frenzy by their statements and acts and writings and directives issued by the Shiv Sena *Pramukh* Bal Thackeray.... Because some criminal Muslims killed innocent Hindus in one corner of the city, the Shiv Sainiks "retaliated" against several innocent Muslims in other corners of the city.... There is no material on record suggesting that even during this phase any known Muslim individuals or organizations were responsible for the riots, though a number of individual Muslims and Muslim criminal elements appear to have indulged in violence, looting, arson and rioting.'

15. Vijay Tendulkar, 'Muslims and I'. The article originally appeared in *Communalism Combat* and was accessed at www.geocities.com/indiafas/India/the_prejudice.htm on 2 July 2004.

16. Within but also beyond the question of the ambiguity of identification, lurks that of identity itself. The violence may not differentiate between Muslims by nationality or sect or even between believers and non-believers, the 'secular' or the 'fundamentalist' and so on. In Baroda, Professor Bandookwala, whose house was savagely attacked in the 2002 violence, said in an interview:

   I was convinced that as I lived my life in as secular a manner as possible, with total commitment to the country, the RSS [Rashtriya Swayamsevak Sangh] would accept me as an Indian first and a Muslim afterwards. Just one day earlier, the Baroda Savarkar Samiti had invited me to speak on Savarkar Day. I was the first Muslim to be ever so invited.... Then the next day disaster struck. I lost my house, my books, my car and, most important, my inner spirit....

('The Day my Spirit Died', *Outlook*, 1 April 2002). Some of these issues of identity will form the theme of a later chapter.

17. He asserts the thesis against the arguments of Feldman (1991) and Malkki (1995). Both hold that violence brutally reduces persons to gestures of ethnicity.

chapter three

muslim marginality and
the experience of violence

In this chapter it may appear at first that we travel a little away from our main theme. Closer attention though will undoubtedly reveal the inner network of associations that links the themes we traverse here and through the rest of the book. There is a need to construct a background against which we speak and alongside of which we have heard and will hear the voices of the individual Muslims who talk through these pages. To whom do we refer is a significant question and this chapter makes it possible for us to locate our speakers a little more attentively. There is a need to consider numbers for here they tell a story that we may not like to confront: the extent to which Muslims are on the margins of the structures of economic, social and political relevance in India. For this reason, there is a deliberate decision to place the numbers at the forefront here, rather than confine them to an appendix or schedule 'attached' to a chapter or the book.

As we shall try to uncover, there are ways in which numbers play on minds, affect decisions and are important for defining courses of action at the level of the individual or the group. Many Muslim groups in Mumbai realized with a start after the violence of 1992–93 that the lack of their representation in the hierarchies of power made them particularly vulnerable to attack. This realization has been at the core of action taken by such groups and individuals to 'reform', as it were, Mumbai's Muslim community. Elsewhere in this book, we will be tracing some of these grass-roots movements, and for that a statistical view of Muslim absence in the higher echelons of power everywhere is extremely revealing.

It has become commonplace for Indian historians and sociologists (Ahmad 1973; Chandra, 1984) to counsel us not to consider Muslims in India a cohesive or structured community. Nevertheless, it is advice that bears repetition for, as we well know, all communal discourse so manifestly refuses to adhere to it. While 'Muslims' are constructed as a monolithic community in both political and communal discourse (there is constant reference to the 'Muslim vote', for example), they are often obliged to see themselves as one, both as an act of ultimate faith as well as due to the compulsions of pursuing common safety in the face of violence.

What are the differences among Muslims? Regional and linguistic differences prevail as do caste and class ones. There are Urdu-speaking Muslims across several northern, central and southern states including Bihar, Uttar Pradesh, Madhya Pradesh, Maharashtra, Karnataka and Andhra Pradesh, there are also Muslim groups in Tamil Nadu, Kerala, Gujarat or Assam for whom their regional language is the mother tongue. Muslims marry according to different regional and caste customs. They are further divided on sectarian grounds. Shi'ism and Sunnism is not the only distinction; there are Aga Khanis and Bohras. There are also Ahmediyas, whom many Muslims do not consider among the faithful at all. Sunnis are, moreover, divided by adherence to a variety of schools of thought. Deobandis and Barelwis may sound familiar; there are also those who call themselves Wahhabis as well as those who belong to the Tablighi Jamaat and to the Ahl-e-Hadith. Some of these differences become relevant during or after periods of strife. Indeed, Muslims in Gujarat and Mumbai whom I spoke to represented a whole range of these distinctions.

It is sometimes surprising even to those who might be expected to know that India has more Muslims than even many Muslim countries. It has perhaps the third largest Muslim population in the world. A little over 12 per cent (2001 Census) of India's population of 1,028,610,328 is Muslim. Indeed, every eighth Indian is a Muslim. Don't we need to learn to live with them, and in haste? It would certainly seem that these numbers alone should be sufficient to denote Muslims not as India's largest minority, but as her second majority and to ensure that Muslims figure significantly in any plans for the future of India, economic, social or political. However, this is manifestly not the case.

From those who adhere to versions of the ideology of Hindutva, of course, we obtain the rather ugly idea that Indian Muslims are somehow a disposable quantity. While Bandukwala may not have his figures completely accurate, he brings out well this dubious notion and why it is so needs revision: 'There are 140 million Muslims spread over every *taluka* of India. Their spread and their involvement at the local level is so deep that the VHP slogan of '*Musalman ko kabristan ya Pakistan*' [For Muslims either the graveyard or Pakistan] can only be laughed at.'[1] Ishaq Chinwala, Sarvodaya activist from Baroda, said:

In these riots there was a loss of Rs 36,000 crores. The number of Muslims killed was 3,500. It cost Rs 10 crore to kill one Muslim. How long can this go on? We have to stop thinking of killing and learn to live with each other.

Subjective assessment aside, the costs of inter-community strife, and that *just* in economic terms, are formidable: for Muslims, for non-Muslims and for the public exchequer. In the case of the 1992–93 Mumbai violence, to take an example, Tata Consultancy Services surmises the loss of gross value of output of goods and services to be about Rs 1,250 crores, the loss of trading business about Rs 1,000 crores, the loss of exports Rs 2,000 crores, the loss of tax revenue for the government 150 crores and loss of properties 4,000 crores. To this may be added the sums necessarily spent in relief and compensation for the victims (Engineer 1995b: 257). The 2002 violence in Gujarat gives us figures even more damaging. The Gujarat Chamber of Commerce and Industry estimated trade loss to total Rs 7,280 crores, production loss to be Rs 2,258 crores and loss to the self-employed to be Rs 700 crores. The state lost each day Rs 20 crores in income from sales tax.[2]

As it flies in the face of some rather glaring evidence, then, the dismissal of Muslims may be assumed to be fed merely by popular prejudice; it does, however, need to be critically evaluated for its worth. When one commences this exercise, it begins to be understood why Muslims may be so easily targeted. Indeed, the contrariness of popular prejudice stands out the more. Muslims are believed to be a 'pampered' minority, yet their exceedingly low position in the urban occupational hierarchy is obviously equally well grasped.[3] The niche position of Muslim labour in the economy may also be read differently. As auto repairman and constituent of the transport industry's ancillary divisions, the Muslim may be disdained, but his absence could be very damaging. Even two months after the Gujarat violence, Muslim truck drivers were too fearful to return to work. They constitute 50 per cent of the total number of truckers, and transporters, often Hindu, were simply unable to resume normal business without them. Vehicles were off the road and even ordinary repairs were frustratingly impossible, for the small businesses, 60 per cent of them run by Muslims—repairing punctures, providing batteries or replacing windshields—had not re-opened.[4]

It would seem therefore that we do need to give more thought to the socio-economic profile of Muslims and its implications with respect to our main subject. The collection of statistics on the social and economic development of different ethnic and religious groups in India has never been given the importance it deserves. It is particularly true that data on Muslims is hard to find. While there is perhaps no intended malice here, it is possible that the ghost of the 'communal' hung so much over politics that sanction for such documentation was not available. It is only in the current census that such data has become available, and has, predictably, been mired in considerable controversy with ideologues of various kinds taking issue with it. The census data came out a little too late for me to rely on it extensively, but I have recorded some of the figures here. For the most part, scholars have relied on the National Sample Survey (NSS) Series among other research resources, which does allow us glimpses into the status of Muslims since Independence.[5] A recent survey on Muslim women conducted by Zoya Hasan and Ritu Menon (2004) and commissioned by the Nehru Memorial Museum and Library (New Delhi) provides some revealing data as does some of the current work of the National Council for Applied Economic Research (New Delhi) in association with the United Nations Development Programme (UNDP). This data was put together in the India Development Report of 1999. This chapter intends to focus on the statistics, to provide what is available and to think about the ways in which such data acts on the minds of Muslims and others in the context of ethnic and communal strife.

It may not be out of place here to give a profile of the spread of Muslims across some of the major states in the country, as documented by the 2001 Census in order to give us a sense of their distribution, which is useful when placed as a backdrop to thinking about large-scale communal violence. (Table 3.1)

Table 3.1
Muslims to total state population (in percentages), 2001

State	Percentage	State	Percentage
Above 20 per cent		Between 10 and 20 per cent	
Assam	30.91	Uttar Pradesh	18.49
West Bengal	25.24	Bihar	16.53
Kerala	24.69	Karnataka	12.22
		Maharashtra	10.6
Between 5 and 10 per cent		Below 5 per cent	
Andhra Pradesh	9.16	Meghalaya	4.27
Gujarat	9.06	Orissa	2.07
Rajasthan	8.47	Himachal Pradesh	1.96
Tripura	7.95	Punjab	1.56
Madhya Pradesh	6.36		
Haryana	5.78		
Tamil Nadu	5.56		

Source: From 2001 Census figures.

This data may be placed against statistics that show the propensity to riot of different states. Utilizing newspaper coverage, Ashutosh Varshney (2002: 98–100) has tried to analyse the Indian pattern of communal violence from 1950 through to 1995.[6] While he does not tabulate the total number of communal incidents by state over this period, his data shows us that Gujarat has the highest per capita rate of deaths in communal violence, followed by Maharashtra, Uttar Pradesh and Bihar. Though recent occurrences may be beginning to bring some shifts in this conclusion, his material for the period under study shows that Orissa, Rajasthan and Kerala can be described as communally peaceful states. What we do learn from placing these two sets of data against each other is that population *per se* appears to have little to do with levels of inter-community violence. Density of population or other social factors must be explored.

As an adjunct to these figures, therefore, it may be pointed out that of the 356 districts of India, only two have a majority of Muslims, when we leave out Jammu and Kashmir. In just about 30 districts, Muslims constitute a little less than a third of the population. Against this, it becomes a little less astonishing the extent to which Muslims can and have been taken for granted in official estimates or public policy-making. One can also begin to gauge the sense of Muslim groups in Gujarat, for instance, scattered across villages and districts and now systematically hounded out of these and not allowed to return. The Islami Relief Committee in Gujarat has made specific attempts to re-house scattered rural households in the always only relative safety (given the overall numbers) of bounded community housing complexes.

employment, assets, income and muslims

Hasan and Menon's survey points out that half a century after Independence, Muslims on the whole have an average standard of living lower than even that of Other Backward Classes (OBCs) (2004: 21). Their standard of living is well below that of upper-caste Hindus. On the whole, Muslims are just slightly better off than the Scheduled Castes, perhaps the poorest section of the Indian population. The immense fragility of Muslim participation in the economy and the low level of their asset accumulation in general as we shall see only further intensify their vulnerability to the displacements, physical and economic, caused by situations of continual communal strife.

Other recent figures confirm the incidence of poverty and deprivation among Muslims. A nationally representative survey of 33,000 rural households conducted in 1994 by the National Council of Applied Economic Research (NCAER) as well as 16 state level reports and 28 village studies completed by the organization during 1995–98 (Shariff 1999; 2000) show the results of relative economic and social deprivation. What emerges from the data is the high incidence of poverty among Scheduled Castes and Scheduled Tribes, followed by Muslims compared to the rest of the population. Fifty per cent or more of Scheduled Castes and Tribes live below the poverty line as compared to 39 per cent of Hindus. For the Muslims, the percentage is 43. The incomes of the Scheduled Castes, Scheduled Tribes and Muslims are 32 per cent, 24 per cent and 11 per cent below the national average.

The India Development Report 1999 (Shariff 1999) shows the average rural household income for Muslims to be below the national average of Rs 25,653. While at 22,807 rupees it is higher than that of Scheduled Castes (Rs 17,465) or Scheduled Tribes (Rs 19,556), it is lower than that for Hindus (Rs 25,712) and for other minority groups. Using this data, Razzack and Gumber (2002) chart the differences between Hindus and Muslims in five states: Bihar, Karnataka, Kerala, Uttar Pradesh (UP) and West Bengal. Each of the states whose data is compared here has a high percentage of Muslims, nearing or above their representation in the country's population. Bihar is 14.81 per cent Muslim, Karnataka 11.64 per cent, Kerala 23.33 per cent, Uttar Pradesh 17.33 per cent and West Bengal 23.61 per cent. Together the five states are home to nearly 64 per cent of the Indian Muslim population. The tabulation shows that Muslims have a lower level of income than Hindus in UP, Bihar, West Bengal and Karnataka. Only in Kerala is it higher than that of Hindus as well as higher than the national average. There appears to be no explicit link between income and literacy, however. While both are equally high in Kerala, UP's Muslims have the second highest annual and per capita income of the five states, but the lowest levels of literacy.

The data also shows the lack of access to productive assets (land, in particular), employment and wage stability of Muslims in relation to Hindus and to the national average (Razzack and Gumber 2002). Khalidi points out (1995: 54–55) that contrary to popular perception, agriculture is the occupation of the largest segment of Indian Muslims. Most Muslim peasants are to be found in the rice-growing areas, which have not been much changed by the Green Revolution technologies. Many Muslims are also involved in non-agricultural rural occupations. When looked at in relation to Hindus, the data begins to show greater disparities. Twenty-one per cent of rural Muslims as opposed to only about 12 per cent Hindus in rural areas are engaged in non-agricultural occupations (cited in Shariff 1995). If one considers data regarding the ownership of cultivated land, a critical resource in an agrarian economy what is found is that relatively more Muslims are landless than are Hindus or Christians. Only 10 per cent of Muslims have land in excess of 5 acres and nearly 60 per cent fall in the category of owning no land or less than one acre. The figures for Hindu in these two categories are 20 per cent and 45 per cent respectively (see Razzack and Gumber 2002; Khalidi 1995). The 1990s is a period of the further marginalization of Muslims in terms of access to land. In 1987–88, 40 per cent of rural Muslim households cultivated little or no land, compared to 34 per cent among Hindus. By 1999–2000 the proportion of households so adversely affected had risen in both religious groups, but more so among the minority community: 51 per cent among Muslims and 40 per cent among the Hindus.

John and Mutatkar (2005) compute and analyse statewise estimates for urban and rural areas of 17 major Indian states. They use unit level consumer expenditure data from the 1999–2000 (55th round) NSSO statistics. Using average monthly per capita expenditure (MPCE) as a proxy for the average living standard of a group, they show that Muslims have the lowest average consumption level in both rural and urban areas at an all-India level. The difference between Hindu and Muslim average consumption levels is but 4 per cent in rural areas; it rises to 22 per cent in urban areas. The prevalence, depth and severity of poverty are highest among Muslims in urban India, while these are highest among 'Others' in the rural areas.[7]

It is worthwhile considering the patterns of employment across religious groups as brought out in the 1987–88 NSS data (Table 3.2). The survey also provides us with information on the distribution of persons by occupation and religion in urban India. Prior to analysing Table 3.2, it is useful to look at that data. In the light of such figures, it is unsurprising that Muslims hold a grievance against the state for rarely considering them among society's weaker sections. While looking at employment and work participation rates for Muslim women, one must be careful to distinguish whether religion per se or the perceived limitations it places on Muslim women's mobility is the cause of the low figures, or some other factors (Table 3.3).

Together these two tables give us a peek at employment distribution across religious communities. What is significant in Table 3.2 is the high number of Muslims who are self-employed in comparison to Hindus or Christians. Muslims are marginalized from the more stable and perhaps more prestigious domain of regular and salaried employment. Forty-six point seven per cent Hindus are involved in

Table 3.2
Patterns of employment by religion in India, 1987–88

	Self-employed (a)	Regular Workers (b)	Casual Workers (c)	All	Work participation rate (d)
Urban females					
Muslims	60	15.7	24.3	100	11.4
Hindus	45	27.7	26.4	100	15.9 does not add up to 100
Christians	34.3	51.5	14.2	100	23.6
Urban males					
Muslims	53.3	29.9	16.7	100	49.1 does not add up to 100
Hindus	39.1	46.4	14.5	100	52.0
Christians	29.7	53.4	17.0	100	48.9 does not add up to 100
Rural females					
Muslims	67.9	3.0	29.1	100	19.6
Hindus	59.9	3.6	36.5	100	33.7
Christians	57.6	9.9	32.4	100	37.3 does not add up to 100
Rural males					
Muslims	59.0	7.5	33.5	100	50.5
Hindus	58.5	10.1	31.4	100	54.2
Christians	52.1	12.0	35.9	100	–

Source: National Sample Survey, 43rd round, 1987–88, Schedule 10. Percentages may not add up to 100 because the non-reported part of the percentage is not represented in the table.

Table 3.3
Distribution of persons by household type (occupation) and religion for urban India, 1987–88 (all figures in percentages).

Occupation	Muslims	Hindus	Christians	Others
Self-employed	53.4	35.9	21.4	44.6
Regular wage/salaried	28.9	46.7	56.1	38.3
Casual labour	13.4	12.1	12.3	10.5
Others	4.3	5.4	10.2	6.6

Source: NSS, 43rd Round, 1987–88. Table 27U; p. S 57.

regular wage/salaried employment in contrast with just 28.9 per cent of the Muslims. Muslims are but marginally more represented than Hindus or Christians in the category of casual labour. Later data (Shariff 1999) also shows that Muslims continue to get a larger share of their income from artisanship and petty trade as compared to other social groups; in contrast, their income from agriculture is far below the national average and less than that earned by Hindus from this source. NSS data (Rounds 50 and 55 for years 1993 and 1999–2000) reveal the unsettling trend of increasing disparity between Hindus and Muslims during the 1990s with respect to consumption, education, employment and landholding, though literacy rates of both communities showed a gradual improvement (Hasan 2004: 248).

In Table 3.2, we get some information on Work Participation Rates (WPR) for the different religious groups. It is not very surprising that the male WPR should be uniformly higher than the female WPR regardless of which group we consider. While the female WPR is lower than that for males in rural and urban areas, there are also significant inter-group differences to be noticed. The WPR for Muslim women is only 11.4 per cent in urban areas, while it is nearly 16 per cent for Hindu women and about 24 per cent for Christian women. Again, the WPR for Muslim women in rural areas is also substantially lower than that recorded for the other groups. It is just 19.6 per cent in contrast to a WPR of nearly 34 per cent for Hindu women and 37 per cent for Christian women. The number of Muslim men in regular work is considerably lower than the number of Hindu or Christian men in both rural and urban areas. Stable and regular work, tied usually with better pay and working conditions, appears to be out of bounds for most Muslims.

The Muslim Women's Survey conducted by Hasan and Menon sampled data from 40 districts spanning 12 states.[8] The socio-economic status of Muslim households was compared with a picture of the Hindu population broken down by caste, using a relative development index. While the data underscored the dismal numbers of women in the workforce, the reasons were seen to be complex. For one, in rural areas, low work participation rates particularly in agriculture link up with the low rates of ownership of land by Muslims as a whole. Further, there is considerable difference across regions, the rates in the south being higher than in the northern or central states. This suggests that there are varying structures of opportunity in place in different regions which constitute Muslim participation in the labour market differently. Thus, Muslim women are disadvantaged not by religion *alone* but by a complex of forces including the play of class and gender. As Hasan and Menon state (2004: 242), with respect to Muslim women:

> The axes of class, gender, and community are contingent on each other for they are constructed and experienced simultaneously, and thus create overlapping and mutually reinforcing forms of disadvantage and deprivation.... [Muslim women] are disadvantaged... as members of a minority community, as women, and as poor women.... Gender discrimination coalesces with class inequalities in perpetuating a *structured disempowerment of Muslim women.*

With respect to ownership of assets and amenities other than land, Muslims again fail to do as well as other communities. While house ownership is high across all social groups in the rural areas, the quality of housing tends to differ. Except in Kerala, across the other states, a much larger percentage of Muslims than Hindus live in *kutcha* houses. Again, access to electricity is imbalanced in favour of Hindus except in the states of Kerala and Karnataka. More Muslims than Hindus in most states have access to protected water. However, access to piped water supply is higher for Hindus (25.3 per cent) as opposed to Muslims (19.4 per cent). Draught and milch animals are important resources in the countryside. Muslims are relatively less well off in the ownership of draught animals and milch animals than Hindus. While less Muslims than Hindus report ownership of draught animals, the number of animals owned by each reporting household is very often higher than that for Hindu households. Thus, there is a greater degree of intra-group disparity: ownership among Muslims is concentrated in fewer hands. Muslims are relatively less well off than Hindus with respect to the ownership of milch animals. Only 38 per cent Muslims (and 38.1 per cent of Scheduled Castes) report the possession of milch animals as compared to 49.6 per cent Hindus or 44.9 per cent of the Scheduled Tribes.

muslims in administration, law enforcement and politics

With respect to Muslim representation in government services, armed forces or the police, the data is equally insufficient. However, the Centre for the Study of Secularism and Society in Mumbai has made a concerted effort to carefully scrutinize available sources to put together some statistical material. Utilizing several publications, including various issues of *Muslim India*, they have obtained a profile, if incomplete and even somewhat dated, of particular aspects of the social and economic development of Muslims in India. Theirs is perhaps one of the few attempts in this area, though the National Minority Commission and State Minority Commissions have been known occasionally to initiate such efforts.[9] Another brilliant piece of work is that by Khalidi (2003); this is a reasoned and carefully researched analysis of the place of Muslims in the armed forces, police and para-military forces leading up to an argument about the relation between these figures and the role of these forces during periods of communal conflict. (Table 3.4)

Table 3.4

Muslims in public employment: All India central services

Service	Year	Total	Muslims	Percentage
IAS	Total in 1981	3,883	116	2.99
Income Tax I	Total in 1981	1,753	50	2.85
Railway Traffic and Account Services	Intake during 1971–80	881	27	3.06

Source: Mushirul Hasan, Legacy of a divided nation, p. 282 from *Muslim India* June 1983, pp. 261–63.

Except in very rare instances, the percentage of Muslims in the central cadres of the Indian Police Services and Indian Administrative Services has never proceeded beyond 5 per cent. The Gopal Singh Report (1983) showed the percentage of Muslims in the IAS in 1980 to be 3.27, while Scheduled Castes were at 9.9. In the Indian Police Service, Muslim representation was at 2.7 per cent

(Scheduled Castes 9.8 per cent) and in the Indian Foreign Service at 3.37 (Scheduled Castes 16.48). During the same period, Muslim share in the Central subordinate services stood at a mere 1.56 per cent. The study further showed that out of 75,953 employees in 150 central government offices in 14 states only 3,346 were Muslim (4 per cent). The comparative percentage for Scheduled Castes was 14.46.[10] In all this, we must remember that figures of success rates of Muslims cannot be simply compared to those of success rates of Hindus or others. We need to understand how many Muslims actually applied for such services and went through the process—examinations and interviews—of selection. What several grass-roots Muslim groups and also individuals in Mumbai, particularly, felt was that not enough Muslims apply to such services, *believing that they will never be accepted*. Clearly, a cycle of lack has set in that needs to be broken. I always confronted these groups with the logic: 'Muslims need to apply, more and more of them. How many will they refuse?' Moreover, Muslims have fallen behind in educational qualifications and this is a reality that they are grappling with in the wake of the pogroms of Mumbai 1993 and Gujarat 2002.

With respect to the number of Muslims in the Lok Sabha, the figures are extremely poor. While there was some rise in the 1980s, there seems to have been a progressive descent since. Moreover, even at their highest (1980), the numbers are not exactly satisfactory. Muslims have, therefore, rarely had adequate position in the spheres of power and decision-making. Under the circumstances, it is perhaps not surprising that there is considerable ignorance about their social and economic conditions as well as a relatively high level of indifference to the question of the improvement of these. No government has been able to put at the centre of their agenda the basic concerns of the educational and socio-economic backwardness of Muslims. Political reticence supported no doubt by a certain kind of Muslim religious leadership has worked to centralize issues concerning personal law while disregarding or suppressing other problems. (Table 3.5)

Several reports, including the Srikrishna Commission Report, on the riots in Mumbai, have made the point that the police are more often than not biased against Muslims and that special efforts

Table 3.5
Muslims in Lok Sabha

Year	Total	Number and Percentage of Muslims in Lok Sabha	
1952	489	23	4.70
1957	494	22	4.45
1962	494	22	4.45
1967	520	29	5.57
1971	518	29	5.59
1977	542	33	6.08
1980	542	49	9.04
1984	543	45	8.28
1989	543	33	6.07
1991	543	28	5.15
1996	543	27	4.97

Source: Adapted from Syed Fazle Rab, 1998: 41 (Siddiqui).

need to be made both to recruit more persons from minority backgrounds as well as to de-communalize the police.[11] We shall pursue further, later in this chapter, the place that diversity in the security forces of a country has in producing greater impartiality and promoting the trust of citizens. It is interesting though not altogether surprising to note that Muslims express strong faith in the army's role during communal conflict, despite the poor representation of their own community in its ranks. The impartiality of the army as opposed to the police or paramilitary forces is further evidenced by the fact that Muslim leaders have repeatedly called for immediate deployment of the army to quell riots. State governments have often delayed such moves. As Khalidi (2003: 95) says: 'The Congress Party and the BJP administrations in Maharashtra and Gujarat, however, both resisted and delayed Army deployment during the riots and pogroms against Muslims in 1984, 1993 and 2002'.

Figures for Muslims in the IPS are predictably miserable, but there is also no marked improvement in numbers when we proceed to consider the representation of Muslims in state level police forces. While there are no neat and accurate figures available, Khalidi has recently judiciously combined a variety of materials to come up with the figures in Table 3.6 with respect to the representation of Muslims in the IPS.

Table 3.6
Muslims in the IPS

Year(s)	Muslims
1947–56	1.55
1957–63	1.05
1965	3.58
1971–79	2
1981	2.85
1982	2.5
2002	3.65

Source: Adapted from Khalidi (2003: 71).

Figures for 15 states in the mid 1980s are compared with the representation of Muslims in each state in Table 3.7.

Table 3.7
Percentage of Muslims in police force by state

S. No.	State	Total Police Force	Percentage of Muslims	Percentage of Muslims in state population
1	Andhra Pradesh	63,147	16.6*	8.9
2	Assam	43,990	8.9	28.4
3	Bihar	83,323	2.0	14.8
4	Gujarat	63,092	6.2	8.7
5	Haryana	30,431	1.1	4.6
6	Karnataka	49,322	7.2	11.6
7	Kerala	34,375	9.5	23.3
8	Madhya Pradesh	88,673	4.2	5.0
9	Maharashtra	158,543	4.2	9.8
10	Orissa	36,995	2.8*	1.8
11	Rajasthan	57,167	5.6	8.0
12	Tamil Nadu	69,021	4.4	5.5
13	Uttar Pradesh	163,875	4.9	17.3
14	West Bengal	59,137	5.8	23.6
15	Delhi	50,798	2.3	9.4

Note: *Only Andhra Pradesh and Orissa seem to have more Muslims in the police force than their representation in the population.
Source: *Towards Secular India* 1 (2), *April–June 1991*.

It is when one looks at this data that one begins to understand the plaintive cry of a Muslim intellectual and social activist in Mumbai who said to me:

When the riots broke out, I looked around and suddenly realized that I did not know a single police constable in the city. I realized that the hierarchy of power is accessed through various levels. In my innocence, I had till then thought—why should I know a police constable? I'm a law-abiding citizen.

Several Muslims, in Gujarat as well as Mumbai, expressed their bewilderment and nervousness at confronting in the time of extreme violence, a police force that stood with and for the Hindus. In Mumbai during the violence of 1993, Additional Commissioner of Police, Aftab Ahmad Khan was taken off duty and verbally abused by his own subordinates, while in Gujarat in 2002 the small numbers of Muslim police officers were efficiently rendered ineffective.

We cannot overlook the menacing connections between minority representation and the question of impartiality. Khalidi (2003: 96–100) offers a reasoned analysis of the issue, which is well worth drawing from here. He divides states into three categories: low minority percentage but impartial performance, high minority percentage but biased performance and low minority percentage with partisan performance, even active hostility. He further acknowledges that under certain conditions—usually political in nature—a state normally not unbiased may exhibit impartiality. In the first category, therefore, he includes Kerala and West Bengal, and the cases of Bihar under Laloo Prasad Yadav and UP under Mulayam Singh. In both Kerala and West Bengal, the percentage of Muslims in the police force is far lower than their representation in the state population. However, the police in these states have typically acted impartially in situations of internal strife. In West Bengal this may be because of the CPI-(M)'s adherence to secularism, while in Kerala communist governance together with the place of the Muslim League in all coalition governments may have exercised some influence. UP and Bihar not otherwise known for the fair conduct of their police forces were spurred into secular behaviour at certain junctures: UP under Mulayam's regime in 1990 when the mosque's destruction was successfully prevented and Bihar under Laloo Yadav's regime in 1992, when he prevented riots from erupting all over the state following the demolition of the mosque.

The second category includes states such as Andhra Pradesh and Delhi (formerly a union territory). While Muslims are over-represented in the police in Andhra Pradesh, all the evidence shows that the force has acted in a manner biased towards the community in every major riot. Similarly, despite Delhi having 21 per cent Sikhs in its police force (as opposed to 6.2 per cent Sikhs in the population), the happenings of 1984 were not prevented. These figures together with the first set do not go on to prove that there is therefore *no* valid relationship between minority representation in the force and impartial conduct. The reverse is in fact true. The deciding factors, according to Khalidi are: *a*) the ideological orientation of the regime in power and *b*) the balance of power held by Muslims. In Andhra, despite Muslims being highly represented in the police force they are uniformly in subordinate rather than command positions. Not unexpectedly, the final category includes most other states. Yet, one must distinguish between active hostility exhibited in certain cases (Moradabad 1980, Meerut 1987, Mumbai 1993, Gujarat 2002) from feebleness and dereliction of duty (Ayodhya 1992).

The analysis must necessarily lead us to think more seriously about the conditions under which the police force may be expected to exhibit neutrality in situations of communal or ethnic conflict. Is diversity the only element that can ensure impartiality? That can surely be nobody's case, as the example of the Indian army so forcefully demonstrates. Non-partisan political regimes, the promotion of pluralism at the level of politics and society and the increase of the commitment of security forces to universal standards in human rights and notions of law, justice and due process are all enabling conditions. Moreover, it is neither possible nor perhaps desirable to seek to make representation the critical factor in employment in every profession. Nevertheless, the experience of India and other countries clearly manifests that non-diversified security forces increase substantially the dangers of discriminatory conduct and the perpetuation of ethnic or communal strife (Khalidi 2003). Ethnically and religiously diverse security forces are an advantage in protecting minority and vulnerable groups. Alone, they may certainly increase the chances of fairness; along with the other identified conditions, they would be virtually invincible.

We turn now to consider how well Muslims are represented in the judiciary. While figures for the Lok Sabha and the Union Cabinet are equally measly, combined with those in Table 3.8—for the bench—they serve to underscore the general invisibility of Muslims in spaces of command and decision-making in Independent India.[12] In the wake of the spate of acquittals that followed the Gujarat carnage against Muslims in 2002, several questions were raised regarding the possibility of Muslims getting justice through the courts when prosecuting lawyers belonged to Hindu right-wing organizations and when police cases were weak and witnesses allowed to turn 'hostile'. In the Mallika Sarabhai vs. Government of Gujarat case in the Supreme Court the point was even made by the plaintiff that a Muslim judge should be appointed as part of the commission of enquiry into the riots. The Court felt that such a plea went too far, but it expressed its unhappiness at the way cases had been dealt with by the Gujarat government till that date. After all this, there are still questions that need to be asked: are other minorities adequately represented? Do they feel, similarly, left out and isolated? Or are their numbers so small that they do not feel the pinch at all?

Table 3.8
High court: Number of Muslim judges (as on 1 September 1985)

Name of the High Court	Number of Muslim Judges	Total Number of posts
Allahabad	2	60
Andhra Pradesh	1	26
Bombay	2	43
Calcutta	1	39
Delhi	1	27
Guwahati	1	9
Gujarat	2	21
Himachal Pradesh	–	21
Jammu & Kashmir	3	7
Karnataka	2	24
Kerala	2	18
Madhya Pradesh	1	29
Madras	2	25
Orissa	–	11
Patna	4	35
Punjab & Haryana	–	23
Rajasthan	1	22
Sikkim	–	3
Total	25	428
Percentage of Muslims	5.8	

Source: *Muslim India*, May 1985.

education and muslims

We need to look at educational statistics for a while, in order to understand the impetus to education that seems to have spurred Muslims, especially in the wake of recent violence against them. Malika Mistry opens up for us another source of possible data on Muslims, the National Family Health Survey, which is conducted periodically by the Ministry of Health and Family Welfare (see Tables 3.9 and 3.10). In this nation-wide survey, for the first time in 1992–93 data was collected on education and exposure to the media, especially with regard to ever-married women of different religious groups. This was perhaps done with a view to understanding linkages between maternal health, fertility behaviour and levels of education and exposure to the media. This data was collected for ever-married women between the ages of 13 and 49. Mistry's collation of the data (1998: 6–8) shows that for India as a whole, 66 per cent of ever-married Muslim women are illiterate. Haryana has almost universal illiteracy among this category of women with 98 per cent illiterates, while Kerala has the lowest level of illiteracy at 21 per cent. 85 to 88 per cent of ever-married women are illiterate in the states of Uttar Pradesh, Bihar and Rajasthan, while 74 per cent are illiterate in Assam, 60 to 65 per cent in West Bengal, Karnataka, Delhi and Madhya Pradesh and 50 to 55 per cent in Maharashtra, Andhra Pradesh and Gujarat.

At an all-India level, only an astoundingly low 5 per cent of Muslim ever-married women have completed high school education and only 1 per cent has completed education above the high school level. The educational backwardness among Muslim women becomes all the more revealing when it is considered against the educational levels of women from other communities. Sikhs, Christians and Jains seem to do better on the literacy and education map in both rural and urban areas than either Muslims or Hindus. Indeed, at an all-India level there is not much difference between the proportion of illiterate women among Hindus and Muslims. While there are proportionately more illiterate Muslim women than Hindu women in most states, the numbers are more or less even in Karnataka and Maharashtra and show a reversal in Andhra Pradesh, Tamil Nadu, Madhya Pradesh and Gujarat (Mistry 1998: 7).

Table 3.9

Distribution of population by education, sex and
religion, rural India, 1987–88 (all figures are percentages)

Educational level	Hindus		Muslims		Christians		Others	
	M	F	M	F	M	F	M	F
Not literate	55.3	75	58.2	76.1	33.7	43.1	45.3	61.4
Primary or below	19.0	11.8	18.6	13.1	20.5	17.8	17.9	15.7
Primary to middle	22.7	11.2	19.1	9.9	35.4	29.2	25.5	19.4
Secondary	5.7	1.7	3.4	0.8	9.3	8.1	9.0	3.1
Graduate or higher	1.2	0.2	0.6	–	1.8	1.5	2.3	0.3

Source: NSS 43rd Round, 1987–88, pp. S 82–83.

Table 3.10

Distribution of population by general education, sex and
religion, urban India 1987–88 (all figures are percentages)

Educational level	Hindus		Muslims		Christians		Others	
	M	F	M	F	M	F	M	F
Not literate	25.3	42.2	42.4	59.5	18.8	22.7	18.0	31.2
Primary or Below	18.8	17.2	20.9	18.5	16.0	17.5	15.6	14.7
Primary to Middle	30.5	25.3	26.3	16.8	36.7	33.4	30.0	8.5
Secondary	17.2	10.7	8.0	4.3	20.1	20.8	23.6	17.5
Graduate or higher	7.9	4.2	2.3	0.8	8.1	5.5	11.7	7.9

Source: NSS 43rd Round, 1987–88, pp. S 85–86.

A variety of reasons have been given for Muslim backwardness
in education. These include discrimination in gaining admission,
the lack of access to languages other than Urdu in some regions,
the biased textbooks and alien school culture as well as the loss of
role models with the migration of the Muslim middle classes to
Pakistan after Partition. These may well have a profound effect;
so too does the economic backwardness of Muslims as a whole.
The India Development Report (Shariff 1999: 121) shows that while
70 per cent of Hindu children in the age group of 6–14 attend government schools, only 49.5 per cent of Muslim children attend these
schools. Again, it appears that the medium of instruction and the
content of textbooks and curricula may be proving hurdles to en-
hancing these numbers. Muslim girls and boys also tend to have
higher dropout rates than Hindu girls or boys, the reasons cited
being failure in examinations, loss of interest in studies and, especially for girls, social reasons.

The Gopal Singh Committee on Minorities set up by the Home Ministry came out with its report in 1983. The report indicated the abysmal level of Muslim participation at different levels of education attainment. Further interesting data was revealed by the report (see Razzack and Gumber 2002). While some 13 and a half lakh students sat for the matriculation examination, only 4 per cent of these were Muslims, even though in the states surveyed the percentage of Muslims was 11.28. The percentage of Muslims who passed the examinations, however, was 59; while the overall pass percentage for all students was below that, at 54. Again, the percentage of Muslims taking the Class XII examinations was only 2.49. Even here, though, the percentage of Muslims who passed (over 59 per cent) was almost as high as the overall pass percentage, which was 60.8. What has come to be clearly established is that Muslims show poorer achievement figures in education even if they are a majority in a particular district or geographical area and even in educational institutions founded and run by Muslims themselves (Khalidi 1995: 104; Razzack and Gumber 2002: 6). It is not surprising except that it should have come so late, that the government in 1986 in its *New Education Policy and Programme, 1986* declared Muslims along with neo-Buddhists to be educationally backward at a national level. (Table 3.11)

Table 3.11
Muslim enrolment in schools and colleges

Category	No. of districts surveyed	Percentage of Muslims in the surveyed districts	Total number of students	Muslim. students	Percentage
Elementary school	45 districts, 12 states	17.32	98.48 lakhs	12.20 lakhs	12.39
Secondary schools	38 districts, 11 states	18.56	19.64 lakhs	2.09 lakhs	10.70
High school	8 boards	12.00	13.44 lakhs	0.54 lakhs	4.00
Class XII	5 boards	10.30	2.26 lakhs	5,645	2.49
Engineering	9 universities	12.44	2698	92	3.41
Medical	12 colleges	9.55	2845	98	3.44

Source: N.C. Saxena, *Political Science Review*, Vol. 22, No. 2, 1983.

On the basis of their detailed analyses, Razzack and Gumber (2002) make out a path-breaking case for the 'empowerment of Muslims in India', a plea the likes of which perhaps has not been heard at any policy-making level and has not been made earlier by any public institution of such stature in the whole course of Independent India's history. Their state-wise study demonstrates that Kerala and Karnataka seem to stand out as states in which Muslims have done better socially and economically than any-where else in India. It is interesting to note that critical among the reasons that Razzack and Gumber forward for this finding is the fact that:

> The south more than the Hindi heartland in the North re-mained largely undisturbed by communal rioting. This has perhaps acted indirectly to the advantage of Muslim in giving them an equality of opportunity. 52.13% of the total Muslim population is concentrated in the three states of Bihar (12.58%), U.P. [Uttar Pradesh] (23.73%) and West Bengal (15.8%) as compared to only 11.83% in Kerala (6.68%) and Karnataka (5.07%). These three states—Bihar, U.P., West Bengal—*have a low human development profile and are also the states which have had a relatively larger incidence of communal rioting* [emphasis added].

I do not stress the remark for its veracity. Ashutosh Varshney's (2002) data suggests the possibility indeed, for it shows that Bihar, Uttar Pradesh and West Bengal are among those states with a much higher record of deaths arising out of communal conflicts, but it also shows that Karnataka is only a wee bit better than West Bengal in its record. The remark is emphasized for being perhaps one of the few explicit statements in contemporary scholarship, reached after a fairly systematic study of social and economic development, endorsing if not completely explaining, *that there is a link between Muslim backwardness and communal violence*. It is not an association that even someone as influential as Asghar Ali Engineer dares to even mention when he argues here (1998: 176–77) as elsewhere that the main cause of the backwardness of Indian Muslims lies in 'their social origin'.

Indeed, as Mishra and Singh (2002: 223) point out, while com-munal riots are 'an irritant to the economic development of Muslim society' and of the nation as a whole, little analysis has been undertaken to estimate the long-term consequences of riots. John and Mutatkar (2005) look at their data on urban Muslim poverty in the context of the history of communal tensions. They argue that the wider differences between Hindu and Muslim backwardness in urban areas needs to be understood against the backdrop of communal conflicts in India, which have been primarily urban conflicts between Hindus and Muslims. While there is no attempt here to read communal violence as *the cause* of Muslim backwardness, one would like to unravel implications of the argument for a while. Narratives of survivors certainly turn again and again to the role played by riots in depressing fortunes, changing around priorities, fracturing aspirations, fostering vulnerability and infusing instability.

The interconnecting trajectories of riots and the economic and social marginalization of Muslims is not a simple story told here (or anywhere) in the full; it will recur elsewhere and in other ways. There is one mode of approaching it that emerges from the proclaimed intentions of those who attack. Studies on communalism have rarely been shy of showing that many riots implicate naked economic rivalries (Gupta 2000). Indeed, violence against Muslims over the last several decades has involved enormous destruction of property and livelihood, apart from life (Engineer 1984, 1995b; Sarkar 2002). To give only one instance, in Gujarat several pamphlets circulated prior, during and after the violence in February 2002. One of them, issued by the VHP, asked Hindus 'to save our country by boycotting Muslims economically and socially' (Sreenivas 2002: 1). A leaflet distributed in Kalol town in north Gujarat asked Hindus to keep away from business establishments that are run by Hindu and Muslim partners (Khanna 2002).

> Recognize them and isolate them and do not buy anything from their shops, because, indirectly the Muslim partners also benefit from their profits. If you stop buying goods from their shops then the Hindu partners will learn a lesson and break away from Muslim partners.

Similar pamphlets have been recorded as circulating in other parts of the country as well (Human Rights Watch 2002).

There is little need perhaps to reiterate the fact that the spate of riots and pogroms in India since the late 1980s that have been linked to the RamJanmabhoomi movement have seen as their main target Muslim lives and property (Engineer 1995a, 1995b; Srikrishna n.d.). We need to perhaps uncover to some extent the pattern and effects of riots in the preceding decades, a task not rendered easy by the fact that accounts are not always clear or yielding of adequate data. For the period between the 1950s and early 1980s, A.R. Desai has to say (1984: 22):

The communal riots during the 50s appear to be more the result of sudden outbursts of group violence. From the 60s communal riots appear to be systematically engineered. The loss of life during communal riots in the 50s was much less. The total number of lives lost during the decade was 316. The loss of life in communal riots after 1960 grows in magnitude.

He further, records, particularly with respect to the more visibly devastating, major riots of the decades after 1960, that every such riot has seen a major loss in lives for Muslims. (1984: 22):

For instance, in the 1969 riots of Ranchi–Hatia, out of 184 killed, 164 were Muslims. In the Ahmedabad riots [also of 1969] out of 512 killed, 413 were Muslims, and in the 1970 Bhiwandi–Jalgaon riots, out of 121 killed, 101 were Muslims.

Drawing his material from various sources, he also shows the enormous losses in terms of property that have been suffered by Muslims over a series of terrible riots. For instance, in Ranchi–Hatia (1969), the Muslims suffered losses to the extent of Rs 14 lakhs. In Ahmedabad, in 1969, of the nearly 6,742 buildings destroyed in the riots, 6,071 belonged to Muslims (Desai 1984: 22).[13] Gupta (2000) dissects the records of a series of riots of the 1960s through to the 1980s. In the Karimganj (Assam) riots of 1968, 150 homes and shops destroyed out of a total of around 230 were of Muslims. In Bhiwandi in 1970, police records showed the total losses to be an incredible Rs 153,20,163. Muslims suffered losses to the amount of Rs 82,80,603 (Gupta 2000: 58).

Jalgaon in 1970 also saw fierce rioting resulting in deaths, injuries and economic losses all around. Taking his data from the Madan

Commission Enquiry which investigated the riots, Gupta (2000: 69) shows that 112 properties of the Muslims suffered arson and of these 87 were completely gutted. 250 properties were looted, while 28 suffered other kinds of damage. Out of the total losses of Rs 34,74,722, Muslims suffered economic losses to the extent of Rs 33,90,997. In Moradabad 1980 there was terrible conflict between the police and Muslims. Over 50 persons were killed when police fired at a mosque. Hundreds of Muslims were dragged out of their homes, arrested and beaten up. Curfew was imposed on Muslims (Gupta 2000: 87; Saberwal and Hasan 1984: 224).

Bhagalpur 1989 has been registered as one of the most violent episodes of post-Independence Indian history. Of some 1,026 persons killed, 876 are recorded to be Muslims. Over 3,000 houses of Muslims were gutted (Gupta 2000: 91–92; Engineer 1995b: 182). Riots in Ahmedabad, Surat and Baroda in 1992 saw large-scale destruction of property. In Surat, 12 small-scale and seven large-scale industries were destroyed and around 1,000 houses and shops looted and burnt. Some 900 of these belonged to Muslims. Similar observations have emerged from the study of other specific post-Independence riots (see Engineer 1984; 1995a; 1995b).

The figures, however disparate, do communicate to us something of the scale of loss for Muslims at a wider level. Mushirul Hasan (2001: 286) also records that since the 1960s particularly after Muslim craftsmen and artisans started competing with Hindu traders and businessmen instead of remaining mere workers in the industry, the competition gave rise to a series of violent conflicts between Hindus and Muslims. These conflicts hit all those cities where Muslims did well and their fortunes were on the rise: Moradabad, Khurja, Aligarh, Kanpur, Bhagalpur, Ahmedabad, Baroda and Surat. The Gopal Singh Report was also to comment on the bitter economic rivalries underlying the disputes during this period. The report said (quoted in Hasan 2001: 286):

The prolonged nature of violence and the target-oriented destruction of property lends credence to the theory that these are not sporadic expressions of communal anger but pre-planned operations with specific goals and targets in mind.... In our view, therefore, communal conflicts are more the result of the economic competition, which has often resulted in the majority community depriving minorities of their economic gains. Innocent lives were taken in this process to instill a sense of insecurity among the victims and destruction of the properties was aimed at uprooting them economically.

It is not the figures of loss of life and property due to communal conflicts, and these from different regions and times, that alone contribute to the making of everyday insecurity, to the extent that some riot survivors expressed it. Fear of the police and of arrest or of being picked up for questioning, these change as well. Several commissions of enquiry into post-Independence riots have pointed out the bias of the police against Muslims (see, for instance, Gupta 2000). Wilkinson, for example, notes (2002: 1579) both the disproportionate losses suffered by Muslims in major communal riots as well as the bias they are subject to. He remarks that in most major communal riots since Independence (including Mumbai in 1984 and 1992–93, Bhagalpur in 1989, Meerut in 1987, Jamshedpur in 1979 and Ahmedabad in 1969) minorities have suffered disproportionately. He points out (2002: 1579):

The Minority Commission's figures on communal riots that took place from 1985–87, for example, found that 60 per cent of the 443 people killed were Muslims and that Muslims had suffered 73 per cent of the Rs 9 crore in reported property damage.

He further elucidates the pattern of bias against the Muslims (2002: 1579).

Commissions of Inquiry prior to the 1980s found a similar pattern [of bias]. In Bhiwandi in 1970, for example, the Madan Commission found that only 324 Hindus were arrested compared to 2183 Muslims, that 'only Muslims died in police firings' and that half of the firings that took place were 'wholly unjustified'.

Interactions with the agencies of the state at the local level are, for Muslims, often fraught with the possibilities of corruption and humiliation. In the narrow slums that Muslims often reside, everyday life is edged with risk. As Sajjid, the young social worker from Jogeshwari (East) told me, as we sat in his narrow office on the first floor in a tiny lane of semi-*pucca* Muslim houses off the main street: 'This place is so *nazuk* (brittle); a riot could break out as we are talking here'.

Indeed, Jogeshwari (East) has seen no less than five riots over the last four decades. The recorded riots took place in 1964, 1974–75, 1984, 1990–91 and 1992–93, the last when Mumbai as a whole was engulfed in violence. Sajjid's words form a sharp contrast to those of secure, well-established Muslims and some Hindus living in Mumbai's prime residential areas, who often insisted, when I spoke to them about this project, that 1992–93 was the first time that *Bombay* saw riots. Clearly, the social space of *Bombay* here is an extremely narrow if fluctuating one, leaving out at will whole areas of the city where the working classes, daily wage earners and urban unemployed and underemployed lead far less secure lives.

Mumbai had seen riots in 1984, when they spread to the city from Bhiwandi. In Mumbai, Govandi, Pydhonie, Kherwadi, Jogeshwari and Kamathipura were affected by riots. In 1990, there were riots in Mahim, in 1987 in Kamathipura, in 1982 in Nagpada, Kherwadi and Dongri, in 1989 in Dongri and Imamwada, Mohammad Ali Road, Nagpada and Bhendi Bazar. As Ashutosh Varshney records (2002: 106):

> Until 1993, when horrible communal riots broke out, Bombay, India's premier business city, was often called an island of peace where local energies were mostly spent on cosmopolitan pursuits and monetary gains. This is simply not true. Bombay's modernity and cosmopolitanism have not precluded communal violence. Bombay was among the most communally violent cities even before 1993.[14]

The world of a majority of Mumbai's Muslims then is one in which the possibility of riot or of other kinds of violence and conflict is always around the corner. In Gujarat, the two cities where I did field work, Ahmedabad and Baroda, are among those most frequently fractured by riots and even Varshney's imperfect data shows that these cities account for three-fourths of the total riot deaths in the state from 1950–1995 (2002: 103). While Muslims in these cities certainly would be capable of making the distinction, without prejudice to the value of lives or property lost, between smaller bouts of everyday violence and the extraordinary violence of a 1969, a 1993 or a 2002, individual life histories and family narratives may not so nicely discriminate among these, for the shadow of death or destruction is not smaller in that register.

life-trajectories, life tragedies

From the macro-perspective of the previous sections, it is time to move into the subjective worlds of survivor stories, for they bring out, at the level of the individual and the family, the strategizing in the face of vulnerability that the larger picture we have drawn necessarily implicates. These accounts may be told again, if in different ways, in other chapters, for in their obvious multi-vocality they bear many tales.

Haji Abdul Rehman lives in a tiny lane in Dharavi, his 200 square foot tailoring workshop, now run by his oldest son, next door to his home. He moved here after 1993, when his home and 2500 square foot workshop in Mazagaon were attacked and destroyed. He says he named the persons involved but none were arrested; on the contrary he and several of his 'people', as he puts it, were charged with rioting and their cases are still in the courts, 10 years after. Because the police kept an eye on him in Mazagaon after his charge, and made life difficult, he had to move. He sent his youngest son, then barely three, back to Uttar Pradesh [his *mulk*] to live with his brother. His older son had to leave school and join the business. It is only this year [2003] that he acquired the financial ease and perhaps the confidence to recall his son to school in Mumbai. Haji Abdul Rehman, as his title suggests, clearly once had the economic and social stature to complete a pilgrimage to Mecca. Those days over, he said, during the intervening years he had had little time to think of anything other than that of an evening his family should have enough to eat [*shaam ko kuch chulhe ke liye ho aur parivar ka pet pale*]. As he said to me: 'Now, if I can feed myself and my family in this country, that itself is enough. Nothing more can be expected'.

Rehman's experience is told very briefly here because he was clearly someone whose social and economic position deteriorated considerably after the 1993 violence. Yet the stories of so many survivors were to recollect similar images of deformed relationships with state functionaries and of strategizing for purposes of economy and sanctuary. Sending a son and sometimes also daughters away protected them in the case of future violence as well as distributed in the wider family or kin-group the costs of re-building life in the aftermath of riot. In so many instances, children were taken out of school for sons had to contribute to the household, while sending daughters outside the house was fringed with an extra layer of insecurity, especially where a father had been killed and a mother struggled alone. This emerges strongly in women's experiences, which we shall turn to at greater length elsewhere in the text.

In Gujarat several persons narrated experiences of multiple dislocations, loss in riot after riot.

Alauddin lives in Gupta Nagar, Ahmedabad, a small *basti* of some 300 Muslim houses surrounded on three sides by largely Hindu localities. He had lived till 1984 in Delhi's Seelampur area. When his Sikh employer's ivory bangle-making factory was destroyed in what he described as the 'Indirakaand' [Indira-episode], he had come to Ahmedabad to attend his wife's brother's wedding. There was nothing to return to. Ivory work was soon banned and he turned to working with plastic. He lived in Lambha (another part of the city) near his wife's relatives, but his house there was burned in the 1992 riots. It was then that he moved to Gupta Nagar. In riots in 1998, his house was damaged but he and his family saved their lives by fleeing to and spending nearly two weeks in a relief camp. In 2002, no one's house was spared. The looting and burning touched all; he showed me the blackened walls of his now semi-restored dwelling. The impact, of every riot, of the loss of working days on this artisan, who lives by his hands, came through again and again in his narration.

Mumbai's Jogeshwari (East) exposes us again and again to stories of successive losses and displacements. One man had suffered from looting, arson and injury in every riot that Jogeshwari has seen. Today he and his family live in a tiny house in the centre of a densely occupied Muslim locality. His house and small factories were attacked and looted in the 1974 riots, when he had to move and resettle elsewhere. In riots the next year, his businesses suffered further attacks. At this point, the family moved again to the Muslim dominated area, where they now reside. Then they had two houses. But riots some nine years later again led to looting and further losses. Abdulbhai, as I shall call him, sold off all his businesses and opened a small shoe factory nearer his house. This was attacked in 1991, as was his home. After this and after the last riots in 1992–93, his Hindu workers refused to come to work in the area. Each time he has tried to start some new venture, but every conflict has impoverished him further.

In Ahmedabad's Akbar Nagar, Salmaben spoke of her experiences. She comes from Indore, but has been in Ahmedabad many years. Her husband used to sell leatherwork items. It was good business and they were doing well. At that time, they lived in Bapu Nagar in what she described as a 'border' area. Their house was burnt in 1985. They returned to rebuild it. It was looted and burnt again in the next two riots. Her husband is now reduced to selling bangles. They live in a tiny tenement, which was burnt along with hundreds of others like it in 2002. They were saved because they had fled across the road to a Muslim majority area. Though their home had been rebuilt now, one year after the riots, with help from various organizations engaged in relief and rehabilitation, their position remains vulnerable. There is talk of the government taking over the land to build, someone said, a hotel and entertainment plaza. As Salmaben said:

> We build up our home slowly, but every four years or so find it destroyed. After each riot, we have to learn to spend less and less. Say, if we have a rupee to spend, we try to spend 50 paise, put the rest away to buy something for the house. We have received no compensation at any point, except this time, when we received just 5,000 rupees.

This time [2002] they got 5,000 rupees, which went towards the construction of the little hut in which she now lives.

The deliberate and imposed scaling down of aspirations is visible elsewhere.

Ajmeri, who is a small-scale industry owner in Vatva, Ahmedabad, saw his factory looted in the 1990s during the violence focused around the Babri Masjid dispute. An educated and extremely capable entrepreneur, he still found the going very tough indeed. He had to sell off the assets to cope with the debts and losses accumulated because of the looting. Though insured, he had the misfortune to have been unable to renew his policy because of the dislocation and violence that went on for quite a time. As a result, he received nothing from the insurance company. Some 10 years ago, he moved from his earlier residence in Shahpur and set up another small business in Vatva in lathe-making. While earlier he had been involved in the manufacturing of a range of machinery, he has consciously contracted his reach. Preparing for violence every five or 10 years, he considers it better to have something going that is small in scale and in which the losses are less and the recovery easier. While his factory remained unhurt in 2002, the insecurity and curfew restrictions played their role in limiting business for several months.

Insecurity may find expression in other ways as well. One of the women I spoke to in the context of the 2002 violence in Ahmedabad mentioned, a little coyly, about wanting to have more than one son because 'who knows what will happen? We will need them to *protect* us' [emphasis added]. The statement jolts; have we previously even considered the relationship between violence and fertility patterns? Let us leave it there, for it is too difficult to assess right now. In Gujarat, a senior political leader was attacked and killed in his own house, sitting judges of the High Court happened to be Muslim found themselves unsafe in their official residences. The poor, regardless of religious affiliation, are unprotected everywhere; in these instances, marginality reached its excruciating peak.

It is not surprising but worth noting that the Islami Relief Committee working with riot survivors in Gujarat has started constructing *pucca* houses even for those poor, who had lived only in insecure tenements. As one of its Ahmedabad members said:

Muslims are easily attacked because they live in plastic sheds, mud huts or other types of shelters that can be easily burnt or broken into. This time we are making them small but strong houses, with bricks and cement and with iron doors and windows with *jaali* [grills]. In the rural areas, we have also built boundary walls.

Conversely, therefore, the most destructive of recent occurrences of violence is leading to a rebuilding of assets, even an enhancement of them. I would like to add a note of further speculation. Perhaps one of the reasons Muslims are peculiarly vulnerable in the face of violence is that they often do not have insurance, either because they cannot afford it or, more significantly, because they hold it to be a challenge to Allah and to the belief that He alone can save and is responsible for property and life, and their protection. But there will be time to dwell more on this at a later stage.

The invisibility of Muslims at levels of power and influence struck them forcefully after the ferocious Mumbai violence of 1992–93.[15] The realization gave rise to several efforts, committed and sometimes creative, at the grass roots to draw Muslims of capability out of poverty and obscurity into the services, professions and various levels of government and public sector employment. Similar efforts now slowly appear to be coming to light in Gujarat as well.[16] In Mumbai, extant organizations also reworked their priorities or enhanced their efforts in the altered environment. These efforts revolved critically around creating greater accessibility to modern education among the urban poor, and we shall be mapping them out a little more closely at other points in the text.

The story of this data is obviously larger than what may be related here. My purpose was not to call on every fact, but to recollect some that may enable the putting together of an argument that I hope is reasonably persuasive. The relations between Muslim marginality and the dynamics of communal conflict in the post-Independence period are complex. Some associations are yet ascertainable and perhaps assertable. Religion alone is not the contributing factor to Muslims' backwardness in literacy and education: class, caste and gender are contributing and intervening factors. Figures for employment, asset accumulation and representation in public office when taken together lead to some realization of the exclusion of Muslims from economic and political advantage. Also manifested is the troubling relationship between lack of ethnic diversity in the security forces and the prejudice countenanced by Muslims, particularly during periods of communal strife. On the whole, Muslims constitute a poor and underprivileged, not pampered minority; this feeds their vulnerability to the destabilizing conditions of continual conflict. In turn, having to prepare and plan for violence must have a suppressing effect on expectations and aspirations in each individual life-trajectory. This emerges more fully when we hear the women speak, as we do in the following pages.

notes

1. *Outlook* 1 April 2002. 'The Day my Spirit Died', and telephonic interview with the author conducted on 30 June 2003. J.S. Bandukwala is a well-known professor of physics at Maharaj Sayajirao University in Baroda, Gujarat. His house was ransacked in the violence against Muslims in 2002 that followed an attack on Hindu pilgrims in a train at Godhra on 27 February. He was, consequently, compelled to sell the house and move to the relatively safer environs of the university campus.
2. 'Disaster Recipe: Floods, quakes... Riots'. *The Economic Times*, Ahmedabad, 18 April 2002, p. 8.
3. Muslims are often stigmatized as '*lungi*-wearing, *paan*-chewing *landiyas* [circumcised men]', thus constructing for them a profile that links them by association with the urban lower classes. They are commonly perjured as butchers, barbers or small-time cycle and auto mechanics, occupations in which they are, for various reasons, very visible. Indeed, in a speech he made during his *gaurav yatra* in the state, the chief minister of Gujarat is reported to have said, without directly naming any community: 'In 5,000 years until Independence, we were only 30 crore. But during the Congress regime, the population shot up to 100 crore.... There were no means of entertainment earlier, but why should the population rise today? When so many children are produced, they grow up to become cycle repairers or pick-pockets'. Both in terms of references to higher fertility and occupational futility the words resonate with popular images of Muslims. In another speech, reference was made to the community of Bohras who, it was said, had fewer educational facilities and so youths aspired to become at best bus conductors (Milind Ghatwai, '25 to 625: Look, Modi is Counting', *The Indian Express*, 23 September 2002, pp. 1–2).
4. Robin David, 'Scared Muslims Break Transport Industry's Back in Gujarat', *The Times of India*, 28 April 2002, p. 3.

5. This data is, however, occasional. It is not based on periodic surveys. It is collected by the National Samples Survey Organization (NSSO), which conducts surveys for samples of households every year, round the year. Each survey usually has a specific focus (see Khalidi 1995: 57). The 1987–88 survey had considerable data on Muslims and this has been extensively drawn on by several researchers.

6. Varshney's data gives us a good indication of trends, which are not elsewhere easily available. Such a large data base, as the one he deals with, offers the potential of enabling us to reach some reasonable conclusions about broad patterns and developments with respect to collective violence in India. As such it is particularly invaluable. While using his data, though, I must emphasize that I do not subscribe to his larger arguments in toto. His use of the concept of 'civil society' in the particular context of the book is defective. His inability or unwillingness to document clearly the role played by Hindu Right organizations in fomenting and organizing violence in contemporary India is patent. I give only a couple of small examples (Varshney 2002: 245) to show the pitifully weak way in which he sets out the role of those he calls 'Hindu nationalists' (is the opposite of this, then, 'Muslim anti-nationalists?'). Talking of communal violence in Gujarat in the 1990s, he says:

> Thus, while cadre-based political parties continue to flourish in Ahmedabad and Surat, the great difference now is that, unlike the Congress, the BJP tries to build bridges only across the various castes of Hindu society. From a Hindu–Muslim perspective, the civic activity of Hindu nationalists is disruptive, not integrative. Their aim is Hindu unity across the various castes, not Hindu–Muslim unity.

Indeed, Varshney (2002: 201–15) has a whole chapter titled with a turn of speech almost too nice to be believable 'Hindu Nationalists as Bridge Builders?' He persists throughout with his analogy of the Hindu Right as builders of bridges, an analogy which cannot but be considered terribly inadequate in India's present circumstances.

7. NSS data classifies religious groups into eight categories: Hinduism, Islam, Christianity, Sikhism, Jainism, Buddhism, Zoroastrianism and Others. In their analysis, John and Mutatkar have used five categories: Hinduism, Islam, Christianity, Sikhism and Others. The Others, who constitute 1 per cent of the rural population and 2 per cent of the urban population, also include the highest proportion of Scheduled Castes and Scheduled Tribes. The data therefore affirms that available from other sources and mentioned elsewhere in the text: that Muslims are among the worst off of religious groups in India, on par with the Scheduled Castes and Tribes.

8. Zoya Hasan and Ritu Menon, *Frontline*, 17 January 2003. p. 88; Zoya Hasan and Ritu Menon, 2004.

9. Interview with chairman, State Minorities Commission of Maharashtra, Mr Amin Khandwani (24 September 2003). The Commission had itself been making efforts to collect such data but responses from government departments were poor.

10. *Report on Minorities*, Volume 2, New Delhi: Ministry of Home Affairs, 1983. The chair of the committee was Shri Gopal Singh and the report is generally known as the Gopal Singh Report.

11. For reports on the role of police and other authorities in Gujarat in 2002 see Human Rights Watch, 2003, *Compounding Injustice: The Government's Failure to Redress Massacres in Gujarat*. 15, 3: 1–72.

12. For Union Cabinet data see Omar Khalidi, Muslims ministers in the Union Cabinets: Half a century of distrust or lack of power', *Radiance* (11–17 February 2001), pp. 14–15.

13. Since this analysis focuses on Muslims, figures for Hindus or any other groups have not been included. Comparisons are relevant but not the only point of significance here. What we need to understand is the way in which the conception of loss reconfigures survivors' strategies for the future, their negotiations of everyday uncertainty and arrangements for the possible recurrence of extraordinary violence. For other groups, the implications of riots for identity and construction of community would require separate study, which, it must be admitted has, for the most part, also not been attempted.

14. The manner in which Varshney (2002) has tabulated his data makes it very difficult for us to tell whether he is collapsing Thane and Bhiwandi (where terrible riots have been seen over a long period). Even if that is so, however, as my own brief data shows, metropolitan Mumbai, or at least parts of it, were routinely considered 'communally sensitive' by the authorities and often saw riots.

15. Conversations with Muslims in Baroda give some indication that a similar reshaping of priorities and aspirations may be emerging there as well.

16. Conversation with Abid Surti. A retired college teacher, he has been trying to initiate some efforts in Ahmedabad and other parts of Gujarat. The aim is to select star pupils from each class and render them extra assistance in order to boost their chances of success and aspirations for future occupation.

chapter four

'i can harden my heart to bear this': women's words and women's worlds

Attention to human suffering means attention to stories...
Cheryl Mattingly (1998: 1).

So do not even ask,
do not ask what it is we are labouring with this *time;*
Dreamers remember their dreams
when they are disturbed—
And you shall not escape
what we will *make*
of the broken pieces of our lives.
Abena P.A. Busia, (*Liberation*).[1]

Men and women speak differently about violence. This is now generally agreed upon (Das 1990, 1986; Kanapathipillai 1990; Ross 2001; Scheper-Hughes 1992), though the ways in which voices differ are not. In his classic study of the *hibakusha* of Hiroshima, Lifton (1967: 367–68) asserts that he usually found that 'women had less capacity than men for expressing their formulations with coherence and completeness'. Formulation, in Lifton's somewhat unhappy choice of term, refers to the process of recovery from violence, the process by which survivors 're-create' themselves and establish the 'inner forms which can serve as a bridge between the self and the world'. His finding may perhaps be related to the particular context of Japanese culture at the time and its demands of femineity; the assertion, as seen in narratives in this chapter, certainly does not hold everywhere.

This chapter explores women talking about violence done to them, their sons and husbands, their homes. Each time I entered a different woman's home, my heart constricted against the things I knew I would hear; I was anxious not to raise memories that women were trying, desperately and daily, to still and to forget. The question of 'what happened' was, as I have said before, rarely deliberately approached; constructions of it emerged themselves, sometimes immediately and often more slowly, when the women spoke. No attempt was pursued to 'promote the rapid uncovering of traumatic memories' (Herman 1994: 184) outside of a frame of more general theoretical and functional concerns, as outlined everywhere in this book.

The most intriguing aspect of fieldwork lay in the ways in which women responded.[2] In Mumbai, the women I talked to engaged, unbidden and almost without exception, in narratives of their lives. Life-story was the self-selected mode of narration and this was in sharp contrast to the way in which women in Baroda and Ahmedabad spoke. Though I was not able to steep myself as fully in efforts in these two cities, my work there provided an invaluable counterpoint to what fieldwork in Mumbai was beginning to reveal. While women in those cities almost invariably juxtaposed their accounts of the recent traumatic violence with recollections of earlier riots, the recounting did not in any way become a self-reflective chronicle registering life's multiple struggles, its costs and compensations conjoined.

We explore these divergences more closely later. Inexorably, they will lead us back to some of the themes we had touched on in the previous chapter: themes about the relationship between trauma and reparation in the lives of communities and actors.

'am I to live by licking the walls?': Tabassum *Appa*'s cup of sorrow[3]

Tabassum *Appa* tells her story with the quiet grace and courage that comes best to women who have struggled and come to terms with a great deal of suffering. When she talked of the violence itself, her story started at another point.

My husband died in 1991. He used to run a workshop for buffing steel. At first, we did not live here, but in another building further across the road. But there was a fire there due to an electric fault, some time in the 1970s, and 11 people were killed. At that time, I had two small children. We were given this place where I am now: this room and the one below it....

My husband lost his business due to falling into too much debt. He remained ill for a while and died of a heart attack soon after. My son Javed had left school some months before he died. He was earning some 15 rupees a day helping in someone's cloth business. I gave the room downstairs on rent as a shop. At that time I could barely think to take a licence for it. After my husband's death, my brother-in-law felt sorry that I had no support and gave my son a job at his workshop for 500 rupees a month. In our community, if there is a death, marriage can take place either within the same year or else three years later. With great difficulty and a lot of help from my brother and other relatives, I managed to arrange my daughter's wedding. She got married in November–December 1991....

Then in December 1992, the clashes started. In January, there was again violence. My son went to get milk on 11 January. He said: 'Everyone is going; I will also go'. He never came back. I went after him immediately. I was just behind him, but he had disappeared. I told the sub-inspector... 'My son has just gone there, come with me'. He refused. He said: 'You go back. He will come. Nothing has happened'. Later, my husband's sister's husband's relative told us that he had been taken across the road, deep into a gully near the cemetery and killed. A tyre was put around his neck and he was burnt. Another boy was with him. They were both burnt. The police simply put him down as 'missing'. We put advertisements in various Urdu papers. It is impossible for me to forget this [*Yeh cheez bhoolna na mumkin hai*].

Later, the narrative continued. Tabassum *Appa* told me about her family and her early years in Gulbarga in Karnataka. She came to Mumbai when she married, some 30 years ago. She still has brothers and sisters in Karnataka, but, through all her troubles, never once saw going back there as a viable option. When Tabassum *Appa* began to talk, in deference to my queries, she spoke first about the struggle for compensation and survival. For years, compensation was out of the question. The running around was enormous and the authorities were unwilling to compensate in the absence of a death certificate. Finally, it was granted some three years ago. To obtain it she had to pay stamp duty of over 6,000 rupees on a bond, indemnifying the government in case her 'missing' son returned. She also had to obtain clearance from the police that she and her son were not implicated in any criminal cases.

The years passed slowly, each day a struggle. Sending the girls to school became an impossibility; Tabassum *Appa* barely let them out of the house. She got some rent for the shop and she and her daughter washed clothes for the drivers of the nearby taxi-stand. For a while, she sold potatoes. When a shop came up which manufactured pins, she assisted with that. Everything was done from her one room. If she went out to shop or pursue officials, she took one of her daughters. 'I fed my daughters with whatever I earned. I never let them go out'. The three remaining girls were young when pulled out of school: two may have completed primary school, the youngest could barely have been educated for a year or two. The youngest daughter is now married, and has a little son. The boy barely two months old has been named and the *khatna* was performed at the time of delivery itself.

Time had brought many changes. Before her husband's troubles started, Tabassum *Appa* had rarely gone outside her home and attended to little other than household chores. Uneducated herself, she had to learn some rapid lessons when life irrevocably changed. She has kept every newspaper cutting and every piece of paper relating to her husband's and son's deaths and to her house, which is now under threat. Taking help to write letters in Marathi, she determinedly fights her way with the officials. Various journalists and concerned social workers have helped through the process. One of her older daughters, still unmarried, has taken on the role of mother's helper. 'We call her *chhoti* now', as she is still at home and unmarried. 'The youngest is now *badi*'.

Tabassum *Appa*'s mistake in not getting a licence for the shop has come back now to haunt her with a vengeance. At that time, with her grief and sudden burden of responsibilities, it did not seem a big deal. It only partook of the casual corruption that easily characterizes urban low-income and slum-dwellers everyday relations with the state, regardless of religious affiliation. The shop also had no commercial electric meter, because the rates were too high for her to pay. When the odd inspector came around to check, she slipped him 50 or 100 rupees to overlook the illegality, which he did, as she said, 'seeing her situation'. Now, the whole slum is to be demolished, to make way for a new development. The slum-dwellers have been promised rooms in another building. Tabassum will have a place to stay, but, thanks to the irregularity of her dealings thus far, her shop is not legally recognized and so she will not be entitled to one in the proposed building.

Her rooms are at the head of a row of ramshackle rooms that is about to come down: her refusal to move has delayed things for a while. While the other, predominantly Muslim dwellers, are ready to move, she has held out. 'Can I live by licking the walls?', she says. 'What will I live on?' The Muslims around her, according to her, are not overly sympathetic; she has had rows with the men. 'You have jobs', is her argument, 'you can move. What will I do?' Tabassum holds the local corporator of her area responsible for creating the riots; a man who is still in power and of whom she says 'Of those who killed my son, he is the only one here'. Yet, she has to address her entreaties about her rooms to him and she does so with barely a falter. As she told me:

> He has said he will help. And I know he will, because the elections are coming near.... He knows I will fight to the end and even he thinks that it is no use fighting with me because I will not give up. That is why I know I will get my way.

Appa, I sincerely hope you will.

I began with Tabassum *Appa*'s story because it has the grains of many of the themes that I would like to explore in this chapter. As with some of the other women with whom I spoke, Tabassum *Appa*'s narrative of the unravelling of her world begins not with the story of the riot itself. The 'riot' is, in her narration, an event that can never be forgotten, for she lost her only son and the 'work of mourning' was made that much more difficult by the fact that, in the absence of the dead body (already cremated in a macabre way), the performance of the last rites was denied her. Nevertheless, as she starts, the slow deterioration of her husband's business and health and his death mark the point of departure.

When the outsider enters the world of enormous social suffering, such as that engendered by a riot, she sees the survivors marked indelibly by that experience. Forgetting is deemed impossible; indeed, time in the narratives is expected to be marked by the event of the riot. The riot fills time, as it were.[4] Certainly, this is true to a great extent perhaps particularly in the shorter term; however, what Lifton (1967) calls avenues of 'transcendence' of the tragic event or what one might prefer, for these women's narratives, to call 'domestication', is possible.

It should be remembered that, wherever we speak of it, the 'event' referred to in this or other chapters is not meant to stand for some unalterably 'accurate' picture of the violence. It is always and everywhere, the *narrated event* that is being analysed here. Narrativity itself directs subjects and episodes, sequencing them in a narratable order. What is notable about Tabassum *Appa*'s narration is that 'event' (specifically *the narrated event* of the riots) does not initiate the thinking about time, it becomes a part of a broader notion of time, *life-time*. This is hardly a process unmarked by struggle or one that is ever, in any sense, finished; it is, though, however grievous the circumstances, critical for survival and continuance. Thus, one begins to understand how a more diffuse perspective is necessary to understand the lives of these ordinary Muslims, lived under the shadow not just of 'riot' but of *violences*, if I may so pluralize the word, of diverse kinds. It becomes more apparent that really lives looked in some ways, as Scheper-Hughes puts it in a different context (1992: 17), 'like roller-coaster rides with great peaks and dips, ups and downs, as women struggled valiantly at times (less valiantly at others) to do the greatest good for the greatest number and manage to stay alive themselves'.

Attention is inevitably therefore drawn towards the uneasy overlaps between the time of extraordinary violence marked by a major riot and the everyday, which is also pervaded by prickling uncertainties, interactions that bristle with the possibilities of conflict and edgy encounters with local representatives of the state that implicate corrosive performances of compromise and corruption. To elaborate a little, *Appa*'s pragmatic use of the 'system' both contributed to her present position as well as promises to improve it. As Fuller and Harriss (2000: 25) argue, 'even the poor, low-status and weak can sometimes benefit from their own adequately competent manipulation of political and administrative systems'. All through, though, we may not allow ourselves to minimize the profound anguish that must accompany her every face-to-face entreaty of a man who is, she feels, the one left out of those who killed her son. Survival shields unfathomable struggles of the soul.

Strained relations with community members, neighbours and kin form another trajectory of tension for many women building life alone for themselves and their children. While *Appa* has a tangible network of support among her own kin, after her son's death her late husband's kin have proffered little. Each daughter's marriage required a stitching together of small gifts and loans from her siblings. The compensation she finally acquired helped her youngest daughter wed. Living within a close network of kin and community both rescued and confined. A family of women was always vulnerable to attack by loose talk and the controlling gaze of male elders. The world of Appa's daughters remained severely limited: she could countenance no education or liberation for them. Appa herself found she was unwittingly embroiled in antagonistic relations with men of the community: holding out against them, despite pressures, for her livelihood.

Najma bibi: 'i could say i am fairly content'

Najma Bibi lives in the heart of Mumbai, in a Muslim-dominated slum that is bordered on one side by the railway lines and on the other two sides by dwellings of caste Hindus and Dalits respectively. 'When any trouble takes place, the only way out is along the rail lines', the people here say. Najma Bibi exudes something of the charming confidence of a matriarch. She has a warm and somewhat dominating presence and likes to talk, but remembering the past is still very difficult.

The first few years were so difficult. There was no one to ask. How did I manage? My children were few days here, few days there. Sometimes with my brother, sometimes with my sister, sometimes with my mother. They grew up this way. I could not send them to school. But you can ask anyone: I brought them up well and they were never left outside the house. Now I can think back. My two sons are earning. One is a taxi driver. He gives me 100 rupees a day for my needs. My other son is in the construction business. He gives me some money as well. They are married now. My four daughters are also married. If their marriages were okay, I could say I am fairly content, happy. But one daughter has come back divorced from her husband's house.

Shall I say how it happened?.... It was 13 January. My son had just come back from school. He put his bag down and went out. The police were firing from all sides; from the top the people were throwing stones. From here also stones were being thrown. The bullet hit my son. I ran. I shouted at the policeman: 'You have shot my son'. He denied it. We were not throwing stones at the police and they were firing indiscriminately....

My husband used to work in a godown. He was an inspector of goods. My father was his colleague. My husband was a Konkani Muslim. He was of a good family. They were educated. My husband's father was a good man. He did not think about education for his son's wife: he wanted me as his daughter-in-law, even though our *mulk* [homeland] was Allahabad and I was not educated. I would keep a good home, he said. Earlier, they used to stay in Bhendi Bazar, but then they sold that and my husband bought this place here. My husband used to talk very little. He was a quiet person....

When this happened, he was in Pune. He got the news and tried to return home. But they sent him back from Bombay from the station itself because of the trouble here. He was not able to come. When my husband finally came, he died in a month or so, from a heart attack. He could not bear it. We all fled to Goregaon, to my sister's house. When we came back from Goregaon, my house was burnt. *Zameen maidan ho gaya tha* [the earth had been flattened]. Hundreds of homes had been burnt. My husband was dead, my son was dead. I was totally destroyed. The relief workers recognized my loss and my house was the first to be reconstructed....

A substantial part of Najma Bibi's narrative related to her younger days, her own marriage and her husband's quiet demeanour and good nature and then to her daughter's unsuccessful marriage. The young girl was married five years ago to a not very well-off Gujarati Muslim, who is a refrigerator mechanic. The proposal came through Najma Bibi's brother's wife's family. However, the boy was, it appears, keen on his own mother's sister's daughter. He ill-treated his wife and forced a divorce on her. She has returned to her mother's home, with her young son. While some money is coming for the child from his father, the woman is clearly unsupported. The return of the daughter seems to have led to some tension in the household, for one of the sons and his wife subsequently moved out to live separately.

While it is not greatly surprising that Najma Bibi's mind should focus on her current difficulty more than on what she had been through in the past years, what is interesting is the intricate narrative that she weaves around her various experiences. There is a story here of continued endurance and of the capacity to bear. Events are part of a trajectory, they have been internalized, learnt from and made part of one's life experiences. Najma was proud of her own strength, which even surpassed that of her husband. Indeed, she surpassed her own expectations; for she had little thought as a young and inexperienced bride that she would have to face all this. God gave the courage. She is proud of holding her family together, of living a full life and reaching a mature age after seeing all her sons and daughters (apart from the one) settled and grown up. It has, after all, been a good life and there is room for contentment, despite the tragedies. Only one wish is left: that she can get her daughter married again.

Past and present interweave in Najma Bibi's tale but the frame that holds the narrative together is her own life, her marriage, her early expectations, her struggles, her coping and preparing for what the future holds, with a certain sense of fulfilment. This pattern was recognizable with other women as well. While all these women appeared to conform to the norms of female deportment imposed on them by the community and while they were usually particular about basic religious education for their children, there were moments of deep discontent with the implications of the way things actually worked for women. Najma Bibi and her daughter, despite opposition to their decision by men in the family, were challenging the *talaq* her son-in-law had given. As she said: 'Men take advantage of the laws among Muslims. My daughter was married in front of so many people; how was he allowed to divorce

her when they were alone?' They had employed a prominent reformist lawyer to fight the case and were determined that the boy
should be made, at least, to pay maintenance for the wife he had
cast off so casually.

Saira: 'we daily dig a well to drink the water [*roz kuwa khode, pani piye*]'

Saira was one of the most articulate of the women I talked to and,
perhaps, the most active within her local community. A scorching
sense of abandonment on several fronts pierces her recollections
of the Mumbai violence of 1992–93. Saira was a little younger than
some of the other women whose narratives are recorded here
and she talked a lot about her growing-up years, her struggle to
acquire some education, her qualifying as a beautician. Her parents
were poor and barely able to educate their large brood, consisting
of six sisters and four brothers. Her father drove a taxi; he had
come during Partition to Mumbai almost empty-handed. She, somehow, managed to finish senior secondary schooling in the Urdu
medium and took a course for beauticians. Today she runs a beauty
parlour, something perhaps unthinkable for a woman of her community in earlier years. Her brothers did not proceed far in gaining
education; living off odd jobs, they barely manage to earn for themselves and their families.

If you talk of coping, let me tell you how it all started.... When
the violence happened, I had a six-month-old daughter. I had
just bathed and massaged her and wrapped her in a sheet. Many
people had left the area by then; I was among the few people
left. I was cooking for the people who were left behind. Bottles
were being thrown, acid bombs and petrol bombs were being
thrown. I had never seen such things in my life. I went out to see
if anyone else was in the nearby houses; another boy went ahead
of me. Suddenly a bomb was thrown. The boy was hit in front
of me; he burnt to death in front of my eyes. People, even women,
whom I could recognize were looting and burning the houses. I
fled back to the house. I had lost the keys in the process. I had to

break my way in. I grabbed my daughter and fled. On the way, luckily, the army was there. They took us to Madanpura Relief Camp. We went with just the clothes on our backs and returned to nothing. I was just wearing a dressing gown. On my way, I managed to grab a set of clothes from a house close by. I returned the clothes later; I had not intended to keep them. But that woman, and she is also a Muslim, registered a case against me with the police. When I came back, the house was destroyed. For some time, I moved back to live with my mother....

Things were bad before that. My father died in 1991. He had cancer. My mother was so poor, we sold a lot of things for his treatment. My brother began to drive the taxi for a while, but did not give much help. I worked in a beauty parlour and helped a bit. It was like having to daily dig a well to drink the water. I was married soon after that....

My husband left me in the riots. He went off to Delhi and married another woman. He is in the leather business. Later, he wanted me back, but I refused. I lost everything in the riots, even my certificates. Later, I did another short beautician's course in Bandra, in order to get a certificate. I worked and brought up my daughter. My younger sister also lives with me. I have a Buddhist friend, who lives abroad. She helped me to start this parlour. It has been running for almost a year now. I am giving my daughter and my sister a 'full' English education....

I try to tell the women here: 'It is not enough to look only at *din* [religion/spiritual things]. *Din* and *duniya* [things of this world and the other world] have to be considered together'.

Saira has views on abortion and birth control that must be strongly disturbing to the traditional-minded in the community, particularly men. As she says:

Poor Muslims create their own problems with their big families. There will be eight to ten children; the father doing barely anything. The parents cannot give education to their children [There is an undercurrent of resentment against her own parents here, who were barely able to or interested in educating their children, especially the girls]. They do not think. Abortion may be wrong in Islam, but a woman has to do something on her own. It is no use asking the mother-in-law. She will not support. If there are so many children, the burden falls on the women, but even they do not listen.

Saira's work among the women in the area has brought her into confrontation with male religious elders. But she persists. Even the women dismiss her: 'You have just one daughter and your husband has left you. So you can afford to talk'. She tells them: 'I could have had more children [her husband wanted her back] but I chose not to'. Her husband has several children from his subsequent marriage.

Saira expressed a deep pain at the betrayals she experienced in and through the *dange* (riots). Her husband's abandonment of her and her daughter, her neighbour's charge of theft against her, her acquaintances' participation in the violence against the Muslims in the area—all coalesced to produce the profound anguish that seared her narrative. Violence left no place for naivete: women like Saira became uncomfortably aware of the tenuousness of familial and kin relations, and of the ways in which social disorder could be manipulated to their own, personal ends by individuals. Suffering could be both painful and humiliating. While men are commonly thought to experience humiliation in terms of defeat or the inability to retaliate (Das 1990; Sarkar 2002), these women abruptly understood their vulnerability not just in the face of outsiders but within their own worlds of familiarity and intimacy.

Saira's account cuts straight to 1993 and makes no mention of the year before at all. Her father's death marks, for her, the point of tangible deterioration in the family's circumstances, though the seeds had been earlier sown in the indifferent education of the children. The males in her family, husband and brothers alike, have been unable or unwilling to shoulder responsibility. She took on a large part of the financial burden of caring for her mother and younger sisters. In her work in the community, she stresses the need for education, especially for girls and for women, by whatever means, to take control of their lives, reproductive or otherwise. The struggle of these women against poverty and ignorance is at the same time a struggle with men within the community.

A deep sense of the divide between communities comes through in her account. She tells of how children, all too early, begin to speak the language of separation. Her brother's son recently ran to tell her, 'A Hindu boy has come to see TV', when a child of about five years of age had come to the house. While individual ties sometimes manage to weather the storms ('I have many Hindu friends. After 1993, there was a lull. Then nature took over and the friendships resumed'), communal separations become sharper. ('The wounds have healed, but the twinge [*takleef*] is still there'). Young boys used to participate in the Ganesh immersions; nowadays, that has become unthinkable. In recent years, the series of bomb blasts in Mumbai, all of which have been viewed as the work of Muslim terrorists, have made members of the community fearful both of the spectre of police suspicion that hangs over them all and of a possible 'Hindu' reprisal.

Hazira Ali: 'our neighbours used to laugh at us'

Hazira Ali has worked hard to ensure that her remaining children did not carry the scars of violence and extreme fear they were subjected to when her husband and elder son were mutilated in front of their eyes and dragged away to their death. Even so she says with sadness: 'The children sometimes remember their father. But they don't talk about it. They just say: "What can be done?" What must go through their minds, who can say?' Hazira Ali was awarded government compensation for the deaths in her family 10 years after the violence, through the sustained efforts of a small group of Mumbai social activists, media persons and some local leaders.

> To get the compensation there was so much running around. People helped a lot. We went wherever they told us to go. I have got Rs 30,000 now.[5] I will get the rest after seven years. In the meantime, I will get interest on it. Even for this, I have to present so many papers, run around a lot. We told the minister: 'People should get what is due to them by right [*haq*]'.
>
> I tried to make sure the children did not miss school. S [her daughter] went to the Urdu-medium municipal school and A [her son] was in a private English school. When we moved,

I had to transfer them. Now, he is in the 10th standard. She has completed BA with geography and Urdu....

We moved several years ago to Kurla. I sold the other place. I did not feel safe. I could not leave the children there, if I went out to work. Here I do not have to worry about the children if I am out. We lived in the relief camp for several months. The neighbours did not allow us to come back. Then the Relief Committee people intervened. I stayed there but the children were frightened. The neighbours used to abuse us. They used to laugh at us. At any instance they would say: 'There is nothing for you here. Go to [pause] Pakistan'.... [She sounded surprised and hurt when she said this.] Earlier they had been all right....

It was on the 10th. We had not expected anything to happen here [in Wadala, where she then lived]. We were just filling water. Suddenly, this started. The mobs came. They had barricaded the roads. No one could escape. They cut off my son's arms in front of my eyes. My husband's arms. They dragged them away. There was blood all over, over the walls. I was thrown down from the roof.... We lodged a FIR with the police. They put them down as missing. But people said they were burnt alive....

I teach *Quransharif* here. I had learnt when I was young in Bareilly. My husband and I were both from Bareilly. He was in Mumbai earlier. He was a vendor of fruits. I came when we were married. Our eldest daughter was married when her father was alive. She lives here, in Kurla. She comes sometimes....

Now I am not strong anymore. My health is not good. Who knew all this would happen? I have done what I could. I cannot do more. Now I have said: 'Enough'. I have told my son and my daughter: 'This is the last year of studies'. My daughter wants to study but I do not have the strength to go on now. I have not thought of her marriage, though people keep prying. Of course, if she sits at home, I will have to get her married. But I want her to stand on her own two feet, have something in hand. I do not listen to people. Who came to help me when I was struggling? I have brought them up with my own hands....

My husband's brother is in Mulund. He is old and very weak. He cannot do much. He does not come here. My sister is in Wadala. She also lost her husband in the riots, but she now has sons to support her. We do not go to Bareilly. My in-laws are no more; it is too costly. Better to spend the money on the children, on their education. We have not called anyone from there either. What do we have here? How can we call anyone?

Despite her difficulties, when I last met her, Hazira Ali told me that her daughter had enrolled in a computer course. Perhaps with some assistance, the son too will continue his education. Both are bright and show an interest in pursuing their studies. As with other women, Hazira speaks almost not at all about *mandir* or *masjid*, 6 December or 1992. Her narrative cuts straight to her personal tragedy and the horrifying images that have not left her. Even so, her recollections enter different spaces that are traversed alike by other women. For all of them, age and the years of struggle are counted, struggles magnified unimaginably by the violence and loss suffered. For all of them, equally, the continuing work of kinship and affinity, reminiscences of early years of marriage, the labour of child-rearing, the struggles of women *as* women weave in and out of their tales of the violence.

Ameena: *'mein itna pathar dil pe rakh sakti hoon [i can harden my heart to bear this]'*

Ameena *Bua* (father's sister; I use it as a term of respect) looks barely strong enough to have coped with all she has been through. However, there is a distinctly reedy toughness to her frail form. *Bua* is, in every sense given to that word, a survivor.

How did I manage? With me, I do what I can. Always have.... It has always been like this: adversity [*sadma*]. I had a shop. It was looted at the time of the riots. When my husband could not work too much, we used to do lock-making in the house. All of us would get together and do the work. I married my eldest daughter when she was only 13 or so. People were against it. She had completed 7th standard in Urdu medium. Her husband was a good boy. He worked as a carpenter and lived close by. When the police were firing, he had gone to the roof to see where the bullets were coming from and he was hit fatally.

We had no information for over a day. The curfew was on and people were not allowed out. People kept giving false information. Finally, next day, in the afternoon I went out. The police were holding guns. I said: 'Shoot. My son-in-law is dead. My daughter's house has been wrecked [*ghar ujad gaya hai*]. Why do I want to live?' Finally, one officer asked me what the matter was. I told him: 'We have not been told anything. Tell me clearly: some say he is shot in the leg, some say he is dead. I can harden my heart to bear this much, but please tell me'. Finally, they took me in a vehicle and I saw the body. My daughter was silent and in shock. She came back to my house....

All my children completed at least seventh or eighth standard. I did what I could. One son is quite useless and just roams around. My other son is the youngest. He was learning the *zari* (gold embroidery) work and now he is employed in that.

Three–four years ago, my next daughter was married. Her husband is in the construction business. She has two small boys: one is two years old and one a year old. She used to teach the *Quransharif* before marriage. Now, I teach those students. Her mother-in-law harasses her. My husband passed away a few years ago. In that year itself, my youngest daughter was married to a Keralite Muslim in Govandi, whose relatives in Jogeshwari brought the proposal. He was supposed to be in the air conditioning business, but it seems to be untrue. He also seems to be impotent [*mard ki takat nahi thi us mein*]. Her in-laws used to beat her a lot and not give her enough to eat. She was married for a year and she told me nothing. Finally, we saw how weak she was and we brought her back about a year ago. We have done the *talaq* now through an organization....

My husband was from Sholapur, but his father died early and his mother brought him to Bombay, Dongri side, and reared him. She also died soon after, and he was brought up by relatives and neighbours. He did the work of carrying *dabbas* [lunch boxes] for office-goers and he was also a watchman....

I was only 13–14 years old when I was married to him. He was 35. I had lived most of my life in Jogeshwari. My mother also died when I was very young. I was fostered by a Memon family and used to help them with their various activities, but not cooking or washing. They helped me out financially whenever I needed. That was how I had started the shop. I married in Jogeshwari and we lived here....

Bua acknowledges the help of various persons at different stages of her life. Her brothers cannot help her very much, but they gave gifts for the marriages of her daughters. She has a step-mother who lives in Pune and is now quite ill. She and her siblings are planning to pitch in and help her out. Her foster family, the Memons, supported her financially at crucial stages. Various social workers, including media persons, have pitched in with information and assistance. Shabana Azmi, who works with Nivara Haq Samiti, personally came and asked her widowed daughter to join the organization. She has been working there some years. Though the pay is not great, the organization has taught her many skills and, more importantly in her mother's eyes, gives her respect [izzat].

That these narratives, and there are others not recorded here, take the form of life stories is of considerable interest. They trace protagonists' lives, their multiple disappointments and tragedies, moments of success and fulfilment. Clearly, these women went through extraordinary violence, but they have also endured, for longer periods and in more diverse ways, the deliberate jagged cuts of economic hardship, everyday injustice and customary coercion. The immediacy of their recollections of the horror of the riots is apparent in the tense, emotionally charged, sensation-steeped quality of what they say: 'I was just behind him'; 'I ran'; 'I shouted...'; 'Suddenly a bomb was thrown'; 'I fled'; 'There was blood all over'; 'I said, "Shoot"'. There is though sometimes a thin line between the extraordinary and ordinary acts of violence which these women have witnessed and experienced. It would have to be someone braver than I to suggest that the agonizing acts of entreaty to her son's perceived killer are obviously less torturous for Tabassum *Appa* than the memory of her lost son.

For reasons that may be interesting to try to uncover, to whatever extent possible, the voices of Muslim women from Baroda or Ahmedabad do not have the same structure or pattern as the aforementioned narratives. To some extent, there are greater silences, there is much more of the narration of the violence as it happened.

The past intrudes more insistently in the present; the present itself seems sometimes emptied of its unique relevance, assuming the shape of a carrier for the past. There is 'an incessant present' as Frank (1995: 99) would argue and, indeed, these are perhaps the 'chaos narratives' that he (1995: 98) speaks of, narratives in which one cannot evade the painfully gaping hole that refuses to be filled in or 'sutured'. While women talk about the violence as well as about previous episodes of violence they may have experienced or heard about, their words do not assume the self-appraising, life-story pattern of Muslim women in Mumbai. Psychology, as a discipline, apparently works with the distinction between two kinds of trauma memory patterns that after Janet (1925: 660–61) and Herman (1994) can be described in the following way:

> Long after the danger is past, traumatized people relive the event as though it were continually recurring in the present.... Traumatic memories have a number of unusual qualities. They are not encoded like the ordinary memories of adults in a verbal, linear narrative that is assimilated into an ongoing life story (Herman 1994: 37).

'Normal' or, aptly, narrative memory, according to psychologists, remembers and recites events in the context of an ongoing personal history, whereas traumatic memories lack verbal narrative and context and make themselves manifest more in the form of vivid sensations or fixed images. It is also entirely possible it seems, according to other psychologists (see, for instance, van der Kolk and van der Hart 1991; van der Kolk and Fisler 1995), that even while traumatic memory *retains* the form of acute sensory and affective perception, it may still be encoded into personal accounts that follow the rules of narrative or semantic memory. Sensations thus transcribed become socially communicable stories that could be condensed or augmented depending on the person addressed or the appropriateness of the social situation.[6]

Before it is possible for us to understand whether or to what extent these or allied categories enable an *anthropological* exploration of these cases, we need to listen for a while to the words of some women from Ahmedabad and Baroda, cities with which I have a small degree of familiarity. It must be clarified here that everywhere, for various reasons, there were some sessions with women which lasted only a brief period, perhaps less than half-an-hour. To lessen the disparity in the material, however, I have here drawn from conversations that took place over longer periods of time, usually about an hour and sometimes over two hours and where I was able to speak to the women as far as possible uninter-ruptedly, even if the presence of others was often unavoidable. In one particular case (see end note 9) I spent several hours talking to a number of women in a group. While such an engagement, it may be felt, probably precludes the possibility of life narration, I have included sections from this particular interaction here for it shows how little it differed from the kinds of voices obtained from women even when they were speaking independently.

From Baroda, an elderly woman, as of August 2003 living with her daughter, Mumtaz, spoke of the killing of her son in the violence that took place in February–March 2002. He ran a bakery and was doing successfully in his business.

How can I manage? My daughter-in-law has taken everything. I don't know how my grandchildren are.... My son was killed in front of me. I was screaming. I begged them to stop. I fell down. I don't know what happened afterwards...his shop, house was burnt. He was doing so well. He had built it all up by his own efforts. He used to take orders from rich people...even Hindus. He catered for parties; his sweets and cakes were so famous. He was so well-known and liked by everyone. We could not even imagine that such a thing would happen....

I gave my jewels to my daughter-in-law. She left me and took the children and everything and went off to her mother's house. The bakery workers brought me here [to her daughter's house]. My daughter-in-law does not let me meet the children.... My son had five children.... I have lost everything. There is no one to help. The government does not listen.

I am living almost like a beggar now. See my state. How long will I live like this. My daughter is looking after me, but for how long. She has her family. All I could bring was a few clothes. My daughter-in-law has betrayed us. The government gave com-pensation. She has grabbed that money, my jewels, my grand-children and now she has cut off from us. My son was my only support. Now I have nowhere to go.

The bereaved mother was obviously caught up in her grief and her daughter was striving to look after her, her own husband and children along with performing all the other household tasks. The old lady managed to mention about the pleas she had unsuccessfully addressed for a new home to various local authorities. She also talked at some length of how the intra-family tensions and conflicts and the separation from her grandchildren in her old age were preoccupying and weakening her further, both mentally and physically.[7]

Again, in Baroda, the speech of Sultana, who had returned to her home a year and a half after the worst of the 2002 brutality, was broken intermittently by deeply disturbing silences. As she took us around, showing us the marks of the violence on the area, she could not keep the emotion and torment out of her voice.[8] She remembered previous riots her mother and grandfather had spoken about, about which some mention has been made in an earlier chapter. She compared those with the present violence. In this attack, her house had been burnt from the back. She came back to the blackened rooms, with a great deal of fear. Sultana began by speaking about her present circumstances and how she has been living in the last few months, but soon (and particularly as we went around the neighbourhood) her account returned to a description of the violence.

> I thought my house was totally burnt down. No one could tell me. For months, I was frightened to come back from my relatives. Some other neighbours had come; they told me my house was burnt. Finally, I plucked up courage and went some months ago. I found the house open. I picked up a blackened sheet and brought some clothes. I was so happy to have the clothes; for so long I had been wearing other people's clothes. People had lost everything but they rejoiced to find among the ruins something that could be used. A blackened but useful spoon. A pan....
>
> My uncle's house was completely looted. The children. They suddenly remember things. They will ask their mother: 'Mummy, where is my doll?' Then, they themselves will say, 'Oh, it must be burnt, no. Okay, leave it'. They remember their toys. I remembered my clothes. I felt bad at having to borrow from others.

When I finally got my clothes I gave many old ones to the relief camp people....

Finally, I came back some days ago. I have someone, one girl, who comes to sleep with me at night. It is very frightening. Whenever something happens [a *bandh* or a festival or the like], we have to go away. Can't stay here....

If the police had been neutral, I feel things would not have been so bad. They said: 'We have got our orders from above'. The police, the government have closed their eyes. Those who did all these things are roaming free. [Silence] Anyway, there is the One above. He cares more about us. He has saved our lives. We did not go out to burn anyone's house. Why did this happen to us? God will not forgive them: they will pay someday for what they have done.... The police only did their combing operations in the Muslim areas. We were forced to stay together with relatives to be safe. They knew. Still they kept asking: 'How do you have so many people in the house. Show us your ration card. Did you bring people from outside to create trouble?'

Apart from the traumatic memories of the violence, Sultana is faced with regular fractious disagreements within her own family. Sultana is unmarried and lives alone with her mentally challenged bachelor brother. Her other brother and his wife have been trying to put pressure on her to marry. Subsequent to the violence, the intensity of their demands has increased. Perhaps the fear of her possible dishonour in the event of another episode of violence is partly behind their wish to get her safely married off. Even proposals from much older men have been put before her. She has resisted with considerable difficulty. Though she earns her own living by teaching, she finds herself sapped by the constant tensions with her brother and, particularly, sister-in-law.

In Juhapura, along with several other women, I met Nasreen, a woman who fled for her life from Naroda Patia's horrors, leaving everything behind, and has not returned in all this long while (over a year and a half) to check on things there. Her mother-in-law lived in Juhapura and she, her husband and children fled here by cover of darkness. Her husband, an autorickshaw driver, was barely able to go out to earn anything for several months on end.

They live in pretty abject conditions, but she cannot think of going back. She could not speak of the savagery, some of which she had witnessed, some of which she had come to know of later. She also mentioned earlier episodes of violence in Naroda Patia.

You can say it is all lost. I cannot go back there. How can we live there? We had lived there so long. It was so beautiful. They destroyed everything. The mosque, the houses...we heard.... Now the *Jamaat* [Islami Relief Committee] I believe has rebuilt the houses. But who will go. I cannot go back.... The houses, we hear, are lying locked and empty....

We are just carrying on somehow...my husband can hardly earn anything. There he was doing all right. Now, I have this work...sewing. Otherwise we would not manage....

There have been riots before. In 1969 there were riots. Then houses were stoned. And looted. People were not touched.... *Auraton ke saath ye sab nahi hua* [These things were not done with the women].... Those women...they are here [in Juhapura]...how will they return?....

She shuddered and her voice trailed off. She did not speak anymore of the violence. Her companions in the room nodded silently and compassionately.[9] 'She has seen terrible things', someone whispered. Later, several women started speaking. Anger was expressed by one of the more articulate, Farzana.

Look at these things. The government now says: 'Forget what happened. Forgive us'. How can we? We want justice. If people had got justice, they would have felt: 'Even if this happened with us, at least we got justice'. They would feel some comfort. But where one woman has been raped by eight–eight people and even after complaint, there is no sign of justice, how will we feel? Because of this, so many do not even speak. They feel they dishonour themselves by speaking and then do not even get justice.... Under this government, nothing is happening. People's compensation for loss has been paltry. They gave people cheques for such meagre amounts, they have even returned them. We have got nothing from the government.

Another woman was pointed out, Rehana, a widow, whose two daughters, married in Chamanpura, fled to safer places, eventually making their way to their mother's house in Juhapura. For days she had not known what had happened to them. She remained ill and anxious. No one had any information. Then, it was God's grace, that they were found to be safe. But they have not gone back; who knows what has happened to their houses?

Again one heard of the terrible death of a school-going boy from Naroda Patia, described by his mother Parveen. The mother has returned to her house subsequently. The return has been facilitated largely by the Islami Relief Committee of Gujarat, which has its activists staying in the area to boost the confidence of the local people. She, her family and neighbours stressed that even the presence of the committee members is not adequate. There is hardly any sleep at night. Financial help has come and the houses have been rebuilt, but there is considerable instability and insecurity. She talked about her son's death.

He had just come back from school. He tried to run. He could not...he was handicapped, you see. They dragged him away. He was crying and shouting. They burnt him to death. These are the atrocities we have lived to see.... He was a good boy....

....He had climbed to the roof. He was trying to defend by throwing stones. He had managed to climb to the roof and was confronting the mobs, defending. But when the stones finished they dragged him down and burnt him.

We have come back. But there is a lot of fear. Every time there is something we are afraid. There is barely sleep at night. One can still hear the screams. These people [the members of the relief committee] are there, but they are one or two. What security is there? The police [from the nearby *chowki*] also tell us to go to some other area [Muslim-dominated area] if there is a *bandh* or any sign of trouble. They say they cannot take responsibility.

The mention of the stone-throwing gave the tragic incident another angle, without however destabilizing the sufferer's role as victim. While clearly Muslims did not always deny active participation in rioting, they saw their role purely as one of retaliation and defence, not offensive aggression. Najma Bibi had spoken of stones being thrown at the police, who were shooting indiscriminately in her area. Saira recalled the bottles and bombs that were being thrown on their houses. Later, she said, regarding the present situation: 'We are not actually preparing by collecting bottles or weapons, but wariness is necessarily there'. Victim and perpetrator must be acknowledged as tough categories to work with in situations of social disorder and collapse; the catastrophic degree of disaster visited on a particular community allows us more ready access to the extensive differences in power or efficiency of attack.

In Akbar Nagar, Salmaben, like many of her neighbours, had lost everything. In particular, her own house was destroyed for the fourth time in less than 20 years. She spoke about each of those losses and the drains they have made on her economic and social condition. Her words appear in an earlier chapter, but I briefly retell a portion of her story here.

We came from Indore originally, but have been in Ahmedabad many years. My husband used to sell leather goods. We were doing well. It was a good business. We lived in Bapu Nagar, in a 'border' area. Our house was burnt in the 1985 riots. When we came back, we slowly rebuilt it....

But every riot it was looted and burnt again. This happened in two more riots. Then, we were forced to move to a little hut here. That also was burnt this time. The whole area was reduced to ashes.

When the attack came, Salma was pregnant. They had mercifully, she said, had enough time to flee to a Muslim-majority area nearby, so no life was lost. Salma gave birth to a bonny baby boy some months after the violence had started receding. The birth was an incredible sign of hope for this mother, till now, of only daughters.

In Vatva, Ahmedabad, Jamila recalled her husband's death. He was killed while out on work, at a distance from his home, near a large public park.

He has gone.... Everything in the house is what he had set up. The television, this house, this sewing machine he had provided everything for me.... We never knew how it happened. He was on his bicycle.... We got the body after some days....

My second son... he was also out... he came home after running, fleeing through the whole city.... The things he saw: burning, bodies, fires... I cannot even say. When he reached, he could not speak. He went crazy. He tried to kill himself by cutting his wrists....

I tried everything. First my husband, then my son. Who can watch their son in this state? I kept two *rozas* (fasts), I prayed. The social workers took him for treatment in the hospital for many months. Now he is better; he is working like his elder brother.

Now again we are facing displacement. They are going to build a road here...our house, which my husband built with his hard-earned money for us, is going to be demolished. I don't know where we will go...when all this will stop.... What is going to happen now.... We have faced so much *takleef* (suffering) already....

Earlier we had lived in Jamalpur. There things were so unsafe. There was some skirmish all the time.... Here we thought it would be safe.... My husband thought we should move to Vatva, built this place.... Who was to know this would happen....

In Ahmedabad again, Zakiya spoke about the death of her husband, in communal violence eight or 10 years ago. This time round, in 2002, they were safer, in the heart of a Muslim-dominated area, but were fully exposed to the trauma and suffering all around them because of the close presence of a relief camp, where Zakiya herself had come to the assistance of the traumatized. Zakiya did not speak much about the hard years she must have spent bringing up her small children alone, though she did mention that she was not able to give them much of an education. Her thoughts returned again and again to the terrible violence they had more recently witnessed.

He was a good man, gentle. Never got into fights. Did not believe in this Hindu–Muslim thing...was always trying to stop violence.... Even this time there was some fight...he went to see what was happening. He did not come back alive....

We moved from there after that; came to this place. The children have been very good, but things are hardly safe.... Who can say, what is a safe place?

Here also, we have seen so much.... Two years ago, if you had seen such things you could not sleep at night.... It was terrible....

In the heat in the camp, the suffering.... We spent whole nights awake...the men patrolling. Who could sleep at a time like that?

Even now there is no real peace. There is a feeling...anything can happen at any time. People did not return to their houses for months. Some even today have not gone back...have permanently shifted elsewhere or the Relief Committee has settled them in other places....

Nearby, Abida, perhaps in her 30s, with several young children, related the experience of coming to terms with her husband's death in the violence of 2002. He was killed in a lane somewhere in the neighbourhood, probably while on his way home from work.

We lived in Dani Limbdi on rent...we had moved here some years ago. My husband made this house.... Before his death, I had hardly gone out even into the next street. He did everything: shopping, getting the things. I knew nothing.... I was in *pardah*. I did not go out of the house at all.

Then I had to learn everything. With the help of the social workers, I got my ration card, birth certificate, death certificate. Opened a bank account.... Then I got the compensation of 1.5 lakhs. Everything was a struggle....

Now I have learnt some stitching, making *dupattas*.... I go to a house down the road.... We work from there. [I gather this work is coordinated by the Self-Employed Women's Association, SEWA.] Three of my children are with my in-laws in Uttar Pradesh. They study there....

My in-laws wanted to take the money that came, when my husband died. But I did not give in. I had to argue with them. I said, now there is nothing, no security. This money is for my children. I put it in fixed deposit for them. I also get some widow pension and SEWA gives some money for the children's fees....

I had to learn all these things after he went. Before, everything was taken care of. *Allah* sent these days also....

Several elements need to be recapitulated with regard to these traumatized voices. Most of these stories, and others, were told in bits and pieces. One might employ the term 'narrative wreck' used by Ronald Dworkin (1993: 211) in slightly different context for the kind of telling one obtains here (see also Frank 1995). Indeed, Frank

(1995) in *The Wounded Storyteller: Body, Illness and Ethics*, describes the elements of what, as I have mentioned earlier, he calls 'chaos narratives'. It is a concept that appears to resonate with the un-stitched tales we have been listening to. He argues that (1995: 98):

> ...those who are truly *living* the chaos cannot tell in words. To turn the chaos into a verbal story is to have some reflective grasp of it. The chaos that can be told in story is already taking place at a distance and is being reflected on retrospectively. For a person to gain such a reflective grasp of her own life, distance is a prerequisite. In telling the events of one's life, events are mediated by the telling. But in the lived chaos there is no mediation, only immediacy. Lived chaos makes reflection, and consequently storytelling, impossible.

This distance may be a function of time, but it is *by no means* transparently so. Referring to Langer's work with the testimonies of Holocaust witnesses collected over 40 years after the end of the Second World War (Langer 1991), Arthur Frank argues that many of the stories of those witnesses are 'chaos narratives', stories which are not really stories at all because they have no narrative sequence, 'only an incessant present' (1991: 99) and a hurried 'and then and then and then' mode of telling (1991: 91) in which each clause is cut off by the next (1991: 105). It is possible to perceive the words of the sufferers just related as being caught in just such a mode of narration.

This kind of telling diverges quite considerably from modes of narration described by Cheryl Mattingly (1998) through which suffering is sought to be endured, perhaps even controlled, if not conquered, through the process of storytelling. Mattingly (1998) defines several modes through which coherent narratives of suffering may be conceived, which may often also overlap. These include the telling of stories as cultural scripts wherein a difficult experience is interpreted and come to terms with by fitting it into 'pre-existing cultural models' (1998: 14), the telling of stories as aesthetic expressions whereby individual experience is connected to a preferred narrative form such as, perhaps, cultural myth, through the appropriate poetic device and, finally, the telling of stories as life histories or life stories. According to Mattingly (1998: 13), life histories, importantly, as a mode of narrating the experience of suffering, tend to emphasize a person's need to try and find coherence and continuity in their lives (see Linde 1993). Thus, telling a life becomes a significant device by which persons try to interpret disruption or pain in the overall context of their lives. The voices we listened to in Mumbai in particular appear attuned to such reflective possibility.

In contrast, in Ahmedabad and Baroda, a climate of unease and trepidation surrounding the *telling*. Once someone said to me: 'You could be arrested for coming to a Muslim area and talking to us like this, about these things. With this government anything is possible'. The discomfort with the government was patent and seemed to have been further magnified with its enormous success in the election that had been held some months earlier. Mention was often made of the hasty acquittals passed by the courts against the accused, usually for lack of proper evidence or investigation, in several cases of the killing of Muslims. So far has proceeded the indifference, that judges have observed the lack of due investigation by the public prosecutors, even while they have had to acquit the accused.[10] In fact, the state government had to admit to the Supreme Court that the high court trial in the case of the Best Bakery violence may have been flawed and that the prosecution's 'hostile' witnesses may have been won over or coerced.[11]

There seems to be, further, among the victims of the violence, a certain mistrust of the capacity of the commission of enquiry into the violence to deliver the truth: mention was made of victims skipping the proceedings and of doctored versions of the truth being submitted before it. More than anything else, the keenness of the government to push on relentlessly with the rhetoric of progress, while burying, without due acknowledgement, the extreme suffering of the victims of the recent past was unbearable. Though there are obvious limits to the comparison, one is reminded very much of the violence of Partition that often would not leave its victims, despite the anxiety of the nascent governments of India and Pakistan to put it behind somewhat unceremoniously in the eagerness of development.

We need to spend some time mulling over what we have heard. While the voices from Gujarat seem splintered and caught up in images of distress, those from Mumbai showed a greater tendency to mould themselves into fuller and more complete narratives. As mentioned before, women in Baroda and Ahmedabad did speak, if sometimes falteringly, about the violence. Most of them, moreover, connected what they had to say with accounts of previous riots and violence undergone or known of. Further, one obtained occasional glimpses into other elements of strain, usually located within the web of kinship and family. Nevertheless, the style of narration could not be said to have taken on the nuance and detail of *telling a life*. There were gaps in the narration; there was a more singular focus on the violence itself. Why should this be so? Can the variance be simply put down to the difference between the time of event and the time of narration in the two instances?

Certainly, this is a considerable difference, though even the Gujarati residents were speaking more than a year and a half to two years after the violence, and, at least one of the women spoke of the painful loss she had suffered nearly a decade earlier. Women in Mumbai could also not, in any sense, put aside the past for several of them have spent all these years struggling with the authorities for the monetary compensation due to them. Psychological studies, moreover, show that it is in the very nature of traumatic memory to ingrain itself within the imagination in the form of vivid sensations that even the process of narrative construction does not usually dislodge. Intense images characterize almost *all* the narratives; while completeness may be the relevant distinguishing attribute. *Duration* per se does not appear, even from a psychological perspective, to be the overarching or only conditioning element of forms of memory construction. In their analysis of trauma memories in victims of childhood trauma and adult trauma, van der Kolk and Fisler (1995) showed how the few subjects in their study who were unable to, even as grown ups, tell a cohesive story of their trauma were all victims of abuse as children. Langer (1991) speaks of the testimony of a Holocaust witness who even four decades later bore his suffering not as a 'scar' which could be said to be a reminder of 'past injury healed in the present' but as a 'festering wound, a blighted convalescence' (1991: 92).

We may bracket then, for the moment, duration as a significant rationale in order to be able to explore the possible *social* conditions that may be relevant considerations. It becomes apparent, as the last chapter has already traced in a somewhat abbreviated mode, that the social environments of distress manifest significant differences. While there is no intent here to enter into a catalogue of comparison between the relief efforts in Mumbai, Baroda or

Ahmedabad, some pertinent remarks about the overall climate of assistance, which also emerge from victims' voices, should be made. The overwhelming discontent of survivors in Baroda and Ahmedabad related to their sense that, this time around, despite the enormity of the scale of suffering, no one seemed to care. As several said in very similar words: 'They say Muslims had to learn a lesson. It is retribution for Godhra. But we are not responsible for what happened in Godhra and they are trying to wipe out the whole community for it'.

There has already been mention of the unabated attempts of authorities to charge ahead without turning back. Such attempts included the decision to shut down the relief camps as soon as possible, the declaration of elections when thousands were yet staying in camps and were afraid to return home and the inadequacy (in contrast to the earthquake relief effort) of civil efforts for reconciliation and rehabilitation. Compensation was meagre when paid at all and further pain was caused by an initial announcement that proposed less compensation to the victims of the post-Godhra violence than to the families of those who died in the Godhra train tragedy. According to several people, the commission of enquiry formed to investigate the violence does not seem to have been able to inspire the trust of survivors. There were stories of witnesses who have stayed away from the hearings.[12]

With regard to the court cases in process, many persons mentioned the Best Bakery case, where the main witness, Zahira Sheikh, asserted that she had retracted on her own testimony in the courts because of threats issued her. The Bilkis case being managed by the CBI and the Best Bakery case, now transferred by the Supreme Court to Maharashtra, have continued to remain in the news and the efforts for justice in these two cases have been yielding some fruits. In July 2004, the Supreme Court ordered that the Bilkis case would be heard in a Mumbai court as well. However, these cases remain somewhat isolated and, further, they appear only to underline the apparent impossibility of justice or the retrieving of 'normalcy' in Gujarat itself. Only a tiny percentage of all cases have even come to trial and activists voiced regret over this paucity too.

Minor skirmishes and violence have continued in the months after the horrors of late February and early March 2002.[13] More than two years after the violence, a central government delegation had to consider the question of security for victims of the violence. As a result, in June 2004, CISF personnel were deployed in places where the victims are resident, particularly Dahod, Godhra Himmatnagar, Vadodara and in Ahmedabad in the Naroda Patia and Bapu Nagar areas. People remain packed and ready to flee at a moment's notice. As one activist said: 'It is virtually impossible to concentrate on peace-building measures, when, as in the area we work, Muslims have fled four times in the past few months alone due to fears of a repeat of violent attacks'. The words of the social activist, 'Nothing is normal', continue to ring in the ears. Restitution *in any sense at all*, as Farzana voiced it, has been ominously elusive. Divine intervention ('He cares more about us') may be the only refuge. An apparently unending series of pressures seems to face Muslims (and other minorities) and those who struggle on their behalf in Gujarat. In the agonized voice of Sophia Khan, a Muslim activist in Ahmedabad with whom we will meet again later:

Here we keep filing PIL [Public Interest Litigation] after PIL... against the inter-religious marriages monitoring cell, the census of Muslims and Christians and on and on. We cannot sit down and think about what we want to do; we just react to things. Even the NGOs tell the Muslims: 'We are prepared to resettle you in other villages'. Why not in their native village? Because the VHP and Bajrang Dal will not allow it. Their writ runs large. There seem to be no laws. All people have sentiment for their native place. So also do Muslims, but they are not allowed. We are creating Indias and Pakistans within our borders. The few Muslims in Hindu areas are not safe, can we blame them for moving? If judges are not safe in their official residences, who can protect the common people?... I feel disheartened and disillusioned. I just keep working on other issues, where I can at least see some results. This keeps me going.

The contrast with Mumbai at first sight does not immediately appear very distinct. While many Muslims I spoke to in the city still had cases being heard against them for apparent 'rioting' in 1992–93, those who attacked them are not only safe but also, quite often, in positions of power. Relocation became an imperative for many families. In many cases, it was by the bullet of the police that death came. The persons accused of killing Tabassum *Appa*'s son were all acquitted; witnesses revoked their earlier testimonies. Cases against the police for indiscriminate firing have been similarly discharged.[14] Compensation was delayed and sometimes denied in the absence of the bodies of the victims. Struggles for financial compensation for the so-called 'missing persons' have taken, in some cases, the whole decade since the violence. The recommendations of the Srikrishna Commission Report on the riots in Mumbai have not so far been implemented. Indeed, many persons I listened to spoke of a climate of uncertainty and hostility being *currently* created with regard to Muslims. They felt that conditions were beginning slowly to replicate if not exceed those that had existed 10 years ago. This was because of the recent series of bomb blasts the city had experienced, each of them attributed to the work of various radical Muslim organizations. As some said, the blasts have forced ordinary Muslims on the defensive, compelled to restate each time their condemnation of such deadly attacks.[15] Policing of 'Muslim' areas, strict at most times, has begun to show some ugly shades in the wake of the 'threat of terror'.[16]

Nevertheless, Hazira Ali and Tabassum *Appa*, as well as the other women, were moved sometimes to say: 'However bad our situation was, theirs [Muslims in Gujarat] is infinitely worse'. They talked of the violence itself: the scale of killings, the treatment of women, the extent of losses suffered by the Muslims, the rumours of persistent economic boycott in some areas and the overwhelming evidence of the large-scale complicity of the administration with the aggressors.[17] More than these, they talked of the 'after violence'. In a deeply shared understanding, their sense of being somewhat better off seemed to lie in the context of support they encountered. They referred particularly to Justice Srikrishna and the work of the commission and to the work of social activists, journalists and ordinary citizens in the wake of the violence in Mumbai. Not one woman professed to feeling abandoned. '*Logon ko kuch laga*': People felt something after the violence, that what had happened was not a good thing. 'Many people helped', is always the way one heard them speak. Indeed, if the women struggled against hostility and inconsiderateness, it was quite often with their own community members and sometimes their kin. While relief efforts obviously reach a crescendo and then slowly peter out, several relief organizations and persons have worked closely with many of these women over the long 10 year period in pursuit of their cases for compensation. These include, very importantly, the *mohalla* committees.

Moreover, as touched on somewhat fleetingly in the last chapter, it is the work of the Srikrishna Commission that, very significantly, gave to these women the public space so crucial to victims of immense social crimes for the expression of their suffering. While saying this, one must not underestimate the work put in by relief organizations and women's groups to encourage the bereaved sufferers to speak. Many of these were women who had barely ventured out of their homes in the pre-violence days and had perhaps never entered such public zones or spoken before unrelated men. Even so, the women showed remarkable strength. Several of the women whose stories are narrated here testified before the commission, some of them courageously named those they recognized in the mobs that came to attack them.

The commission formed a secure space of public listening for these women, of shared acknowledgement of their torment. Justice Srikrishna showed himself remarkably open to pursuing and recording what he quoted from the *Ramayana* to describe as the unpalatable, 'bitter' truth.[18] His recommendations included the prioritizing of compensation cases of those 'missing persons' who could, by all the evidence received, be presumed killed. There were, of course, other enquiry committees and fact-finding missions that probed the violence in Mumbai and Gujarat. In the latter case, certainly, the number of such committees, national and international, and their reports has been enormous. Nevertheless, in the eyes of a people crying for their rights as citizens, it is the official commission set up by the state from which the expectations tend to be the highest and from whom redress is most insistently sought.[19] Moreover, in the case of many of the persons I spoke with, the onus of relief and rehabilitation was left to religious organizations, rather than those of the state or non-religious social activist groups. This has further isolated Muslims from the public sphere; religious organizations are concentrating on issues of survival and faith, and are not encouraging of the act of witness of the survivor as wounded 'citizen' in the public domain.

While social activists perhaps more than survivors themselves continue to reiterate the need for *justice*, the women I heard in

Mumbai appear to have forged an uneasy truce with the reality.[20] No attempt must be made to minimize the need for justice to be done as well as for justice to be seen to be done in the case of great social atrocities. Nor should I be perceived at all to be suggesting that the families of those killed would not like to see the conviction of the murderers. This is definitely not the case. Nevertheless, for the survivors, justice in the courts is manifestly not *everything*. The fact that a space was created in which their wounds were publicly admitted and grieved, the fact that their testimony was taken seriously within this space, the fact that they were able to name the evil-doers and expose their crimes, the fact that the commission appointed by the state *confirmed* their evidence at its conclusion—must all be held to be critical moral victories for the survivors. The claims for compensation of some of these women took years to resolve; however, success has been achieved in most cases and, importantly, the battles kept on. Further, in Mumbai, in the aftermath of the violence, the police and authorities were keen to be seen as non-discriminatory and several efforts, including the setting up of the local-level *mohalla* committees, were made to work with people to address issues of conflict.[21]

It might, indeed, be suggested that the process of coping (for I would hesitate to speak of recovery) for women in Mumbai signalled by their ability to narrate their experiences and, critically, integrate them into accounts of their lives has been, to some extent at least, rendered possible by the secure context of public listening and acknowledging that embraced them. The evocation of this argument would not leave unacknowledged the fact that the capacity to resume the work of everyday living, day by day, as well as to learn to negotiate gradually the longer term, in the wake of great social suffering, must necessarily be processes that remain fragile and always unfinished. The narratives, even when they assume the shape of telling a life, always remain 'interrupted narratives', lives told *through* disruptions. Even so, the suggestion actually proceeds a little differently. The tentative intimation here is not that recovery has been achieved but that the social conditions of support spoken of render possible the active surrender of pain through the constant struggle of retrieving or repossessing a disrupted life in story.

As Das and Kleinman (2001) have already been recorded as saying in the last chapter, communities and groups are not chained to a fixed notion of justice. The setting-into-motion of processes of public owning of pain create the possibilities for resuming the life of the everyday. The attempts to silence trauma by putting it behind or forgetting it, on the other hand, and to surge ahead without due space for remembrance or some form, however flimsy, of public restitution, tend to unravel the speech of victims, induce silence and fracture conversation. According to Farzana, 'The government now says: "Forget what happened. Forgive us". How can we?' As Herman has argued, in the absence of a supportive social environment, a victim, especially one who may be always already socially devalued, such as a woman, 'may find that the most traumatic events of her life take place outside the realm of socially validated reality. Her experience becomes unspeakable' (1994: 8). The silence delays, indeed denies, recovery. Though publics may wish to forget, survivors demand remembrance and engagement. In the absence of these, events may remain 'unredeemed and unredeemable' (Langer 1991: 200); trapped in 'unreconciled understanding' (Ibid.), witnesses are unable and unwilling to relinquish the immediacy of their suffering for they perceive no worthy vision of survival or the future.[22]

We may perhaps now return to recording some of the other significant themes and threads pursued through the course of this chapter. For one, we have become aware of the tenuousness and fragility of the boundary between the violences of everyday life and extraordinary violence. Women faced tensions within and outside the circles of kin and community. They had to struggle to maintain their own under the not particularly benevolent scrutiny of male community members and elders. Deceased husbands' relatives were often not willing or able to assist beyond a point; moreover, women must have faced their own tussles to secure what they received from the state for their own children and ensure that these meagre resources were not captured by husbands' kin or others within the kinship circle. Such tussles are often referred to only indirectly; occasionally specifically, as in Mumtaz's mother's case or in Abida's case. In and, indeed, beyond every voice may be captured the pitiless daily battles of survival. It is impossible to attempt to minimize Tabassum Appa's relentless preoccupation to find some work she and her daughters could do from home, Najma Bibi's labour of providing for her children being shared among her close natal kin but only through the painful device of dispersing the family over long periods, Ameena and her children's multi-tasking to cope with an aging husband and brutal losses due to the riots or Salmaben's herculean efforts, mentioned in an earlier chapter, to save half of each meagre rupee earned to rebuild what has been ruined.

Fraught encounters with the police and state officials constitute another trajectory of pressure in ordinary or 'riot' time. Whether it is the neutrality of the police at stake or the complicity of attackers with lower-level political leaders, law and government appear in treacherous garb in the imaginations of the Muslim women heard here. Painful periodic interviews with the attacker to whom appeal must be directed deform the everyday with the grinding reminder of one's powerlessness. At the same time, for the poor and marginalized, the corruption of the system has been seen to be sometimes both enabling and insidiously ensnaring. Several women make reference oblique or direct to their disagreements with the norms of behaviour imposed on them by community or kin-group. For most, tense compromise has been imperative; the costs of open disregard—isolation or ridicule perhaps— is too excessive to bear. However muted, though, confrontations, as in *Appa*'s case or Najma Bibi's or Hazira's or even Sultana's, are inevitable and demand careful manoeuvring and management.

It is perhaps unsurprising that our women speak hardly of religion, of their Muslim identity or of Muslim politics to do with *mandir* or *masjid* alike. Do we simply write off this silence as indicative of the ignorance of women wrapped in domesticity with no knowledge of larger complexities? I would be cautious. Living under the shadow of the savage reality of violence, all the women here are excruciatingly aware, whether or not they make reference to it, of the bitter politics of Hindu–Muslim identity that has rent their lives. Hazira's surprise when her neighbours told her to 'Go to Pakistan' did not arise from her unawareness of what they meant when they said it; it arose from a deep pain at being alienated by those she thought shared her small world. Rather, I would reiterate what I said in the previous chapter: men speak more in terms of larger narratives of community identity and politics. Constantly grazing against community norms in the small and big strifes of everyday life, women perhaps incline less towards this language, for they understand too surely its insidious capacity to recoil on them.

notes

1. Abena P.A. Busia, 'Liberation' (1983) from *The Heinemann Book of African Women's Poetry*, Heinemann Educational Publishers, Oxford, 1995. Edited by Stella and Frank Chipasula.

2. Since I was not expecting such a mode of narration, it intrigued me and led me to think about possible explanations, which form the basis for the analysis in this chapter. All anthropological reasoning being necessarily unfinished, I submit the thesis of the chapter cautiously, though it seems to me one which makes sense of much of the data. Men also talked in terms of their lives, but most often with a slightly different focus. Life histories of men more typically interwove with explanations of suffering in terms of cultural myths or social scripts (see Mattingly 1998). Most of these conversations took place over an hour and sometimes over two hours. I usually began by telling the women that I would like to understand how their own experience of violence had affected them in terms of economic circumstance and occupation (particularly battles for compensation), in terms of losses with regard to their children's education and in terms of possible physical displacement (temporary or permanent) they may have had to undergo. I also asked about how recent violence has, in general, affected the identity of the Muslim community, adding that I would be happy to hear whatever they had to say on these or related issues. Beyond these initial questions as my introduction, I rarely said or had to say much more. Men often took up the second question—of identity—a lot more; women rarely, as we shall see. While the questions were obviously open and positively *encouraged* narration, they did not immediately invite life stories.

3. Almost all names in this chapter have been changed.

4. This is clearly the view taken by Mehta and Chatterji (2001) in their analysis of riots in Dharavi, when they seem to argue that narratives crystallize the event, evaluating future and past from the point of view of that which happened.

5. This was the common compensation package. One lakh rupees was paid in two parts. Rs 70,000 was locked for seven years in a national savings scheme and only interest on it paid during the interval. The remaining amount of Rs 30,000 was awarded by cheque.

6. I am aware of recent critiques of the theory of traumatic memory, especially those coming from Hodgkin and Radstone and the contributors to their volumes (see Radstone and Hodgkin 2003 and Hodgin and Radstone 2003) as well from Paul Antze and Michael Lambek (1996). Antze and Lambek's work and the authors in the volume offer a critique of Herman and her interpretation of Pierre Janet's theory. In so doing, they seek to underline the importance not of remembering but of forgetting in the process of psychological healing. It appears to me, however, that the volume's critique is somewhat reductive of Herman's own understanding and is not convincing in its argument that Janet invoked 'forgetting' rather than narration in the process of recovery. Herman certainly is not unaware that the final process of healing

involves that of the gradual erasure of the traumatic event, at least in all its sharpness and pain, from the memory. Hodgkin and Radstone (2003: 97) argue that the interruptions and elisions of traumatic memory bear no specific relation to an event but are the characteristic of the 'workings of memory in general'. They also find it hard to pin down the traumatized. Is it those who bear the loss or also those who witness the loss? There is too much sliding, they argue, and it is difficult to know where to draw the line. The politicization of loss is a very real danger in contemporary times. The difficulty of locating the traumatized is not limited to trauma theory. While politicization is a problem, it is not restricted to questions of trauma and cannot be considered an adequate argument for ignoring the theory. Moreover, for our purposes, it must be noted that the differences in types of memory emerging from the data are sharp and real and call out for explanation; the theory of traumatic memory indeed affords a good location from which to comprehend them.

7. It is difficult to ascribe 'merit' in such disputes, in the absence of any detail about the previous state of relations in the family. However, some of the critical angles may be considered. The woman clearly felt the pull of kinship norms, which delegate the care of the mother to the son and his wife. It should, in her understanding, be the mother, not the wife, who receives the compensation. The daughter-in-law's depravity is measured by her taking the money and her mother-in-law's jewellery, abandoning her, and denying her contact with the only thing she has to remember her son by—his children. Given the totality of the divide, it is likely that relations between mother-in-law and daughter-in-law had shown strain even before the violence. Perhaps the daughter-in-law perceived the opportunity to de-link herself; perhaps she just needed, in the traumatic circumstances, to return to the natal fold. We cannot be sure.

8. I was accompanied on the visit by a local social activist. It might be mentioned here that I find the categories 'walking narrative' and 'sitting narrative' carved out by Mehta and Chatterji (2001) in their article mentioned earlier somewhat contrived. The situation created by a riot or other forms of large-scale devastation *necessitate* such 'walking' narratives, for mapping out the visible or remembered destruction of places and even persons. It does not seem to me that this mapping or imagining of spaces is not also sometimes attempted, through gesture, pointing or naming roads, junctions or buildings, when people are speaking within homes or other enclosed places. Many such walking narratives tend to be narratives of men, which Mehta and Chatterji do not seem sensitive to. There are some exceptions, though, as in the case I describe. 'Sitting' narratives must be of all types, surely. Again, men and women render different 'sitting' narratives.

One must also mention those who did not speak. Can our argument apply to them? I tentatively suggest that in terms of where the Muslim community in these different areas finds or locates itself at the present time, it should. There were indeed some cases of persons and families I approached in Mumbai at least who would not talk with me. However, these were very few in number. Almost all those I approached consented to speak and *did so in the particular narrative style I have mentioned*. Therefore, as said earlier, the pattern that began to emerge is sought to be understood here. Given the fraught nature of the subject, the analysis may well be partial; I put it forward as a possible lens through which to view the material.

9. These were women who belonged to the Mahila Patchwork Cooperative Society started in Juhapura some decades ago. It is a haven for women with few resources and those who have lost their husbands or their homes in disasters of all kinds. Nasreen had just joined the society and was beginning work there. Several survivors of violence were together when this conversation took place over a few hours.

10. See, for instance, 'Prosecution did not Examine Eyewitnesses', *The Times of India*, 17 October 2003, p. 9.

11. 'Trial may have been Flawed, Admits Gujarat, *The Times of India*, 20 September 2003, p. 1

12. The press also had such reports. See, for example, 'Vatva Victims Skip Riots Probe Hearing', *The Times of India*, 4 November 2003, p. 5.

13. See, for instance, reports such as 'Victory Marches end in Riots, Curfew in Vadodara', *The Times of India*, 16 December 2002, p. 7; 'Violence mars Id in Gujarat', *The Times of India*, 13 February 2003, p. 5; 'Violence mars Ganpati Immersion in Vadodara', *The Times of India*, 10 September 2003, p. 5.

14. For example, the case against former Police Commissioner R.D. Tyagi and eight others for firing against Muslims in the infamous Suleman Bakery episode. The accused were discharged on the grounds that they were doing their duty, though the Srikrishna Commission had found the firing to be unnecessary and excessive.

15. See, for instance, interview with the well-known Mumbai actor Farooque Shaikh, from which I have quoted in the last chapter. He argued that Muslims should not have to necessarily rise up as a community to condemn every act of terror. Their condemnation must be 'taken as a given', taken for granted. ('Minority Report', *The Times of India*, 2 September 2003, p. 14). Also see the prominent photograph of Muslim women praying at the site of a recent bomb blast on the first page of a national daily (*The Times of India*, 26 September 2003, p. 1).

16. Reports of police atrocities and abuse of power emerge regularly. A man who was arrested for playing a role in a bomb blast that took place in December 2002, disappeared under mysterious circumstances from police custody within a few weeks. The family claim that he was beaten to death in custody; the police's claim is that he escaped from the police vehicle while being taken to Aurangabad and met with an accident ('Mother of Blast Accused says Police Killed her Son', *The Times of India*, 14 June 2003, p. 3). Witnesses have testified that screams were heard from the room where the man was being interrogated and that he had vomited blood subsequently. In another well-known incident, Mohammed Altaf, also arrested in the blast cases, alleged that the police had made him sign a bogus confession. Recently, two young men lodged a police complaint that an officer wrongly accosted them and wrongly accused them of being associated with the banned Students' Islamic Movement of India. They were beaten and taunted. (see 'Youths Accuse Police of Bias', *The Times of India*, 29 April 2003, p. 3). Various human rights groups as well as the Minorities Commission have cautioned against the use of such

brutal methods by the police ('Human Rights Activists Advise Restraint', *The Times of India*, 4 December 2002, p. 3).

17. The involvement of the police and administration in the violence has been corroborated by the several reports brought out afterwards (see, for instance, Dayal 2002; Concerned Citizens' Tribunal-Gujarat 2002; Human Rights Watch 2002 and 2003; Varadarajan 2002). Recently, a top police official is reported to have said that persons in the government ordered the 'elimination' of members of the minority community (Leena Misra, 'Modi and his Aides Ordered 'Elimination' of Minorities', *The Times of India*, 14 April 2005, p. 1).

18. *Sulabhaah purushaa rajan satatam priya vaadinah*
Apriyasya cha pathhyasya vakta shrota cha durlabah
[Persons pleasing in speech are easy to find; it is difficult to find one who speaks or listens to the bitter, but wholesome, truth]. *Srikrishna Commission Report.*

19. The intensity of expectations of law and the government can be seen elsewhere. In Gujarat, such was the implicit faith of Muslims in the law, such their trust in democratic procedure, that raped and assaulted women, tortured and almost naked, trudged to police stations in remote areas to file First Information Reports (Nandini Manjrekar, Baroda, personal communication). Medical assistance was sought afterwards, the reports filed first. Of course, we now know that many of these reports were not properly filed by officers; the accusations were toned down or minimized (Human Rights Watch 2002). As Khilnani has argued, the post-colonial state lies at the very core of India. It has 'etched itself into the imagination of Indians in a way that no previous political agency had ever done (1998: 41).

20. Social activist Teesta Setalvad maintains that the wounds of Mumbai will not heal until justice is done. ('For Healing, you need Justice', *The Times of India*, 4 December 2002, p. 3.) Another social activist who spoke with me, Shakeel Ahmed of Nirbhay Bano Andolan also stressed the need for justice, as did Sophia Khan working with the Vikas Adhyayan Kendra in Ahmedabad.

21. We might recall the words of Dharavi's Waqar Khan from the last chapter: 'The police needed to remove the stain of blood that had tainted their uniforms in the violence. Hence, they set up the *mohalla* committees and made efforts to build communal harmony'.

22. This was written before the general elections of 2004. With a Congress government at the centre, some of this dismay has been no doubt mitigated. However, a lot will need to change in Gujarat itself, including the way in which POTA has been used, in order to bring a more discernible shift in community sentiment. Even now, there is little possibility of that happening without something of a struggle. While the 'Best Bakery' case was shifted out of the jurisdiction of Gujarat a while ago, very recently (July 2004) another case, the case of Bilkis who survived rape and the carnage of her family, was also transferred to the jurisdiction of the Mumbai High Court. This move by the Supreme Court, made because Bilkis herself felt that she would not receive justice in Gujarat, only underlines the continued weakness of trust of Gujarati Muslims in the administration and the State. The battle did not end there. The public prosecutor appointed by Gujarat to hear Zahira Sheikh's case

was criticized by the Supreme Court for opposing the issue of arrest warrants against the accused. He was subsequently removed and the Supreme Court appointed public prosecutors, who had the confidence of the victim, from Maharashtra, P.R. Vakil and Manjula Rao. Each step, therefore, is embattled and progress is slow and not achieved without great effort and enormous tussles along the way.

chapter five

fissures in a time of crisis

It will obviously not have escaped notice that the word 'community' has been employed quite freely through the course of these chapters. There is considerable justification for its use, I would maintain. For the kind of assertive Hindu identity-based politics that has emerged around the issue of the Babri Masjid–Ramjanmabhoomi in recent decades has, in many ways, thrust on Muslims almost everywhere a sense of belonging to a single, and threatened, community. In Mumbai certainly the slaughter of hundreds of Muslims in the violence of January 1993 and the injury and displacement of thousands of others ensured that all would afterwards bear a collective scar. The patterns of displacement which, as we have already seen, increasingly confined Muslims to certain spaces and areas of the city, have entrenched separation and the sense of 'Otherness'. Similar enforced patterns of spatial division have been perceived emerging in Gujarat cities such as Ahmedabad and Baroda.[1]

Nevertheless, as all good scholars have warned us, splits of sect, caste, class or language manifest themselves everywhere (Chandra 1984; Pandey 1990) and may never be disregarded. Certainly, when it comes to marriage alliances as well as to questions of custom and tradition, one can hardly speak of a 'community'. It is the some-times highly localized, sect and caste groups that form the relevant universes. Some of this good advice, particularly with respect to sectarian divisions and differing schools of thought, continued to lurk in my thoughts even as I came across everywhere the real feeling that 'Muslims' are under attack. Perhaps it was the precise sameness of this language that was itself an alert, language that

I soon began to appreciate was, more often than not, spoken by men. It required little to scratch beneath the surface of the all-encompassing category to find, perhaps not quite as paradoxically as it may at first sight appear, both urgent claims of unity as well as fierce assertions of difference. Having been thus sensitized, it was a short step to the realization that I needed to talk with some of the religious leaders among the Muslims, especially those who had worked, and sometimes continued to work, with riot survivors. For clearly, the ideas must be under fashion in spaces other than the unassuming homes in which survivors conversed with me.

Thus, in this chapter (as well as in the one that follows), I attempt to enter a little more closely the worlds of the survivors of extreme violence by going beyond to embrace some of those community members and leaders who have worked closely with the survivors in at least some of the processes of rehabilitation and recovery. Some of the organizations at work have wide influence within the community as evidenced by the readiness with which their names are recognized, by the extent of relief work and other social and religious activities that they engage in, the prominent banners which proclaim their ideas in Muslim-dominated areas or by their ability to come together and bring people together for certain kinds of protest movements, such as one which took place some months ago against the proposed visit of Ariel Sharon to Mumbai.[2] Indeed, one has also now and then come across a degree of grumbling against them by survivors of violence who claim that they extract religious loyalty before offering or handing out aid. Their presence, moreover, at the sites of rehabilitation evidently serves two purposes: first, to raise the morale of the survivors and second, to give *talim* and teach the people about correct practice in Islam. Not all such members of religious organizations or movements are clergy or Ulema; several are lay persons specifically trained or educated to work for the cause of teaching proper Islamic practice. They come into contact with large numbers of people and are fairly well-known in the local communities.

Through the interweaving narratives of this chapter, then, the Muslim tryst with pain takes on another dimension. In listening to men's voices, the strenuous efforts to re-fabricate honour and reconstruct a historical narrative of Muslim pride become apparent. In some cases, the language and ideas used by male witnesses and survivors of violence appear to bear the imprint of thoughts articulated by different religious leaders. One must definitely suggest that strains of a common ideology find their expression here, though it is virtually impossible to receive from anyone an open admission of membership of a particular religious organization. The intermittent emergence of such ideas in the field, however, is of some interest.

The chapter bends to trace the intricate formulations of stoicism and forbearance, challenge and defiance that may be discerned in the utterances of men. Narratives bleed here; they also expose alarming rifts that the context of violence seems to have unfortunately deepened if it has not, in fact, created. In a discussion of this nature, it seems to have become almost impossible to avoid reference to those exceedingly treacherous categories 'fundamentalist' and 'liberal'. I will not wholly attempt to keep away from the mention for while popular labels certainly blur understanding, their use unhappily often has significant implications for those thus marked. Indeed, Indian media reports are frequently noticeable both for their overuse of such categories as well as for their haziness in such usage. We may well enquire how leaders and Muslims view such categories, against the background of increasing aggression in ethnic politics in India today. Though, when one employs an anthropological perspective in the field one would immediately be on the look out for the fissures and the fragility of categories conceptualized as rigid and supposedly impermeable.

In view of my current location, it may not be an altogether bad idea to repeat the words of the Prince of Wales, spoken on a visit to Oxford in 1993:

> We need to be careful of that emotive label, 'fundamentalism', and distinguish, as Muslims do, between revivalists, who choose to take the practice of their religion most devoutly, and fanatics or extremists, who use this devotion for political ends (1993: 16).

In the Indian context, the issues are much more complicated. Given the minority position and the geographical dispersion of Muslims, 'devotion for political ends' has, right from the outset, very little potential of fulfilment regardless of the ambitions of individual persons or particular sub-groups. Such ambitions may not, however, be non-existent. I will return to this discussion later. Moreover, certain orientations driving persons towards tradition-alism in the face of modernity do emerge. How may we understand these? Further, what we are particularly interested in pursuing are the undoubted if tormented ways in which the growing context of hostility towards Muslims and the increasing violence they have seen in the areas where I worked, has riven the community, sowing strife among sects, causing boundaries to be drawn in the face of uncertainty. This is a process that is simultaneous with the stress on oneness, the expression of which also crops up in diverse places. Further exacerbation of this process has taken place in the wake of terrorist strikes in Mumbai and, more recently, Gujarat. Attributed to militant Muslim groups and individuals, these strikes have the increasing potential of strength-ening antagonism towards Muslims as a whole.

muslims and the question of 'fundamentalism'

Fundamentalism like many other terms in the social sciences is one which has a life both within academics and outside of it. We need to consider both lives; and perhaps to supplement (maybe even subvert) the academic discussions with the complexities and contradictions of the field. Critically, since this is an anthropological analysis, it tries to avoid abstract categories used in a generalizing way. Rather, the effort is to take more seriously what people, and their leaders or elders say, in a particular context; one moves behind abstractions to explore the negotiated intricacies of the 'real'. While our understanding cannot be uncritical, for we have to be aware of people's positioning with respect to what they say (or don't say), there can as well be no easy conflation of the Islamic with the fundamentalist, an inference which newspapers and popular jour-nals are all too easily inclined to reach. As one Muslim said: 'What is wrong with being fundamentalist? It only means going back to the purity of one's roots. It cannot be confused with terrorism'. On the other hand, some sections among the Muslims find the stress on religious purity incompatible with the demands of modernity and negotiation within a plural culture. In order to understand these expressed concerns, therefore, we need to spend some time looking into the ways in which fundamentalism has been variously interpreted in the literature.

The word is these days used almost invariably in connection with Islam, though it has its first connections with Christian movements of an earlier century (Hallencreutz and Westerlund 2002). Today, in fact, there is a very unfavourable understanding of the term. However, in its first phase, the word was self-applied as 'a proud epithet used by and of those who saw themselves as defending the fundamentals of their faith' (Caplan 1990: 3). With respect to Islam, anyway, some writers are inclined to view fundamentalism as that orientation in Islam which propels its adherents towards particularly defined political goals (Tibi 1998; Ali 2002). Accordingly, fundamentalism is perceived 'not as a spiritual faith, but as a political ideology based on the politicizing of religion for socio-political and economic goals in the pursuit of establishing a divine order' (Tibi 1998: 20). Indeed, the term 'political Islam' has been used equally widely (Beinin and Stork 1997; Esposito 1998; Karawan 1997). This perspective differentiates 'puritanism' in Islam per se from its channelling towards the set up of a distinct society and polity running on Islamic principles (Ali 2002).[3]

Anthropologists in particular as well as most of the authors associated with the 'Fundamentalism Project' have tended to a slightly more diffuse definition of fundamentalism believing, first, that it is a bundle or complex of orientations and, second, that like an 'ideal type' all its attributes are rarely found together in a single person or group (Antoun 2001; Caplan 1990; Marty and Appleby 1991a, 1993a, 1993c; 1994; 1995; Munson 1993).[4] Rather, one must conceptualize a continuum of characteristics and those that adhere to them. This is a perspective that seeks to use the term fundamentalism comparatively and to draw its definition from those characteristics that manifest themselves whatever religious tradition or regional context may be under examination. In this view, fundamentalism inescapably emerges as plural, as *fundamentalisms*.[5] Thus, while examining possible opposition to the use of the term, Marty and Appleby hold (1993b: 2):

As a comparative construct encompassing movements within religious traditions as rich and diverse, and as different one from another, as are Islam, Judaism, Christianity, Hinduism, and Buddhism, 'fundamentalism' is a useful analytical device. The title of...the project...is not meant to indicate that every movement examined within it equally qualifies as a fundamentalism. Rather, ...there are 'family resemblances' among disparate movements of religiously inspired reaction to the aspects of the global processes of modernization and secularization in the twentieth century.

Again, Richard Antoun (2001: 153–54) defines fundamentalism as:

a cognitive and affective orientation to the modern world focusing on protest and change. The fundamentalist's protest and outrage is against the ideology of modernism: the emphasis on change over continuity, quantity over quality, and production and profit over sympathy for traditional values such as long-term interpersonal relations, visiting with neighbours and kin, nourishment of home and children, and the pertinence of the religious life over many domains. The fundamentalist's protest is also against the secular nation-state, which it regards as instrumental in pushing religion to the margins.

Fundamentalism's engagement of the modern has been critical to social science's understanding of the term. As Marty and Appleby (1991b: 826) record, fundamentalists:

reaffirm the old doctrines; they subtly lift them from their original context, embellish and institutionalize them, and employ them as ideological weapons against a hostile world.... [In] remaking the world, fundamentalists demonstrate a closer affinity to modernism than to traditionalism.

Clearly, then, fundamentalism is viewed as a peculiarly modern phenomenon and as quintessentially encompassing a critique of the modern. By no means is there ever a complete rejection of the modern. Cultural modernity is usually the target of attack; on the other hand, technological and scientific modernity can be adapted with enormous fruitfulness to fundamentalist causes. While a political stance may lie at the heart of fundamentalist discourse, the loci of power as well as the level of aspiration for it may be very different in varied contexts. And there can certainly be no a priori allocation of fundamentalists to particular positions in political affairs, though they usually take strong right-wing positions on most issues (Caplan 1990: 8; Marty and Appleby 1991b: 837). The return to the purity of a usually mythical defined past is characteristic of many fundamentalist movements and often involves separation from a milieu defined as contaminated because pluralistic.

Thus, according to Antoun (2001: xii), among the various aspects of fundamentalism are the search for purity, the attempt to make ancient truth relevant to the present, the effort to spread the influence of religion across various domains of individual and social life including, for instance, education or economics, selective modernization, controlled acculturation as well as an attitude of confrontation and protest, perhaps even violent, towards political or religious establishments. Munson (1993) has distinguished between types of fundamentalists in accordance with whether they view their struggle as moral or political. Moral struggles confine themselves largely to a focus on a strict Islamic way of life, while political ones aim towards the ultimate establishment of an Islamic state. He conceptualizes a continuum from the mainly moral to the radically political. Another aspect of fundamentalism appears to be the fact that it defines itself explicitly or implicitly in terms of what it abhors or is in opposition to (Antoun 2001: 56; Caplan 1990: 21).

While the concept might suffer somewhat in precision when looked at in this way, it may also be argued that, from this perspective, fundamentalism sheds its frightening image and gains in usefulness in comparative analysis. One can understand the argument put forward by some Muslims that there is nothing wrong inherently with fundamentalism, for it simply implies a return to a purified religion. At the same time, we must be aware that there are those who might see a dilemma in the desire to wash clean the fabric of faith from its immersion in India's deeply syncretic traditions, for this process necessitates, in different contexts, the separation of Muslims from various local cultures, Hindu or other. These processes, in turn, may only increase the distance between ethnic groups and contribute to cementing the conditions for possible future violence. Some of these issues will emerge in the course of the discussion in this chapter. While there will nowhere be the attempt to employ fundamentalism as a *label* in our analysis, we will be on the look out to try and comprehend how the term 'fundamentalism' and its correlates are variously construed, how their meaning is deeply contested depending on the experiences of different persons or groups and how such terms are able to assume negative or positive associations hinging on who is employing the usages and the particular context of reference.

when community fragments

It is both expected and disconcerting to come across the dis-integration of even a presumed sense of unity of a 'Muslim community', accentuated certainly by the crushing pressures of the experience of systematic targeting and violence, particularly over the last decade or so. Differences, particularly sectarian ones, which are of special relevance for us here, have no doubt at different times been stressed or remained submerged depending on the historical context, and this section should not be read as suggest-ing that they have recently emerged. What we want to explore over the next few paragraphs is the somewhat menacing mano-euvrability of margins, the ways in which they are drawn in or pushed back in accordance with the exigencies of association (or dissociation) in the recent intensifying economy of violence. One may initiate the discussion by listening to the voice of Hyder, a prominent Shia of the Khoja community, who has been involved in the dispensing of aid to victims of violence both in Mumbai and Gujarat.

... Shias are in a minority, Sunnis are in a majority in India. Every-where in the world, terrorism and gangster activities, whether we are talking of Afghanistan or the Bombay blasts, are all the work of the Sunnis. There is not a single Shia involved in all this. We believe that life is so important, even the life of an animal. Before prayer, a Muslim performs *wazool*, ritual washing. But there is a teaching that if there is very little water for *wazool* and a thirsty dog needs it, we must give it to the dog. Life is more

important, even if one then has no water to perform the *wazool*.
One can perform *wazool* with dust....

Bal Thackerey has also declared in *Saamna* that Shias are not
involved in terrorism.[6] But we remain afraid. We are helpless.
Our property is also looted. We are also attacked. *Gehun ke saath
ghun bhi pista hai* [Along with the wheat, the weevil also gets
crushed] . We keep aloof from these things. We do not believe in
taking life unnecessarily.... After the riots people have started
living in 'safe' areas for their own security. The effect of world
events can be seen on the Shias. They are also affected. Everyone
is looking only at Muslims. But what is happening happens.
Our religious leaders have told us to keep aloof. We should not
go out and shout slogans or get into conflicts and fights. We
must not without any reason put our lives in danger. The state
will do well by us. *Hum matam karte hain* [We ritually grieve] the
martyrdom of the grandson of the Prophet. The Companions of
the Prophet, the Sunnis, killed Hussain and his followers. They
were murdered in Karbala. We run several charities, for those
affected by riots or other calamities—for widows, for orphans,
for the homeless. We constructed houses in Mumbra after 1993;
we sent a mobile dispensary to Gujarat's remote areas....

Selling liquor is not legal. Music is also *haraam* (taboo) among
the Shias. You will find *qawwali* only among the Sunnis.... Interest
is *haraam*. The Sunni Pathans give and take money in interest.
There is permission to put one's money in banks. For the banks
earn money through trading and one can therefore take that
money. It is profit, not interest. There is no wrong done in this.
One cannot take advantage of someone's position: *jowar de kar,
gehun nahi le sakte hain* [for a debt of sorghum, wheat cannot be
taken]. All the Mughal kings, and Babar and so on, were Sunnis.
This Babri Masjid, no Shia is involved in all this...Sunnis and
illiterate people have brought about the defamation of Islam.
Shi'ism is pure Islam. It emerges right from the Prophet and his
family. The Shias pray with open hands; the Sunnis pray with
hands over their chests. Yet they know that the Prophet is said
to have prayed with open hands. The practice of *teen talaq* spoken
privately all at the same time is not followed by Shias. The Shias
can give *talaq*. It must be for a genuine reason. It must be in
front of the priest. This has to be done three times. The Sunnis
have no proper rules. We believe in 12 imams. So many have

been martyred. They have been killed by the Sunnis for nothing. The Shias have been tortured and killed right from the time of the death of the Holy Prophet. From that time, they have been prey to terrorism. Almost no imam died a natural death. The killers were all Sunnis.

Islamic history and that of the violence on the subcontinent has been rewritten in this narrative as an embittered and everlasting battle of Shias and Sunnis. In fact, it is a struggle in which Sunnis are the archetypal aggressors, Shias the eternal sacrificial lambs. The image of sacrifice, both intense and malleable, surfaces once more; one becomes acutely sensitive to its polyvalent possibilities for thinking about the Muslim past. The utter volatility of imagery is also revealing, or concealing perhaps, of the considerable tension that must lie behind the anxious separation of oneself in the painful knowledge that to the outsider the Shia is simply part of the Muslim 'Other'. The simplicity with which the ills of not just the Muslim present but also its past are projected onto a particular sect would be merely caricature if there was not a shade of pathos about it.

Other younger Khojas, with greater involvement in relief efforts in Gujarat, had, not surprisingly, come away with a somewhat different perspective, one pierced more deeply by the sense that sectarian difference was not adequate shield from the ravages of religious animosity of recent times. Nevertheless, painless recourse to the 'secular' or liberal position was not possible for it fused too easily with a trivializing of Islam's central principles; one had to understand the true Islam. The following narrative is actually put together from what two young Khojas whom I spoke with had to say.

One should understand the true Islam. The Taliban is fanatic. But 'secular' Muslims are just namesake Muslims. After September 11, things have become very different. Islam has been demonized. Bush, Togadia, Modi make bad statements about Islam. What Muslims are doing, they say Islam is doing. What the Taliban teaches is not Islam. In Islam we are taught not even to harm an animal. The Taliban follows Wahhabism. The Saudi Arabs are Wahhabis. One cannot interpret the Quran by oneself. One must look at the commentaries. The Wahhabis interpret the Quran themselves....

The biggest *jihad* is with one's own soul. The war of Ali was a defensive war. Since Mohammad's time, all the wars were defensive, not attacking. We have to go for *bada jihad*, struggle with oneself. The struggle in Kashmir is misled. Fighting for a piece of land is not *jihad*. One can fight to save oneself though....

The minorities are frightened. Such terrible things happened in Gujarat, but there is no justice. Muslims feel they will not get justice, though this is wrong. But they should not provoke or attack by coming onto the streets. That would be revenge, not *jihad*. Muslims are frustrated after the Mumbai riots; but they do not seek revenge. Mainstream Muslims do not want revenge; only a few do these things. We need to isolate the few within each community that instigate these fights. Muslims have been ghettoized after Mumbai, Gujarat riots. Nowadays, they are trying to push themselves as patriotic. That is wrong. We did not come from Pakistan. Pakistan emerged out of India. We have got nothing to do with its making or with current politics....

The Babri Masjid is a mosque; once a mosque, always a mosque. But we should not keep fighting about it. Religious people should sit and decide; we should remove politics from the issue. We are ready to accept the court's verdict. There will be no riots if the verdict goes against us. But if it goes against them, this issue will not end. Masjids are not Shia or Sunni. They are the house of God. Wahhabis however are different from both Shias and Sunnis....

Another rewriting; the bearer of Muslim aggression becomes much narrower and more specific, as the strain towards the achievement of a larger unity seems to emerge more strongly. It is now the Wahhabis, a particular sect of Sunni Muslims, who carry the responsibility for fuelling violence and strife.[7] As Shias are increasingly not spared the hostility and the terrible violence that at one point of time they barely experienced, their need to draw closer to the majority Sunnis becomes palpable. Issues that might once have not concerned them—such as Babri Masjid or Muslim Personal Law—now implicate them as well, ever more deeply.[8] There is possibly the growing realization that they sink or swim with all Muslims.

Like Khojas, the Bohras too have always projected themselves as 'peace-loving' and quite different from 'those other Muslims'.[9]

In earlier times, in fact, their leader thought it necessary for them to demarcate themselves from other Muslims by the use of the cap for men and the veil called the *ridha* for women, so that Bohras were not attacked by Hindus in communal riots. In any case, the wealthier members of these communities were often spared violence, which in the past tended to confine itself largely to low-income slum pockets, working-class areas and shanty towns. Khoja and Bohra leaders have always held their communities back from street-level conflicts and demonstrations and have encouraged them to loyalty towards the government in power at any point of time. This position has been supported by the idea that Muslims must be loyal to the leadership of whichever country they reside in. In fact, Engineer (1989: 63) recalls a Bohra who maintained that if a Muslim opposes his country's leadership, he should migrate to another country and conduct his struggle from there. This person gave the example of Ayatollah Khomeni who migrated to France, from where he engineered the rebellion against the Shah of Iran.

As a whole, the Bohras are known to keep aloof from other Muslim castes (Engineer 1989; Kettani 1986). In fact, several Shia groups are haunted by a history of oppression and persecution as the hands of Sunnis (see Khan 2003). As one Kutchi Memon who lives in Mumbai and who had been deeply involved in local riot relief in the wake of the Mumbai violence said:

> The Bohris are different. They are disciplined. They keep themselves aloof and distant. They will not come out to fight. They were not much affected in the Bombay riots. They live in Muslim dominated areas like Bhendi Bazar and so on.
>
> They don't come out of their houses. They will avoid trouble. They are cowards [*kayar*] in this respect. The Bohris were badly affected in Gujarat. After the Gujarat violence, a big group rushed down to Bombay. They wanted people to help. They talked of how all Muslims must come together to help each other. But if they meant it, they should be with all the other Muslims. They should join them in their sorrows and joys. But it was just a passing phase. Once the initial panic had gone, they went back and forgot about it.

On an earlier occasion too, the Bohras had dramatically appealed to and received the support of other Muslim groups and organizations.

This was in the late 1970s when a section of the Bohras, the 're-formists', rebelled against the apparent authoritarian dispensation of the Bohra religious leader, the Syedna. The government took the part of the reformists, but other Muslim groups stood with the Syedna, arguing that the matter was internal and should be left to the community to resolve without political intervention. It is also true that the Bohras find representation on the Muslim Personal Law Board and seek to speak in the name of Muslim interests thereby. However, such assertions of unity have their limits, as the words of the Memon seem to suggest, petering out when the crises have been somewhat controlled. It is rather the 'reformists' among the Bohras who tend more towards the framing of alliances to fight communal hatred with other Muslims, regardless of their sectarian affiliation. A prominent Bohra of the reformist persuasion included all Mumbai's Muslims in his claim when he spoke:

When we went around doing relief work, after the Mumbai violence, we found that the fear factor was great. Many families fled to their *mulk* [places of origin] and did not return. Now, however, Muslims as a whole feel that this will not happen again in a 1,000 years. Both sides have learnt a lesson. The Muslims have perhaps learnt that the Babri Masjid is no concern of theirs: they know nothing about it and they will never go there. The Hindus learnt after the bomb attacks that these people retaliate very badly. Muslims were happy after the 1993 blasts; they rejoiced. However, that feeling is not there now. After the recent blasts [in August 2003], Muslim ambulances and volunteers were there in large numbers. Muslims were saying that this sort of thing should not happen. It gives Muslims a bad name. They were upset.

The question of strife certainly engages the Sunni consciousness much more, for as one young local leader in Mumbai put it: 'The Shias have only recently started being attacked. It is really the Sunnis who suffer the most in violence. They bear the brunt of it, since they are more numerous'. I spoke with prominent persons of different conviction among the Sunnis, in Mumbai and in Gujarat. All have been intimately touched by the violence of the past years, by experiences of suffering and of working with those in distress. Much more strongly does one hear the desperate declarations of accord, then, though traces of difference, sometimes even wrangles over terrain, filter through. Shia and Sunni have been known to come to blows in Mumbai and cooperation has to be hard fought for.[10] Barelvi and Deobandi barely acknowledged each other in the past, but the violence of 1992–93 brought them together.[11] As a prominent Maulana of the Jamaat-e-Ulema-e-Hind said in Mumbai:[12]

> Barelvis were more numerous in the past. The last fifty years have seen a shrinking. They are still in large numbers in Mumbai, Ahmedabad and so on. Only *jahil log* [ignorant people] conform to it. They don't know anything about *roza* [fasts] or *namaz* [prayer]. They believe in *babas* [holy persons] and in making vows. After being beaten, then they all came. Before 1992–93, Barelvis would not do *salaam* [offer greetings] to the Deobandis. They were taught that the Deobandis were *kafir*. After the riots, there was a concerted effort by Maulana Bukhari, who was later killed, to bring all the Muslims together. Everyone was in trouble; till when would they fight like this? All came together to form the Ulema Council. It tries to bring together all the persuasions of Muslims. The Barelvis were also in it; some still come. Some remain outside, such as the Shias. To a very large extent, however, the enmity is over. This has helped the community a great deal.

One cannot take too seriously the claims of diminishing numbers; these are statements often made by all sides. Each time, it is the 'other side' that is apparently experiencing a decrease in strength. And indeed the predominance of Barelvis among Indian Muslims has been attested to by most earlier scholarship. The pressure for unity in the face of attack has been something that Muslims have no doubt felt earlier as well. A range of Muslim organizations attempt to bring together Muslims from all over the country and represent their interests; their claims must have varying degrees of veracity. The All India Muslim Council held its first Muslim convention in 1953. Additional efforts for cohesion were spurred by riots in Jabalpur, Madhya Pradesh, in 1961. The 1970s saw further enhancement of efforts towards unification

(Kettani 1986), which, of course, reached culmination in the struggle over Muslim Personal Law in the wake of the Shah Bano case in the 1980s.

Both the Maulana and M.H. Daimakumar of the Jamaat-e-Ulema-e-Hind from Baroda echo the idea of the *masjid* (mosque) as a space eternally dedicated to God that we have heard earlier. The impasse over the Babri Masjid therefore is one that can be resolved only legally, for Muslims are bound to adhere to the decision of a court of justice in the country in which they live. For Daimakumar: 'We [Muslims] will accept whatever the Supreme Court's verdict on the Shah Bano case is'. The terrible trail of violence set in motion by the Babri Masjid controversy was perhaps something Muslims would ever want to avoid. The Maulana said:

> There is only solution to the Babri Masjid issue. At the time of the initial trouble, Muslims were frightened. Our elders told us to keep away from conflict with Hindus and, instead, to fight our case in the courts. Our struggle should be with the state, not Hindus. We have been fighting the case in courts. Whatever the court decides is all right with us. Some Muslim political leaders took up the issue to gain popularity. So many mosques have been broken, cattle go into them in Punjab and other places. Shall we spill so much blood for one mosque? We should not be doing this. Now the issue is too hot to handle; it cannot be resolved easily. We tried to explain to Shahabuddin, but he did not listen.[13] Once a *masjid* is established, whether it is used or not, it is called a *masjid*. So we cannot give it to build a *mandir*. But we can go to the courts to decide. If we fail, it is our destiny. We will call it a *masjid*; that is our call. Whatever the courts decide is up to them. They may make anything of it. It is in their power. But we do not have the right to give it to the Hindus even if some people have that idea. The courts may say give it to the Hindus or build a monument to communal harmony or a garden or whatever. We leave it to them; we don't interfere.

While Sunni leaders differ on various other predicaments generated by the context of violence, as I shall discuss further later on, there seems to be greater consensus among them on certain themes. A Barelvi leader, while articulating the differences between the traditions, spoke of the Babri Masjid issue, in much the same words as we have just encountered and also inclined to the view that Muslims as a whole have been affected by developments in India and across the world.

In 1992, the riots were spontaneous; then in 1993 they were well-planned and systematic. The Babri issue is a political one no doubt. But a *masjid* is always a *masjid*. No one, not even *ulema* can change that stand. Even if someone says 'We are prepared to build a hospital'. It cannot be done. This is the property of the Almighty. No one has a right to change it. From the land till the sky, it is a *masjid*. It would be against Islamic law; only sinners would do it.

Deobandis don't believe that the prophets and saints have any power. We believe they have powers given them by the Almighty. So, they don't accept the tradition of supplication at *dargahs*.... They are not Sunnis; if so, why are they called Deobandis?.... But what happens to Muslims affects all of us. After September 11, after the Gujarat riots which has its effect all over India, Muslims feel they are second-class citizens. An atmosphere has been created to make Muslims feel that they are not part of the country. After September 11, Islam is being shown as terrorist. Whoever believes in Islam is a terrorist. This is part of the worldwide procedure of the Jews who are dictating the policies in America and Britain.[14] The biggest enemies of Islam are the Jews. And this enmity is not recent. It began 1,400 years ago. Indian policy has been with Palestine; we [our organization] are against friendship with Israel. What Israel has done to Palestine, they [the attackers] are trying to now do with Muslims in Bombay and Gujarat. Israel has been doing it for the last 50 years; ours, the RSS and the like, for the last 25 years or so.

It is Deobandis more than the Barelvis who try harder to communicate the idea that the differences between the two schools of thought are lessening. Barelvis both acknowledge the separations, while speaking the language of political unity of Muslims. This is perhaps because Barelvi Islam is the dominant tradition in the

Indian region but one which has come under growing competition from the increasing spread of less syncretic and more exclusivist approaches from within the Deobandi, Wahhabi and Tablighi strains over the last decades.[15]

A preacher associated with the Islamic Research Foundation in Mumbai, which appears to have a strong Wahhabi leaning, for instance, liked to specify:[16]

Both the Barelvis and Deobandis follow Hanafi Sunni Islam.[17] The Barelvis believe that one can get help from a dead person; the Deobandis argue that a dead person is dead. They do not encourage hard structures on graves. Most Muslims in India are Barelvi. The Wahhabis don't call themselves Wahhabi; they call themselves pure... plain Muslims. In Saudi Arabia, they are called Salafi.[18] Mohammad Ibn Abdul Wahhab tried to revive pure Islam. The Ahl-e-Hadith are Wahhabi. Wahhabism is a fast-growing movement. Even the chief minister came out and said that the Ahl-e-Hadith were moderate.[19] The Taliban are Deobandis; most Pakistanis are Barelvi. The Wahhabis are the most moderate. They are against grave-worship. They believe in revival of pure Islam. They are against suicide bombing and terrorism.

Here while Deobandi and Wahhabi are brought together in terms of certain theological concepts, they are also irrevocably parted. The taint of terror works quickly to distinguish the Afghani Sunnis from the non-violent Wahhabis. It is perhaps instructive that the voice of a political leader of the party in power at the time (Congress Party) is brought in to underline the disconnection of the Wahhabis from any extremist act of violence.

Tablighi and Jamaat-e-Islami differences emerge simultaneously.[20] While Imran, the Tablighi Jamaat ideologue with whom I spoke clearly tried to separate 'politics' from 'spirtuality' and claimed no interest in the former, Jamaat-e-Islami members in both Ahmedabad and Mumbai argued that their organization addresses all aspects of Muslim life: social, political, cultural and religious. Under the circumstances, then, the Tablighi Jamaat ostensibly has no interest in issues such as that of the controversy over the Babri Masjid and sees violence as implicating the corrupt use of power, the solution to which, for Muslims at least, lies in greater immersion in the faith and stronger belief in the Almighty. According to Imran:

Differences between Shias and Sunnis are clashes of mind that developed at the time of Ali. Ali and the Prophet appreciated each other. Between Barelvi and Deobandi, things have slowed down; there are no sharp differences. We believe that we can bow only to Allah. If I bow to anyone else it is *shirk* [attributing to created beings qualities that belong only to Allah]. It cannot be excused. Other sins can be excused. God has created the Prophets and the saints. There is a basic difference between the created and the Creator. The Jamaat-e-Islami wants the country. If the country is ours, we will be fine, according to them. But the Deobandi don't need the country. We have all the freedom here to practice Islam. There is no need for country or political power. Mohammad said he feared Allah the most. He knew the greatness and power of Allah. The basic principle of Tabligh is being appreciated and inculcated. If people have hurt you, you forgive. There is a teaching in Islam regarding retaliation. One may retaliate in the same measure, but it is far better, according to the teaching, to *forgive*. Because I am a Muslim, I don't have the right to burn somebody's shop because somebody else has burnt mine. We can't take law in our own hands; the law of the land is there.

To emphasize the differences of position, Tablighi ideology here seeks to separates the Deobandi tradition from the message of the Tabligh. In core, they are similar, however, and certainly have strong historical associations (Sikand 2002). However, the Tabligh does concentrate on six principles: the *kalimah* (article of faith), *salaah* (prayer), *dhikr* (knowledge of principles of Islam and remembrance of God), *ikram-i-momin* (respect for Muslims), sincerity of purpose and donation of time, even by ordinary Muslims, for the preaching of Islam (Haq 1972: 66).[21] In doing so, it apparently keeps itself at a distance from political thought. This is a position that must, though, be considered much more critically; an attempt will be made further on. Violence is, in a sense, interiorized here; it is a force the source of which, in terms of a discussion of Muslim–non-Muslim relationships, remains relatively under wraps. The underlying source of the violence unspecified, the emphasis turns rather to religious internality: Muslims must contain violence by spiritual self-control and surrender to the law.[22]

The Jamaat-e-Islami has been involved in considerable social and relief work in different parts of India, which has, according to its members, never been properly recognized. While it has a radical political position that slants it towards a critique of democracy and secularism in favour of aiming ultimately for the setting up of a state according to Islamic principles, on the ground it seems to negotiate its stance far more pragmatically.[23] Akram in Ahmedabad said:

> Muharram is not there in Islam. We should remember the values and principles people fought for, not do *matam*. It is not in Islam, crowning one's own son. Rather one must crown the person most full of character. That is the principle for which Yazid fought.

Straightaway, the separation between Shia and Sunni is marked; while with Wahhabi too, with the reference to Saudi Arabia dynasty politics, there is obviously a neat split drawn. Akram felt that the kind of ritualism being promoted in Hinduism as well as in Islam, as he just mentions, is detrimental to the promotion of better relations between communities. Hasan, from Mumbai, saw the Deobandis as following only some of the Quranic thoughts, not others. For him, the Jamaat-e-Islami looks at Islam as a way of life, having the answers to all questions, whether on education, health, diet, economy or whatever. These attempts to subtly trace boundaries, which are essentially boundaries between the Jamaat-e-Ulema-e-Hind and the Jamaat-e-Islami and which translate unfortunately into turf battles when groups come together for social action particularly in times of crisis, are interesting.[24]

Though these groups are far closer than say the Barelvis and Deobandis in terms of religious teaching, their differences lie in the postures adopted towards the State. The Jamaat-e-Ulema-e-Hind was strongly opposed to Partition and did not believe that Muslims needed their own political unit. While the perspective of the Jamaat-e-Islami has been shown to differ, their everyday interactions combine the attempt to slowly rework individual lives and practices in terms of Islamic principles and the mediation with non-governmental organizations and non-Muslims for the purposes of social and aid activities and 'living together [with non-Muslims] in the *mulk*'.[25] Hasan also appeared keen to separate the modern-day Jamaat-e-Islami from too close an association with its founding father, Maulana Maududi, perhaps because of the knowledge of a current tendency to associate Maududi's thought with various forms of militant Islam (Choueri 2004). 'We do not follow Maulana Maududi, but through him, we follow Islam. The Quran is from God, not from man'.

This section has attempted to trace through the material the remarkable agility of boundaries as they are raised and reduced on the competing terrain of contemporary Indian Islam. It is not an effort at entering into religious disputations or chalking out in detail the nuances of theological distinctions between movements and groups. Rather, what is interesting and perhaps somewhat alarmingly illuminating to discern are the ways in which contemporary challenges and struggles call forth core Islamic images such as of the battle of Husain and Yazid and of sacrifice, grief and suffering, suffusing them with dramatic new significance.[26] Long-standing divisions of ideology between groups are reiterated, now overlaid with the added implications of culpability for present-day tribulations.

Locating ourselves in the specific context of an anthropological inquiry, listening to the voices of positioned actors speaking in a situation of disquiet, our analysis reveals both the tentative, perhaps even reluctant, groping towards commonality as well as the passionate contentions of distinctiveness. The charged edginess of these fluctuations might bespeak a foxy pragmatism, but that would imply a consistency of control even if not of position. What one gets a sense of most, however, is the frightening concession of control as an overreaching spectre of the 'Other' appears to cast a dark shadow on the only *apparently* volatile mergers and separations of identity surfacing through the narratives. While for most this is irretrievably the Hindu 'Other', for some the conflicts reach much further into the past, today's Hindu aggressor simply holding the baton for a charge initiated by others (Christians or Jews) way back in Islamic history.

strategies for coping in a conflict regime

In the violence of Mumbai and Gujarat in recent times, destruction and loss had by no means been confined to the city slums; it visited commercial pockets and middle-class neighbourhoods.[27] Further, for some certainly, the experience of violence has been repeated. In the light of this, conversations with community leaders working with survivors of riots raised several questions for me, some of them seemingly mundane. However, it appeared that such issues tormented them as well, though resolution was not always obtainable and differences of judgement inevitably emerged. What was the Islamic standpoint on insurance? Did the fact that so few Muslims appeared to insure themselves place them that much more at risk in conflict situations?[28] How did a community, exposed more frequently to violence contend with rehabilitation at the very sites of harm? Coping with violence might raise queries for gender roles and expectations. How are these contended with? These are not themes that have not appeared earlier; here, however, they are addressed through alternate routes. While ordinary Muslims no doubt negotiate their own way through such concerns, they are also exposed to the teachings of their community or *jamaat* on them. An adherent of the Deobandi school of Islamic thought, for instance, spoke explicitly and at some length.

> We have to understand how to behave as a minority, or if one is in majority, how to behave then. If one is in majority one has to behave with compassion [*reham se*].... The 1992 Babri Masjid incident has hit Muslims' identity. Before that, there was loss of life or possessions. Muslims feel pride [*fakr*] at giving life for their *watan* [land, country] or for Islam. In 1947, several Ulema were sent to the Andamans. They gave their life for their country. For Muslims, life is not so important [*jaan kimti nahin*]. But when overall a community is being talked of, its identity was hit. When small things happen, Muslims are willing to endure [*sabr*]. But [recent events] have shaken the Muslims [*poora hila diya*]....
>
> Property and life insurance are big questions. When thousands of Muslims are destroyed, and they have no insurance. In these circumstances, can one insure property? For years, no one had

considered this question. The teaching of Islam is that Allah alone gives and he alone is the protector. But one must think of the teachings in terms of the conditions. God gives to Muslims and non-Muslims, but we are also taught to be futuristic, spend less, be careful. After 1992, there was a *fatwa* from the Deoband school that one can insure one's property. Life insurance, however, is a different question. It is a challenge to God.

There was a somewhat different viewpoint. As a Barelvi leader said:

Debate is going on among the Ulema about insurance. Our lives are in the hands of the Almighty according to one set of Ulemas. The time of death [*ane ka samay*] is written. However, insurance may be allowed. The issue is still being debated. The problem regarding insurance is: if one doesn't die, the money gets wasted and we are not sure about what will happen in 10–15 years time. Wastage is not permitted in Islam.

On the Shia side, however, from what one can gather, these do not appear to be problematic concerns. Perhaps Shia groups involved hugely in trading and commercial activities cannot afford such risk. Moreover, it would be argued that the money paid into insurance is in turn invested by the companies; one is therefore sharing in those profits when one gets an insurance bonus and this is acceptable in Islam. Clearly, there is no overall consensus; however, what draws attention is the fact that there has been, in some quarters, renewed thinking on the subject. Repeated violence has indubitably cast its shadow on those who live in its dread.

More and more is the issue of rehabilitation assuming significance for Muslims. While individuals and families make their own decisions, as we have traced earlier, and follow their own trajectories of movement and resettlement, increasingly religious leaders have begun to try to influence and direct such arrangements. Their capacity to thus get involved arises chiefly out of their close involvement with riot relief operations, particularly in recent times. The Barelvi leader was painfully clear:

After the Gujarat riots of 2002 we held a press conference by the Ulema to appeal to Muslims to come back to places where

there were more Muslims. Wherever Muslims are in a minority, they are targeted the most. After 1992–93, people moved
individually but now the heads have announced it and want
it to happen. Earlier, they had thought it [residential patterns]
should be cosmopolitan.

Again, one would be hard put to find, if one were searching for
it, total agreement across lines of sect and tradition. Moreover, the
concern is probably not as much appreciated by all. For Shia
groups, for instance, living in communal neighbourhoods has long
been a preferred custom. Nevertheless, certain members of these
groups, often highly educated and wealthy enough, sometimes
deliberately chose to live along with others in their social class in
cosmopolitan, affluent neighbourhoods rather than in the more
socially heterogeneous and usually crowded ethnic quarters
(Engineer 1989). In 2002 in Gujarat, many such families were the
conscious target of violence and they therefore came in for ridicule by religious leaders. Further, in the wake of the violence, some
religious organizations worked specifically to relocate Muslims at
new sites, away from mixed neighbourhoods. From the Jamaat-e-
Islami, Hasan said:

Most of the rehabilitation has been done in the same areas.
We have not worked to displace people. Morally, we try and
give them courage. Tell them it is their *zameen* [land], *basti*
[village], they should not leave it.... In some cases, we bought
land and rehabilitated them near by at a new site, complete
with surrounding walls, *pucca* houses and so on.

One of the relief workers in Ahmedabad was to elaborate:

People should not give up their place. We made *pucca* houses,
where there were *kuchcha* ones. We also built houses for Hindus,
in places where houses of both communities were destroyed.
We ensured that people could reach their fields or work sites,
so they could have their livelihood.

It is when we touch upon the issue of gender that we find ourselves abruptly in extremely fraught territory. It is true that cataclysmic violence, such as that of Mumbai 1993 has had a share

in awakening Muslims to the need for education even, if not especially, of daughters and women. There is more than ever a growing interest in education in English, particularly for boys. Several grassroots organizations working with Muslims in the cities have noticed these trends. However, the increasing pressure that the Muslim community feels itself under, with the growing virulence of the violence of the last decade and more, also works to hedge the troubled questions regarding gender equality or gender identity. The common understanding appears to be that when the community is being battered from outside, such questions only destabilize and enfeeble it from within. Thereby, certain ideas are calcified; critically those relating to *hijab*, for instance.

Some communities which had almost no previous tradition of donning the *hijab* have increasingly begun to do so. The Konkani Muslims of Maharashtra, with a strong presence in Mumbai, are a case in point here. Women of this community have over recent years begun to don the full black *burqa*, which was not conventional earlier. Multiple influences are no doubt at work in these processes, in which reaction to the violence faced by Mumbai's Muslims may be just one factor. Men who migrate to the Middle East, especially Saudi Arabia, return with ideas of social mobility and female deportment that run contrary to community custom. Someone who obviously disapproved, from a well-established Gujarati Memon family, put it disparagingly: 'They have taken to wearing what we call among ourselves the *ninja burqa*'.[29]

The memories of trauma leave their mark though. 'Things have changed', said a Konkani Muslim.

Earlier, in the village in our childhood we were never aware of differences between Hindus and Muslims. As children we all played together and took part in each other's festivals. Things began to change with the coming of the Shiv Sena. 1992–93 was nightmare. A rift has definitely formed. If people have taken to *burqa*, become more religious it is because they feel the need to stress their identity. If one is going to be attacked, simply because one is Muslim, then why not behave like a Muslim.

Religious leaders and preachers have sometimes been criticized for preying on, indeed for setting off, such vulnerabilities.

For certainly, they appear to converge with remarkable regularity on the theme of appropriate conduct for women within Islam practised as it should be. As a result, a unified image of proper Islam is constructed and preached, one which has little respect for the diverse and customarily syncretic practices of local communities.

From all sides of the spectrum one gets the view that *hijab*, indeed full *hijab* and not just covering the hair or breasts, is good Islamic practice and that, moreover, importantly, it prevents any kind of misbehaviour or mischief by non-Muslim men (*ulti sidhi harkatein*) which could become the cause of riots (*fasad*). Tensions emerge when attempts are made to enlarge the scope of Muslim girls' roles. One can recall the troubled efforts of a prominent Muslim woman educationist, who took charge of rebuilding the lives of Muslim women and girls in a particular locality in the aftermath of the Mumbai violence. She, a self-confessed religious believer of the Deoband school and descendant of the family of the founder of that school, decided to train women for employment and financial autonomy. Almost immediately, conflicts with Ulema erupted. Girls were being trained as journalists and textile designers; they were even being trained as beauticians. She faced the charge that this was *haram* (taboo) in Islam—*shakal surat badalna* (changing one's natural, God-given features). As a believing Muslim how could she condone it?

The emphasis was shifted, though the beauticians' course was retained. From teaching techniques of altering features (shaping eyebrows, for instance) the training moved to coaching in other practices such as aromatherapy, acupressure and the like. As she argued, it was possible to stay within the limits defined by Islam as well as innovate to suit the contemporary times.

For Muslims, even portraiture is *haram*, a sin. It is a challenge to Allah. Will we be able to put in the soul, spirit [*ruh*] also, as we paint the face [*rukh*]? But can't we control it.... I discussed with the Ulema. We can take steps to ensure that we do not infringe on the teachings. We can make our own paths, otherwise Muslims will be going backwards.... *Haram aur halal ke beech ka rasta kya hai*? [What is the middle path between what is taboo and what is fine?]. If we have to stay away from *haram*, how do we proceed?.... My girls have been taught personality development and communication in English. They can hold their own in their jobs. Some of them are working with newspapers and magazines, even fashion magazines. They say: 'We write about the film industry, but we wear *hijab*'.

These difficult themes related to gender identity and expectations will presently resurface when we discuss the embattled relationship between grassroots activists working with women's and social work organizations and religious guides and leaders. Inescapably, the theme of Muslim educational backwardness that was uncovered in an earlier chapter comes again into view. It is, as we shall explore a bit more later, not an untroubled one.

sabr and the internal struggle of control

> *The bodies fallen in the bush*
> *the roofs, the roofs of men*
> *destroyed by the storms*
> *of incendiary flames*
> *the burnt lines*
> *they now form an unusual court of justice*
> *and cry for revenge...*
> Alda do Espirito Santo[30]

I did not anywhere have any significant difficulty in meeting or conversing with Muslim men. The degree to which they would confide or the extent to which they would talk differed considerably from women; nevertheless, at various places I have been able to consider the ways in which they articulated their struggle to cope with the multiple hurts of violence. I do not wish to repeat here an analysis in terms of the recollection of life stories, as in the previous chapter. As I said then, some men did use that narrative mode; however, the emphasis of what men typically dwelt on was different and it is the knot of concerns centred around community pride, self-control and suffering that I wish to try to unravel to some degree in the following pages. Indeed, men's narrations of personal lives intertwined often with rationalizations of community suffering which bore the stamp of social and cultural scripts (see Mattingly 1998). It is manifest moreover that for many men and women faith in their religious beliefs provided a firm support against buckling under the weight of trauma.[31]

Yusufbhai is elderly and leads a semi-retired life, only visiting his automobile repair shop once in a while. Soft-spoken and gentle, he conducts himself with much dignity and is well-known in the neighbourhood. He carries his faith lightly. He has never been able to afford to go on pilgrimage, or celebrate any religious functions with lavishness. Yusufbhai had never encountered communal violence in his native Uttar Pradesh. It is the Babri Masjid issue, an essentially political issue, that according to him made the Muslim the ultimate 'Other' for Hindus and created these tensions and frequent riots. *'Logon ke dil me kaala aa gaya hai'* [People's hearts have been tainted with black] he says. This was never the case before. 'Being a Muslim is a problem [*takleef*] today.

> I have a beard. After the *dange* [riots] since the Babri Masjid episode, if I am on a bus the conductor will shout: 'Go in front' or 'Move back'. Or he might say irritably: '*Chacha*, why can't you bring change?'

When Yusufbhai's eldest son was killed in 1993, and another son died soon after (out of shock, as he said), he and his wife received great support from the neighbours and social workers. For the most part, though, they turned inward searching for some means to cope with tragedy. The demands on the aging father were tremendous. There was barely time to grieve. There was the automobile repair shop that he owned and that his eldest son had been running for some time to be managed. There was his daughter-in-law and there were the son's three children to be looked after. There was the struggle for compensation to be waged. Where the strength came from he finds it difficult these days to imagine. However, Yusufbhai's faith in God and the presence of his other children held him on.

> For the other children's sake, we had to be strong. We had to endure. When some big event like this happens in one's life, God sends endurance [*sabr*]. It is his gift. But we have to live and carry on for the family's sake.

Sometimes, the search for meaning to make sense of great tragedy leads to nothing other than one's destiny. However, even this may provide a certain frame for one's experience. As both husband and wife said in very similar words: 'There have never been riots in Bombay. Just this once and...this happened. It was our destiny [naseeb]'. The sense of suffering in isolation, and perhaps therefore as a result of some particular failing on one's own part, is however quickly denied. 'So many suffered. It was a terrible time'. The suffering is made bearable through generalization and through location in a recognized theodicy made suddenly intensely real through personal experience. For Yusufbhai, ultimately, the tragedy was a test from God. 'It was our test from Allah. He also gave us the strength to bear it. Even if no one is there, God is there'.

Sabr emerges again and again in the voices of survivors and victims of violence. Farhan in Baroda spoke of his next-door neighbour, a member of the Bharatiya Janata Party.

> The house was burnt. But this room which shares a wall with his house was left as it was—locked and untouched. Recently, he had a heart attack. None of the neighbours visited him, not even his Hindu friends. Only I went. He was touched. He said: 'Only you came.... Forget the past, what happened. I have forgotten it; now you forget it'. His hand was definitely in the riots. But we have to see his face daily, rising and retiring. We must have endurance [sabr] or else we cannot continue to live.... I reopened my shop. For the first few days, the Hindus were hesitant to come, but now they come again.... One of my children said: 'Abba, don't talk to them. Don't sell to them. They are Hindus. They burnt our house'. We scolded them. Islam does not teach us this. We do not want our children to learn to think like this.

In men's voices sabr sometimes emerges as particularly urgent and out of a sense of tension, perhaps because it must strain against the inclination for vengeance. In Haji Abdul Rehman's words:

> Even if we feel anger at the atrocities that we have experienced, the love of my family and the prohibition in Islam will hold me back.... If you kill there is no place for you in jannat (heaven). You will go straight to jehnum (hell).... There is a teaching in Islam: 'Take things with patience, endurance. Everything will eventually work out for the best'.

Sabr appears to have some of its own compensations for God is just and He will ultimately hear the voice of the afflicted. Ishaq had his warehouse burnt in the Mumbai violence; his largely Muslim residential neighbourhood was also under considerable threat. Regular watch had to be set up to prevent violence. Several deaths and injuries took place, particularly of those who ventured too far out to the borders with the Hindu areas or, being away from home, found themselves unable to return safely. Ishaq was firm in asserting:

> I believe strongly in Allah's justice. Of course, we are human: we feel the need for revenge. But we are taught to have patience [*sabr*]. There is this Hindu woman [from the Hindu neighbourhood nearby]. She was so proud [*fakr tha*] that her sons had burnt Muslims and set fire to their property. Now both her sons are dead. One died in a road accident; another at an accident at his workplace.

Without setting aside in any way the fervent faith of these witnesses of violence, it may be allowed that perhaps powerlessness merges to some extent with religious belief in containing anger. For the forces are just too strong to oppose and loss of face or honour may only be prevented by turning the responsibility of justice altogether onto another power: a power exterior, superior and abstract all at once. Certainly, revenge has no hope against the combined forces of the police, the majority community and the government. As a survivor and witness from Dharavi acknowledged quite openly:

> There will never be justice. We have to learn control [*sabr karna*]. Apart from *sabr*, there is no option [*aur koi chara nahi hai*]. We have to live together and keep our peace. The politicians will never give justice. They are fighting for their *gaddi* [seats in power]...

Even mild-mannered Yusufbhai was by no means imperceptive when he said: 'Muslims are nothing in front of the political leaders, the government and the police'.

Occasionally *sabr* is encoded, as I have mentioned earlier, in a particular narrative of the Muslim past, which perceives this past as one of continuous suffering and awaits a future renaissance. It is possible that such a formulaic account emerges out of or through negotiation with interpretations offered by religious leaders. Haji Abdul Rehman thus opines, and we have quoted him speak earlier:

> What is happening is a conspiracy of the government.... Countries that support the Jews (*Yehudi mulk*) are giving the signal. America is giving the signal.... Muslims have been targeted for 1,400 years. The Jews have been after them for all these years. America supports the Jewish cause. India has only been following in the footsteps of America and doing the work of the Jews for them. If you suppress Islam it will rise again.

As I had pointed out earlier, some religious leaders had used very similar language and expression to explain the suffering of and the violence against Muslims in India. Haji Abdul Rehman admits his attendance at the mosque as that of many others may have become more frequent for finding the chips down. 'Now [after 1993] Muslims are going to the mosque, after being beaten.... There is a realization.... They have no hopes from the government; they have made their application to God', he said.

Hope in a future resurgence of Islam expresses itself in his words as well as the anger at the worldwide silence against the injustices being done to Muslims.

> Atrocities upon atrocities are being committed everywhere. The world is silent. The people who are calling Muslims terrorists, they are creating terrorism. If you kill a son in front of the father or a father in front of a son you will have feelings of revenge. They expect Muslims to see that and remain in the house. Is that possible? Some people will react, but not all. There is a teaching in Islam: 'Take things with patience, endurance. Everything will eventually work out for the best'.... The time is coming soon. Everywhere, government is unjust. America is ruling in Iraq and Afghanistan. After this, peace will come.

A certain undercurrent of menace if only expressed in terms of the considerable self-control needed to contain the urge for revenge emerges:

> Even if we feel anger at the atrocities that we have experienced, the love of my family and the prohibition in Islam will hold me back....

However, later he was to add:

> That is why *inquilab* [change, revolution] is not taking place in India.... But to suffer injustice (*zulm*) is also injustice in Islam....

Muslim past and future are here constructed on rather slim historical foundations. It may be mentioned that Haji Rehman's *bete noire* is the police. False cases, he claims, were filed against him and his family for rioting in 1993, while those whom he named for burning and looting his house and factory were allowed anticipatory bail and are today still free. He was even put in jail for eight days. The police kept an eye on him after he filed his case, for he had claimed in his charge that certain police officers were implicated as well. The police made life difficult for him, so he finally decided to shift from where he was residing then. At first he was a regular participant in *mohalla* committee meetings to promote communal harmony with Hindus but stopped going, he says, when he realized that the persons on these committees acted as 'informants', conveying back to the local police station the name of anyone who raised uncomfortable questions and was therefore a potential source of 'trouble'.

For all this, Haji Rehman expressed little hatred of Hindus in general. There was a degree of sadness in what he said about Hindu–Muslim relations: 'People feel bad, after they have hurt you. They see you wearing good clothes earlier, later you are wearing old and tattered ones; they feel bad. They feel: Why did we do this?' From what we noted earlier, it appears to be much more with the police and perhaps with the State that Haji Rehman has his more bitter quarrels. For certainly, his are rather grim pronouncements and there is a somewhat dubious historical sense employed in a lot of what he says. His words are a forbidding reminder of how the sense of being hemmed in by injustice, fed by personal experience and magnified several times over by parallels drawn across space and time, if not redressed or reduced through other channels may so easily produce a climate in which reprisal may come to be justified, perhaps even lauded.

in search of identity

It would be hazardous and plainly untrue to argue for any necessary correlation between the experience of communal hatred, however bitter, and the leaning towards a rigidity of faith, in whatever way defined. No assertion of the kind has been ventured. All I have tried to do in the previous few paragraphs is to place before the reader the voice of a person whose individual trajectory bears witness to profound religious transformation. In this section, I trace the story of a young man who a few social workers in his neighbourhood insisted I should meet. He was described by them as having undergone a complete change after 1992–93, of having, indeed, turned 'fundamentalist' (*kattarpanthi*). While the person they spoke of would himself possibly pick no quarrel with the notion of fundamentalism understanding it simply to be a 'going back to the purity of one's roots', these particular social workers from the community found his conduct extreme and their employment of the label 'fundamentalist' carried unmistakeably the implication of censure.[32]

Yousuf, the son of well-to-do parents, dabbled in journalism while assisting in the family business. He was courteous and charming and willingly spent several hours talking with me. When we spoke about Muslim identity in the backdrop of their current situation, he carefully elaborated differences between sects and schools of thought. His own inclination was towards the Wahhabis, the most moderate, he claimed, of all Muslims. He was to say:

> I call myself plain Muslim. Perhaps I could say I am closer to Wahhabism or the Ahl-e-Hadith. After the Babri Masjid incident and the events that followed [Yousuf's father's shop was burnt down in the violence], I started religious studies. I wanted to understand how this thing could have happened.

I was a Muslim, but I became a better Muslim. Muslims were broken at that time.... I used to go for *namaz*, now I study more and talk [on Islam] in the slums.

Yousuf left the eclectic company of the Fourth Estate and his Western garb, adopting instead the loose *salwar-kurta* as preferred wear. He started a book shop, stocking Islamic religious literature and was influenced by and is associated with the Islamic Research Foundation, mentioned earlier.

'Islam is the best religion there is' is his firm contention and he argues that conversions to Islam have been increasing since the September 11, 2001 attacks in the United States. His own position on the Babri Masjid refers to Saudi practice. 'There should be justice; it is the decision of the court whether the mosque is built or not. One can shift a mosque. Saudis have shifted mosques. But why should there be violence and destruction [*khoon kharaba*]?' The literature he gave me to read included tracts on the rights of women under Islam and the scientific discoveries to find mention in the Quran. Again, the images of the extended tussles between Jews and Muslims emerged. The anger against the United States targeting of Islam is evident, though he was to clarify that France and Germany had opposed the attack on Iraq desiring as he put it 'justice, wholeheartedly'.

Americans helped the Israelites to take the land of the Palestinians.... The Jews are also monotheistic but their God can get tired, can make mistakes and have regrets. In Islam, Allah cannot do any wrong. We give respect to all the prophets of the Jews and Christians. They are mentioned in the Quran. Therefore the Bible and the Quran have similarities. Yet, Jews are unable to respect just one prophet in Islam: Mohammad'. Today's global battle over faiths is between Christianity and Islam. Islam is increasingly spreading, according to him. 'Hinduism is not spreading; only Christianity and Islam are in the race. In Muslim countries, however, Christianity is not spreading.... Islam has the solution to all problems—corruption, economy, theft. People are realizing that they need Islam.... Muslims themselves should convert [to the pure faith].

He continues:

Is *purda* really such a rigid concept? *Burqa*-wearing women themselves feel safer. They feel there is no problem of being teased in a *burqa*. In Islam, men are also advised not to look at women indecently. They must lower their eyes (*nigaha niche rakhe*). In Saudi Arabia there are plainclothes policemen to catch people who are misbehaving with women.

The title of this section emerged out of what a Muslim in Mumbai at one point averred: 'The destruction of the Babri Masjid really hit me. It set me off on a search for identity'. In the lives of some men (and women) the cumulative crises of recent times appear to have led to a search for meaning in terms of a stronger religious identity. It is in particular the voices of men, the few murmurs available to us, that we have begun to listen to here. Yousuf's is clearly one such voice. It is not possible for me to label his transformation straightforwardly as one from the 'liberal' to the 'fundamentalist'. There is, of course, much in the literature we have reviewed earlier that would perhaps support the application of such categories. There is the fierce protest against political establishments, there is the effort to return to some definition of the 'pure faith', the desire to increase the influence of one's faith over all domains of life and a strong anti-West or at least anti-America strain.

We must contend with the fact that for Yousuf, his choice fulfils an inner search for meaning and identity set off by the sudden critical undermining of his world. His alternative may, however, be laid against that of, for instance, Ashraf (see chapter two and next chapter), a man for whom the events of 1992–93 were equally shattering and transforming, but whose path took a very different turn, or even against that of Yusufbhai who turned to the support of an inner spirituality not reliant on any form of implacability. Ashraf found Yousuf's path evasive and dubbed it frankly 'fundamentalist'. It had no solution for the real issues: Muslim backwardness and poverty. It allowed further the immurement of women, at a time when gender equality had emerged clearly as a critical component of human rights discourse.

This disagreement, worked out here in the lives of specific individuals, is definitely one that is critical for many Muslims today.

It seems to be tearing the community from within, forming battle-lines which seem at first sight to be clearly drawn but reveal themselves, on closer scrutiny, to be rent by ambiguity and paradox. These contradictions are very much the stuff of later discussions. My own discomfort with both sides of this dispute lies elsewhere: with the way in which the one side reduces religious belief and practice to a set of rigid components, while the other appears to dismiss them altogether.

notes

1. In Gujarat's rural areas, the situation is even more treacherous. In the wake of extreme violence, Muslims have entirely left certain villages and resettled elsewhere. The extent to which this has changed the demographic profile of particular districts still needs to be more closely studied.
2. The material under scrutiny therefore emerges out of interviews conducted with personnel and affiliates of a range of organizations or movements in Mumbai and Ahmedabad which include the Jamaat-e-Ulema-e-Hind, the Jamaat-e-Islami, the Islami Relief Committee (Gujarat), the World Islamic Network and the Najafi Trust (both Shia organizations), the Tablighi Jamaat, the Raza Academy, a well-recognized Barelvi group, and the Mumbai-based Islamic Research Foundation. The activities of these organizations tend to have a considerable spread; several of them are pan-Indian in reach.
3. In a highly illuminating and opposed view, Marty and Appleby (1993d: 6) argue that political involvement may in fact alter the exclusivist character of fundamentalism and make it more pragmatic. Attempts to alter personal relations or educational institutions are usually much more narrowly defined and eliminate compromise. On the other hand, 'when they play politics to influence the policies of the state, however, fundamentalisms are... necessarily involved in some measure of compromise and accommodation'.
4. The Fundamentalism Project which resulted in six definitive volumes published by the University of Chicago Press was a major, interdisciplinary, cross-cultural study of worldwide religious resurgence. The project was sponsored by the American Academy of Arts and Sciences and directed by Martin E. Marty and R. Scott Appleby.
5. Each of the volumes of the fundamentalism projects bears the word 'fundamentalisms' in its title or subtitle.
6. *Saamna* is the mouthpiece of the Shiv Sena. Despite efforts, it was not possible to trace this particular reference to Shias apparently made by Bal Thackerey, the leader of the party. However, what is interesting, if somewhat redolent of desperation and excruciatingly aware of the inequities of power distribution, is the legitimation sought, as it were, from the heart of the opposition.

7. Wahhabism takes its name from Muhammad Ibn Abdul Wahhab (1703–92) born in the Arab Peninsula in the town of Uyayna. He began to preach a return to the pure Islam of times past. He opposed the worship of the Prophet, castigated Muslims for worshipping at the shrines of holy men and criticized the custom of marking graves. He stressed belief in the oneness of God and considered all non-Sunnis to be heretics (see Ali 2002). His alliance with Muhammad Ibn Saud led to the foundation of the dynasty which rules Saudi Arabia today. Popular understanding in India as well as these Shias tend towards a confusion of the Wahhabi tradition with another conservative cult, that of Deobandi Islam, which derives its name from the small town of Deoband, where a Deobandi Dar-ul-Uloom came to be established. The movement itself precedes the setting up of the Deobandi Islamic school of learning. It was an anti-British movement, which also espoused a literal and austere interpretation of Islam. The Taliban have had their training in the Deobandi tradition of Islam. Some Indian Deobandi Muslims lean towards an admiration of the Saudi Arabian religio-polity. Deoband teachings manifest a distrust of other cultures and seek to purge Islam of Western and modernist influences and to establish the Quran and Hadith ('sayings' of the Prophet) as the sole sources of tradition. Deobandi schools have sought to purify Islam of such popular practices presumably borrowed from Hinduism as the veneration of idols and visits to shrines and graves of saints. The Wahhabi and Deobandi Sunni traditions have much in common with each other as well as with the Tablighi Jamaat movement in south Asia; it is likely that Saudi Wahhabism supports and allies itself with Deobandi Islam in south Asia. Nevertheless, we need to recollect their differing historical trajectories in order to understand their varying manifestations in the different regional contexts. In India, the Tablighi Jamaat follows Deobandi tradition and there are strong genealogical links between them (see Ahmad 1991; Jeffery, Jeffery and Jeffrey 2004; Mayaram 2004; Sikand 2002).

8. Though there is some Shia representation on the Muslim Personal Law Board, which tries to unify various sects and organizations to work for the legal protection of Muslims as a minority and their rights to be administered by their own religious codes, several Shia groups express disinterest in its efforts. This is because they tend to be ruled in familial and marital affairs by their own caste/community leaders.

9. The Bohras consist of various groups: Suleimanis, Alia Bohras, Dawoodi and Nagpuri, at least. It is the Dawoodi Bohras, by far the most numerous Shia group, that is usually referred to, and it is the most prominent in Gujarat and Mumbai. The others are in comparison extremely small in numbers.

10. While there does not appear to be evidence of actual street fights between Shias and Sunnis in Gujarati cities, in Mumbai there have been such battles. One such infamous clash took place in 1988 arising out of the fact that the Bohra Syedna had made some comments in his Muharram discourse that hurt Sunni sentiments. The Raza Academy brought together the Sunnis for a protest march against the Syedna, while on the streets there were riots. Reformist Bohras openly dissociated themselves from the Syedna, asserting they were not to be blamed for his remarks. There was even a call for the boycott of the Syedna.

11. Barelvi Islam is a school of thought founded by Maulana Ahmed Raza Khan Al-Qaderi, a contemporary of Maulana Ashraf Ali Thanvi of the Deoband school. Unlike Deobandis, Barelvis believe in the powers of the Prophet and the saints and in supplication at *dargahs* [tombs of saints]. The Barelvis are influenced by a variety of Sufi practices, including the use of music (*Qawwalis*) and intercession by their teacher. Barelvis believe in the intercession between humans and the divine through a chain of holy *pirs* [saints] ultimately reaching the Prophet.

12. An organization of Islamic clergy formed during the British period and strongly anti-imperialist. It was against Partition. Its successor organization the Jamaat-e-Ulema-e-Islam functions in Pakistan. The organization follows the Deobandi school of Hanafi Islam.

13. Syed Shahabuddin is convenor of the Babri Masjid Coordination Committee, member of the All India Muslim Personal Law Board and a former member of parliament. He has argued that the Babri Masjid should be rebuilt on the very site it stood prior to its demolition.

14. This posture would explain the notice pasted outside the Raza Academy office off Mohammad Ali Road, in the wake of the attack by the United States against Iraq in 2003.
    AMERICAN AND DOGS
    BRITISH AND PIGS
    ARE NOT ALLOWED.

15. In a recent episode, in 1998, Barelvi Sunnis clashed with members of the Wahhabi inclined Ahl-e-Hadith, over the sighting of the moon. There was violence and stabbing in the streets of Mumbai's Crawford Market. The dispute was over the fact that the Sunnis began their fast on the New Year, having apparently sighted the moon on 31 December. The other side sighted the moon a day earlier and began the fast on the 31st. A meeting to try and resolve the issue failed to reach a compromise solution and with tempers frayed, clashes broke out in the vicinity of the Juma Masjid. See also Ahmad (1991) for a description of the Barelvi's competition with the Tablighi Jamaat.

16. He was an interesting person, having developed a serious curiosity about Islamic learning and theology out of the crisis and struggles initiated by the Babri Masjid demolition. We shall be listening later to the story of his transformation. The apparently well-funded and well-managed Islamic Research Foundation (Mumbai) was started in 1991 by a Dr Zakir Naik, a celebrated preacher, who has travelled all over the world to teach. Its orators appear to have a strong incline towards a Wahhabi/Salafi interpretation of Islam. The Foundation presents regular lectures on the local cable television network and its teachings and ideas are thus accessible widely to a large number of Muslims. Many highly educated Muslims are attracted by the teachings.

17. The Hanafi school of Islamic thought is named after Imam Abu Hanifa born in Iraq in about 700 AD. The Sunni Hanafi system depends a great deal on reason and opinion in the making of legal decisions and is, consequently, decentralized in approach. Most Sunnis follow this tradition. The other Sunni traditions include the Hanbali, the Maliki and the Shafii, each named after its respective founder.

18. Salafis are those who stress the following of pure Islam in accordance with the ways of the Prophet and his companions. Salafi ideas base belief and practice on the Quran and the Sunnah (Sayings of the Prophet) with no additions or deletions. Wahhabi's teachings based on exactly such an understanding of the uncontaminated Islam falls precisely within the Salafi definition and Wahhabis often prefer to call themselves Salafi.

19. The reference here is to the chief minister of Maharashtra, Chagan Bhujbal. After a recent bomb blast in 2003 in Mumbai, the Kurla offices of the Ahle-Hadees were raided for the police suspected the hand of its believers in the violent deed. Subsequently, members of the Ahl-e-Hadith met the Chief Minister to deny any association with terrorism and to stress that their activities were related purely to Islamic learning. The Ahl-e-Hadith may be described as a sect or a movement seeped in the Wahhabi tradition. It inclines towards a highly conservative and austere interpretation of Islam.

20. The Jamaat-e-Islami was formed in 1941 in Lahore on the initiative of Maulana Syed Abul Ala Maududi. The organization split up on Partition into the Jamaat-e-Islami which continued to function in Pakistan and the Jamaat-e-Islami Hind, which functioned in India. The Jamaat-e-Islami opposes itself to the separation of religion and politics and claims to strive for the ultimate installation of a polity based on Islamic principles. Efforts at Tabligh (preaching) have been made from the late 19th and early 20th centuries by Jamaat-e-Ulema-e-Hind, Barelvis and Deobandis of the Dar-ul-Ulum. The institutionalization of the Tablighi Jamaat took place under the M. Mohammad Ilyas in the second decade of the twentieth century. The unit of preaching was the 'jamaat', which consisted of a small group of teachers who went around from place to place educating Muslims in correct Islamic practice. The jamaats consisted not necessarily of religious clergy, but ordinary Muslims, who could be trained to preach and participate in the work of Islamization. The growth of the Tablighi Jamaat is linked with the rise and spread of the influence of the Hanafi Islam seminary at Deoband in north India (Haq 1972).

21. The Islamic Article of Faith: *La ilaha illa'llahu; Mohammadun Rasul-u'llahi* [There is no God but Allah; Mohammad is the Apostle of God].

22. Mumtaz Ahmad (1991: 520) also records that even on the issue of communal riots, the Tablighi Jamaat refuses to encourage Muslims to protest or complain. They should rather leave the matter to God and concentrate on rectifying their own moral lapses thus building around themselves a protective barrier composed principally of moral qualities.

23. In the late 1970s, the Jamaat-e-Islami ruled that its members should not exercise their vote because the Indian state is *taghut* (anti-Muslim and despotic). The organization was banned during the Emergency and for a period when the Babri Masjid was demolished. Its members speak straightforwardly of the failure of secularism and their desire to see a 'trial' of the Islamic system of rule in India.

24. In Baroda, M.H. Daimakumar critiqued the Jamaat-e-Islami and the fact that the enormous amounts of money it had received for relief work in the wake of the 2002 violence had not yet been adequately accounted for. In Mumbai, the Maulana had similar reservations. Their own work on the other

hand was, it was claimed, transparent and available for all to see. In Baroda and Ahmedabad, the Jamaat-e-Islami perhaps precisely because of such allegation both from within the community and without, had started putting up notice boards advertising their activities wherever they worked or built houses and shelters. Akram said:

> Our society has been engaged in social activities for very long. We did not publicize these earlier. We had housed so many people after the 1969 and 1984 riots. Now we put up boards. The government is also strict. Our accounts and audit are transparent in any case; but now we also publicize with these boards.

25. Such activities include running commercial establishments, educational institutions and the like. Organizations like these have no difficulty in coming together with like-minded political parties or non-governmental organizations to stage demonstrations or protests. In recent times, in Mumbai for instance, there have been protests against the bomb blasts of August 2003, the proposed visit of Ariel Sharon and the staging of a 'Mumbai Resistance to Globalization' campaign during the World Social Forum.

26. The images of suffering as well as *sabr* [self-control; endurance; patience] appear to be very important in Islam. In the core concept of *jihad*, for instance, it is the lesser *jihad* to actually wage war against the enemies of Islam. The higher *jihad* is the struggle over the self, with one's own soul and sinfulness. Allah allows suffering because it is a test of human beings; life itself is a test. Human beings have to strive to live it in accordance with Islamic guidance and to avoid the temptations of Satan. While for Shias, the concept of suffering is undoubtedly critically linked to the martyrdom of Husain and remembered in many regions in the physically painful flagellations of Muharram, *sabr* is a significant Quranic concept and its many meanings have a deep resonance with other Muslims as well. The concept of pain, self-control and suffering also implicate a particular notion of Muslim masculinity. Mehta (1997, 2000) argues that for Muslims circumcision is linked both with belief and *mardangi* (masculinity). The body is said to acquire strength through the pain of the ritual wound; the wound is a mark of the endurance of pain. With circumcision the body is said to recognize pain, a distinct pain, which enhances belief. Thus, the circumcised man has no desire to masturbate; circumcision turns him to the remembrance of having 'heard the Quran and voluntarily recited it' (Mehta 1997: 203).

27. Among others, middle- and upper-class Muslims also often tend to hold the view that riots (at least in the past) only affected the poorer and congested areas of the city. Contrary, however, to this kind of popular belief, it must be pointed out that there have been notable instances in the past of rioting in posh neighbourhoods and even of the middle classes participating in violence and looting. In the unforgettable riots of Ahmedabad 1969, newspaper reports show that riots spread beyond the walled city to 'fashionable, usually peaceful' areas such as Navrangpura, Ellisbridge, Shahibaug, Usmanpura and Vasana (*The Times of India*, 20 September 1969, p. 1).

28. Of course, all too often, as with so many whom I spoke to, Muslims are far too poor to have anything to insure. However, here I am interested in understanding how the issue is considered, in relation to cases where the situation may be different.

29. Here is an astonishing image capturing vividly the dizzying jostle of influences within which the Muslim community in modern India is perceptibly perched. Technology and the media, children's entertainment on television, global images, Cartoon Network and traditional trappings coalesce to create a strikingly novel and, by the juxtaposition of contrariness—the power of the Ninja versus perhaps the submissiveness of the veiled woman—amusing picture. There is also the clear contempt of a group apparently trying to achieve social honour through the procedure, rendered cruelly comic here, of covering its women in black.

30. Alda do Espirito Santo, 'Where are the men chased away by that mad wind?' Translated from Mario de Andrade's French version by Jacques-Noël Gouat. *The Heinemann Book of African Women's Poetry*, Heinemann Educational Publishers, Oxford, 1995. Edited by Stella and Frank Chipasula.

31. While the previous chapter was concerned with somewhat different aspects of women's voices, and it has been suggested that they were not easily drawn into discussions of Muslim political identity, they did speak of their faith in God a good deal. We can, as one instance, remember Sultana's words: 'Anyway, there is the One above. He cares more about us. He has saved our lives. We did not go out to burn anyone's house... God will not forgive them: they will pay someday for what they have done'.

32. In one of the talks I heard on cable television by a speaker from the Islamic Research Foundation, the message was clear. To be *kattar* [rigid or fundamentalist] in faith is a good thing, not a bad one, for one is adhering to the Quran and the Sunnah strictly and this is the essence of *salafiyya* [being *salafi*]. One is cleansing the faith of influences from outside (such as Hinduism, perhaps).

chapter six

breaching boundaries: experiments in remaking the world

It is in everyday life that human beings are tested as to whether they are—in Goethe's words—'grain or husk'
Agnes Heller (1984: 7)

Altaf lives in Vatva, Ahmedabad. When the violence of 2002 engulfed his home city, he was no longer the young boy he had been when his father, a textile mill worker, died in riots in 1985. He had told this son to go home, while he went on to try and stop the battles on the streets. He did not return alive. Altaf's grandfather, a staunch Communist, also died in communal violence in 1969. The boy grew up with stories of the courage and social activism of his father and paternal grandfather. His mother moved to Vatva, an area considered safer for Muslims, from Rakhial near Bapu Nagar, where her husband had been killed. Altaf acknowledges his anger and the hatred he had felt against Hindus. He felt like killing and cutting them down [*unko kaat de*]; but his mother brought up her children explaining to them that riots were not the work of Hindus or Muslims. Some people, often, some politicians, sow the seeds of violence. When the violence started, two years ago, survivors started coming in into the Muslim-dominated Vatva. Altaf, despite not having a great deal of formal education himself, was instrumental in re-gistering the area's relief camp and in organizing assistance. This involved opening a bank account and negotiating with govern-ment officials, whose rules transferred to the local organizers the responsibility for any deaths that might take place in the camp. The elders of the community were consulted with. Their view was: 'Sign the documents. At least this way these people will get some relief. Afterwards, we will see what happens'. Through his work in the camp, he encountered and engaged with the hard-working members of a prominent non-governmental organization. They helped to train him and others like him in providing psycho-social support to the victims of this trauma; his training, he said, built on the foundations his mother had already laid.

Two years after the violence, Altaf retained links with the non-governmental organization as part of a community of women and men working for communal peace and justice, but his engagements as a grassroots social activist took him much beyond the call of duty. Altaf worked with both Hindus and Muslims, but the efforts were definitely a bit of a struggle. A visit to the families of the Godhra deceased ended in failure; he and his team were looked on with suspicion and turned away. The second time, he went with the district collector and helped with the process of application for educational scholarships for the children. When some children succeeded in obtaining the financial assistance, trust in him increased a little. Later, a programme was organized to bring together the victims of the train crime and the violence that followed.

Altaf talked about how he learned slowly that communal peace could only be a part of a complex of engagements; some of these involved dealing with a range of activities that residents found difficult to negotiate. Following up on compensation cases, helping people acquire ration cards or voter identity cards, making them aware of available grants and benefits of the government and assisting them in availing of these—this was the stuff of daily activity. On the ground, it was trust constructed gradually on the basis of these myriad tiny actions that alone could feed the larger projects of building political discernment or links across communities. There was a new sense though in this young man, as in others I met in different places, of empowerment and of the imperative to translate this into a direct political asset through contestation, in the primary instance, of elections to local-level bodies.[1] Work at this level could involve a fair amount of negotiation, in fact confrontation, with local police and state officials. When Altaf was helping run the relief camp, the police visited daily—to count the survivors and record deaths. They usually could not match the numbers to be found in the camp with those on the records because without much shelter to protect them in the heat of the day, the survivors would disperse to wherever they could find some shade. This caused daily friction with the police for the camp organizers and had to be constantly sorted out.

Altaf however found that his own gradually garnered success in organizing his neighbours as well as the backing of a well-known non-governmental organization could begin to have enormous potential. It was not without a degree of calculation, that he was on the odd occasion tempted to test it. In a recent incident, two young Muslim men were taken to the police station on the grounds of stealing electricity. They were kept there, though no case was registered against them. When Altaf went to the police station, he protested that they should be released or charges immediately framed. They could not be held without charge. Indeed, he argued that electricity purloining was such a wide-spread occurrence that cases should be framed against all those involved. The police refused to release the two men and dared him to bring others involved. He returned to the police station at the head of a large procession of men, feeling that the challenge could not be left to rest. The police released the two men unconditionally; further, a very senior officer, on being informed of the incident, was led to visit the *thana* [police station] and meet with Altaf, to discuss with him the grievances that had led to the *dharna* [protest]. Altaf's sister, a young widow and mother, is an outspoken co-worker with her younger sibling in the area. She is one of very few women who would venture out into work of this nature, and faces, obviously, her own set of difficulties along the way.

In the previous chapter, we had ventured beyond the world of riot survivors to including those Muslim religious organizations, leaders and elders who have worked with the survivors on a level of considerable and often continuing intimacy. Here, we listen to more ordinary members of the Muslim community, who categorically do not identify themselves as 'religious' leaders, for whom work in relief and rehabilitation has woven into a wider concern with social activism and improvement within the community. Many, though not all of them are young and their stance towards some aspects of their faith cannot but be described as ambivalent, but they are often called upon to interact with local religious leadership and these interactions can be lively if not troubled by a degree of tension.[2] In this chapter, we will find ourselves in engagement with several such persons who, it may be possible to term, after Agnes Heller, 'individuals' (elaborated further on). Some of them would appear to fit neatly the category favoured powerfully by historians of the colonial period, 'reformist Muslims', and might indeed refer to themselves in this way. In particular, several of them would posit rather starkly their difference from the kind of person we encountered in the previous chapter for whom religious identity was assuming paramountcy. As a local-level Muslim activist said in Mumbai: 'We cannot think only of Muslims. Everything is not a community issue. Many larger and more critical issues are at stake: fundamental rights, justice and so on.'

Some of these grass roots workers would systematically distance themselves from those who pursue exclusively the cause of religion. Sajjid from Jogeshwari (East) was clear:

We do not involve ourselves with religious activities at all. Ours is the only organization in the area that is engaged in social activities within the community. Apart from religious activities, there were no organizations that were involved in social activities. Today, on our own strength, we have set up several such local-level organizations that do not run *madrasas* [Muslim religious schools], are engaged in the work of communal harmony, building community-based associations and bringing out protest marches on the streets in connection with different issues.

While the circumstance of a certain disdain towards *all* matters religious could raise its own set of concerns, the sources of this apparent unease may be certainly clearly comprehended in sociological terms. It appears to me that Agnes Heller's work on the social construction of the life of the everyday and the radical political possibilities inherent in it offers a remarkable perspective from which to approach the themes of this chapter. The next section attempts to briefly chart out her argument and some of her central concepts before returning to connect them to our initial subject matter and to develop a little more elaborately the themes of this chapter.

the everyday world, rationality and the concept of the political

What does Heller mean by the concept of the 'everyday'? According to her (1984: 6), everyday activity involves the process of growing into a 'ready-made' world. It is the internal process of accommodation to the world's requirements. Therefore, the everyday includes not only what one has learned from one's parents, but also what one teaches one's children. The anthropological worlds we are exploring through much of the course of this book lie in that changeable yet constant terrain that would be coeval with Agnes Heller's definition of the everyday. As she says, 'Everyday life always takes place in and relates to the immediate environment of a person' (Heller 1984: 6). It is aimed at the solution of everyday problems and is therefore primarily pragmatic. Everyday knowledge does not constitute itself into a specific or separate sphere, but remains a 'heterogeneous amalgam embedded in everyday life' (1984: 197). The work of Muslim social activists in their neighbourhoods and communities partakes of just such heterogeneity and requires a wide diversity of competencies: helping people obtain ration cards or voter identity cards, assisting them with compensation or benefit claims or school admissions or even troubles with the local police.

It would appear at first though that for Heller everyday life, in which individuals reproduce themselves in order to reproduce society, is so highly objectivized as to be inalterable. However, and this is of vital significance, Heller is a firm believer in the capacity of persons to transcend, indeed to change, their environments. This becomes evident from her own words (1984: 15):

It is a tough world into which we are born and in which we have to make our way. In this tough world, people work, eat, drink... and make love (usually by the rules); people rear their children to play a part in this tough world and timorously guard the nook they have managed to corner for themselves; the order of priorities, the scale of values in our everyday life is largely taken over ready-made, it is calibrated in accordance with position in society, and little in it is movable. There is little opportunity to 'cultivate' our abilities beyond, at best very narrow confines. Where life is comparatively full, it is obtuse or 'narrow-minded'.... Where it is not narrow-minded, it is no longer protected by a solicitous community. What is surprising is not that the alienated development of human essence creates persons with particular motivations, that it fosters particularity, but that free individuality can—as it does—develop at all.

Some of the concepts introduced in previous paragraph require elaboration, in particular Heller's idea of the 'person' and the 'individual' as well as her understanding of 'particularity'. For as has been mentioned earlier, the protagonists in this chapter seem to measure up to, to a great extent, Heller's idea of the 'individual'. Implicit within all these ideas, of course, is her definition of objectivation itself. Objectivation is simply the practical creation of an objective world; it may be material or ideational in nature. 'Objectivation-in-itself' is clearly the base of, though not constitutive of the whole of, the sphere of the everyday and it accounts perhaps for its alienating character. For though human beings need to learn all that makes them a functioning member of their society, in terms of skills, values, language and custom, and though they all develop this knowledge to varying degrees and in terms of their own unique personalities, the knowledge is generally taken for granted and not reflected upon. It is also knowledge that is, as said earlier, ready-made and given by society, rather than the creation of actors themselves. To quote Heller (1985a: 82):

> The sphere of objectivation 'in itself' is the social *a priori* of human experience. It has three constituents: ordinary language, man-made objects (with rules for their use, including the use to which the natural environment is put), and customs.... A newborn is thrown by fate into a world of a *particular* sphere of objectivation 'in itself'. 'Growing up' means the transformation of this accident into a defined 'being in a particular world'. This happens via the appropriation of the objectivation-in-itself'.

Objectivation-for-itself is a different thing altogether. It is the sphere of homogeneous knowledge, of formalized and specialized knowledge, which provides human life with all its meanings. It consists therefore of the religions, science, arts and philosophy. The Muslim activists in this chapter clearly have access to the wider worlds of, for instance, law, social philosophy and social science, worlds opened out to them through their interactions with non-governmental organizations, academics or the media. With these definitions in hand, therefore, we may have the rudiments essential for distinguishing between 'persons' and 'individuals'.

Every human being is a person and develops particularistic motivations, intents perhaps, out of the engagement of his unique qualities and capacities, opinions, skills and position within the social matrix. It is worth quoting straight from Heller, for the clarity of her observations (1984: 8):

> Every human being is a particular person who comes into the world equipped with a given set of qualities, capabilities and aptitudes. From the person's point of view the qualities and dispositions with which he is born are natural gifts. They accompany him throughout his life; he must reckon with them whenever he takes stock of himself.

And further (1984: 11):

> Man is born equipped with particular properties and with a particular viewpoint, but not with particularistic motivations. Certain particularistic motivations unfold and develop from the matrix of inborn qualities and viewpoints.

There are those who are more than mere persons, however; they develop into 'individuals'. Individuals are motivated to reform both themselves and their world. They engage with higher-order objectivations—philosophy or art or science—and turn these to illumine, perhaps to change, aspects of everyday life. In doing so, they transcend 'rationality of reason' and attain 'rationality of intellect'. While reason essentially constitutes the faculty of discrimination, there are different ways in which it may be manifested. The uncritical observance of norms and values, which are internalized and regurgitated repetitively in a largely unreflective manner, makes for rationality of reason. Rationality of intellect involves a more reflective approach to everyday life, its norms and rules. It entails the capacity to employ higher-order norms, values or meanings to reflect critically on the norms and rules of the sphere of 'objectivation-in-itself', within the domain of everyday life.

Thus, an 'individual knows when to abandon repetition in favour of an innovatory approach to a problem.... He knows when the customary has to be questioned, and when a value taken for granted needs to be devalued' (Heller 1984: 259). Moreover, the individual knows 'when, where and why it is time to drop the pragmatic approach and adopt a theoretical attitude' (1984: 259). He knows when to drop the everyday habit of 'over-generalization' before it turns into a prejudice. In other words, 'the individual relates in a relatively free fashion to... objectivations 'in itself', and to the customary system of requirements and norms as a whole which he receives as a datum in everyday life' (1984: 260).

In several references to the kinds of transformations wrought by individuals in their everyday lives on the strength of their engagements with objectivation 'for itself', Heller appears to adhere to something of an apolitical aesthetic. For instance, in *Everyday Life*, while speaking of the ways in which higher-order objectivations ('for itself'), or what she also refers to as 'species-essential' objectivations, could infiltrate everyday understandings of the world, she says: 'The (social) sciences, philosophy, art, can bring experience into conscious focus, can prompt us to see our own person in a new light and in this way they can influence everyday perception itself' (1984: 192). The illustration she offers of this kind of 'awakening' or 'illumination' is of how an understanding of the Impressionist painters could, for instance, help us appreciate better or teach us more about 'colour' in our day-to-day, mundane world.

We need to pursue her writings further to obtain glimpses of a far-reaching political philosophy. In *Can Modernity Survive?* (1990), Heller argues that the concept of the political inheres in the contrast of the 'Is' and the 'Ought', thereby enabling the possibility of critique. It is not essential for everyone to become an artist, philosopher, scientist or statesman to participate in the philosophical endeavour. Individuals may acquire the vision that enables them to comprehend the practical/political implications of philosophy. Thus (Heller 1990: 120) says:

> What hitherto has happened only in philosophy can and does now happen in political practice and life. Men and women constantly juxtapose Ought, that is, universalized values, to Is, to their political and social institutions, which fail to match or live up to Ought. Men and women interpret and reinterpret those values in their daily practices and they go about using them as vehicles of critique and refutation, of realizing philosophy or philosophy's ultimate end.

In other words, we may surmise that everyday life can become the terrain for the acting out of an activist politics by individuals who believe in something beyond the mundane and in the possibility of transformation and who opt to initiate the work of change in their own environments, neighbourhoods or communities.

the making of a grassroots muslim activist

We began this chapter with an introduction to Altaf. It is time now perhaps to bring him back into the picture. Altaf did not have a great deal of education and is certainly not a fluent speaker in English. His spoken Hindi is passable; his education has been largely in his local tongue, Gujarati. His initiation into a larger social vision than that which may normally be associated with a boy growing up in a largely Muslim environment in one of Ahmedabad's ethnically-limited pockets certainly commenced with stories and maxims from his politically-aware father and, later, his mother. His mother is, indeed, with all her almost complete lack of education, an intriguing individual. She spoke of the making of revolution [inquilab] which has to come from within, when people want it and are ready for it.

> It is like the *chip-chip-chip* sound of the chicken trying to break out of the egg. If one gets impatient and tries to speed up the process by cracking the egg deliberately from the outside, the

chicken will emerge sooner but will be weak or disabled. It has to come out in its own time, out of its own effort from within, and then it will be strong.

With a mother who has such passionate ideas, it was not surprising that Altaf should be interested in social and political activities. This bundle of heterogeneous ideas that he gathered during his growing-up years did not however achieve any level of coherence, even though it probably formed the basis for his facilitative work in the setting up and running of the relief camp in 2002.

At his own admittance, it was Altaf's interaction with an international non-governmental organization and the training and theoretical inputs he received thereby that helped his disaggregated and somewhat hazy social ideas fuse into a more highly conscious and developed world-view.[3] He and some of his co-activists in the community have indeed proceeded to think beyond their acquired ideas and to contemplate the possibility and course of action required in taking their involvement to the next level: formal engagement and participation in local-level politics. Activists such as these have a deep-seated interest in turning around the trend of low political representation of Muslims at all levels, which we have documented earlier. Feroz Ashraf from Jogeshwari, for instance, believes that the reversal of the trend must commence from below, literally out of the slums. According to him, once a few Muslims from the deprived and backward classes stand up as candidates from their local areas (preferably women as Independent candidates or with the support of parties committed to socially progressive ideas) the true empowerment of Muslims will have begun, for they can work to bring about change more effectively.[4]

In an earlier chapter, I had briefly outlined Ashraf's story of his involuntary journey from a comfortable middle-class existence in an ethnically-mixed neighbourhood to one of Mumbai's Muslim-dominated areas. It is perhaps best to allow Ashraf's own speech and silence into the text.

In 1985, communal riots broke out in Bhiwandi that also engulfed a part of Mumbai. There was fear that the riot would spread to the rest of the city too. Fortunately, the tension abated. But what

I will not forget is the advice of a very close friend—Anand Mohan Sahay. He told me to move out from my present Hindu-dominated location to a 'safe' Muslim place. Of course, I did not agree. At that time I never thought that one day Anand's words would come true and I would be compelled to heed his warning.... Then came 6 December 1992 followed by January 1993. At that time I was living in Malad. I had been living there for 18 years. I had begun my married life here. Both my son and daughter were born here. A lot of friends gave us assurances, came to see us and inquired about us constantly. I can't write what happened. I have never written about it, just experienced it. The result was that I changed my house. I had to leave the four walls that I had decorated with almost two decades of memories. Now I live in Jogeshwari, a suburb in Mumbai which is probably safe. But who knows?

This enforced dislocation, which Ashraf continues to fight in spirit, led gradually to a different turn—a move towards engagement with the problems and concerns of his local area. A retired employee of a major Indian oil company, Ashraf spent a large part of his time writing for a number of different journals and newspapers. As we shall see later, his life-long bent towards leftist politics clearly framed his critique of Muslim local religious leadership as well as his understanding of the issues that ailed the community. While a number of the activists engaged in the work of ethnic amity are from the younger generation, there are clearly some who have spent decades in these efforts or, like Ashraf, been drawn in at a later point in their lives. Pyar Ali Khapadia was a postal employee for most of his life; today, at 70, he lives with his wife in the heart of Ram Rahim Nagar on his meagre pension. Thirty-four years ago, he moved to this river-side location, after his house was destroyed in the communal carnage of 1969. That experience sensitized him irrevocably to the dismal danger of persistent inter-community aggression. Ram Rahim Nagar itself started coming up in the 1960s along with other slums and shantytowns on the banks of the Sabarmati as poor Muslims and Hindus moved there with every recurring spurt of violence. Growing up as a Muslim in India in the early years of Independence, Pyar Ali developed a definite predilection for the political figures and ideals of that period, particularly Nehru and Gandhi. He heard and read them as much as possible.

Not surprisingly, almost immediately after he moved here, Pyar Ali worked to set up the Ram Rahim Nagar Jhopadpati Nivasi Sanstha, bringing together Hindus and Muslims of the area with a firm commitment to keeping aggression away. It was no easy task, and there were always those who defied persuasion; nevertheless the central thrust of his message was clear—that violence must be prevented in people's own interest—and, finally, worked to bring others in the neighbourhood around. In 2002 as in many preceding years, Ram Rahim Nagar remained an isle of quiet in a city torn by communal strife. As Pyar Ali had to say:

> We put in the effort all these years. Now things are better and people understand. We have explained to them: Riots do harm to us. Ours is a poor neighbourhood. We work for daily wages. If there is violence, we cannot earn. At the time of violence, no one comes to help us. We have to help ourselves, ensure that there is peace. We have to deal daily with conflicts that could flare up. Take each situation apart and make people understand the manipulations of the politicians and ensure that they are not taken in by false propaganda.... If the property of a Hindu or a Muslim is destroyed, national wealth is destroyed.... Why are Muslims targeted today as if they are anti-national? When people say all manner of things against Muslims, I let them speak. Then I ask: 'Who killed Mahatma Gandhi, Indira Gandhi, Rajiv Gandhi? Were any of the killers Muslim? Then why do you give *dosh* to [blame] Muslims?'.... Now our message has got through. It is like if you hear a song many times, then it becomes common; you automatically remember it, without thinking. Our work is now like that, people remember automatically. As a result, everything is open here— shops, restaurants—even if there is violence in the city, despite curfew. Even the police are surprised.

Pyar Ali's is clearly an education sustained and augmented by active engagement with the everyday issues and politics of his neighbourhood, rather than one obtained in the classroom. His understanding of the need to contain ethnic conflict appears to have emerged not from any direct engagement with the realm of 'objectivations for itself' but from the realization that the new society, the new 'nation', as he put it, required novel thinking with regard to social relationships. As Heller would recognize, the expansion of everyday knowledge does not have to emerge, as it were, from 'above', through interaction with philosophy or social science; it may well materialize when a 'nexus of social needs and personal experiences' translates into new knowledge (1984: 191). With Pyar Ali, the constant effort to re-interpret broader, national events and concerns in the context of the daily life of the neighbourhood appears to have been worked deep into the strategy for containing local conflicts. It is not benignly unstructured communities that Pyar Ali addresses; there is the unambiguous assertion that the interests of those most at stake are the deprived sections. Communal violence brutally implicates class and privilege, with the underclass and the disprivileged perceived as bearing the brunt.

For a Muslim woman, the engagement with difference may implicate an even greater degree of friction. Sophia Khan in Ahmedabad comes from a background she self-consciously describes as orthodox. Her father is an extremely religious person, a businessman, whose faith did not permit him to insure his property or even maintain a savings bank account. When he retired, he simply kept his cash in the house, inducing an even greater degree of vulnerability in a household with no sons. Sophia completed her education, including an advanced degree in law, in the face of constant pressure from her family and their exhortations that she should abandon her studies for matrimony and the home. Her tentative interest in social work was fostered by her teachers and, later, her interaction with Ila Pathak of the Ahmedabad Women's Action Group. It was this initial work that steered her towards a greater concern with gender issues. The awareness of being 'Muslim' and, therefore, 'Other' remained, reinforced rather than reduced by well-intentioned educators who continuously urged her to work for 'her community'.

Sophia's initial forays into work with unions and in the villages sharpened her awareness of the deep divisions of caste and community, divisions which she gradually came to appreciate had to be worked into the analysis as well as the plans of action for all social issues. The realization was strengthened by her perception of particular discriminatory practices of the provision of relief following the shattering earthquake in Gujarat in January 2001.

When I stressed caste and community issues, people laughed at me at first and thought I needlessly brought these in everywhere. One of my acquaintances... who dismissed my claims earlier now finds himself *gheraod* [under siege] by the tribals. He started an NGO [in the wake of the earthquake] and now he himself has been removed from it. The tribals say: 'We want no Muslims here'. Such is the hatred and hostility to Muslims in Gujarat.

Sophia's arguments were glaringly underlined in 2002, when she had to assume a Hindu name and make an identity card in that name to even allow her, despite her position as a social activist, to move through the city to help in the relief work. She had to carefully strategize: adopting a non-Gujarati name so that she would not encounter questions about her caste identity and would be able to explain away her frequent lapses into Hindi when she speaks. Her own neighbourhood in Shahpur was bound by curfew, but on the western side of the Sabarmati life appeared to be proceeding fairly undisturbed. Sophia fits no 'stereotype', according to her, of the Muslim woman. She does not don the *burqa*; she speaks Gujarati fluently and wears her hair short.

No one knew I was Muslim. But I know that I am Muslim. On 3 March, we were short of medicines [in the Shahpur relief camp]. I rang a Hindu friend and asked her to come with me. I came to this part of the city [West of the Sabarmati river]. I was amazed to see things were normal. Life as usual. Girls going around on two-wheelers. Only we were under siege. I felt, no words can describe it, humiliated. I could not look my Hindu friend in the eye. To what have we been reduced? We are nothing. I was frightened because I knew I was Muslim.... My driver [a Hindu] did not want to work for me. One of my junior colleagues... was asked [by her family] to leave, not to work for a Muslim. She told them: 'Sophia is not *like that*'. I have kept her on despite the fact that the project she was working on is at an end. Perhaps she will influence her family to see Muslims in a different light.... There are major waterworks where I live, so the authorities were afraid of trouble. They dispersed the mobs that came, though they did not arrest them. At that time, we were grateful even for that.

With both Ashraf and Altaf, the trajectory of involvement in community activities and, particularly, communal amity is one in which a painful intimacy with violence has been established somewhere along the way. All the men and women here share that fateful knowledge of the sudden shattering of familiar worlds of neighbourhood and community, and sometimes, far more acutely, of family. All the while that Sophia was working in the relief efforts for Muslims in 2002, her own household, she said, was strategizing for its security.

We had nothing.... We had only some stones from broken walls. These would not protect us from the mobs.... We were 10,000 but the mobs were as far as the eyes could see—crying Jai Sri Ram and carrying gas cylinders and weapons.... At night there was no sleep. We would strategize at home. Perhaps we can run up if they burn the house from below. That was one way to save. Or we could run in any direction, not wait for each other, can catch up with each other later. My sister who is a heart patient said: 'Don't wait for me. I will not be able to run fast'....

One of the aims here is to sketch some of these particular lives, to listen to specific individuals rather than to record a harmony (or cacophony) of distant sounds. While many of these individuals are or have come to be associated with particular groups or non-governmental organizations, their voices are here located as individual voices. Their views are undoubtedly shaped by their particular group and its ideology; this is recognized here, particularly in the following section. Nevertheless, their experiences are also very personal.[5] There is no suggestion that any particular 'event' marked the defining moment of change for any of these protagonists, though there is excruciating evidence that memories of violence deeply entwist with the way these men and women understand the work they are engaged today; there is a scar whose erasure is perhaps impossible. Its tracing need not be framed in a narrative of vengeance however, but in one whose trajectory perhaps leads to a different future. There must be no impression allowed that a halo of sanctity wraps these fledgling efforts; rather, the constant reflexivity and re-interpretation required by Heller's model obliges us to recognize their sometimes contradictory and always incomplete character.

subplots and skirmishes: gender, modes of struggle and forms of leadership

Multiple skeins of discomfort unravel as we enter into conversations with 'Muslim' social activists, beings that Sophia's experiences certainly impel us to recognize the existence of. It is not of course a matter of surprise that the question of gender immediately surfaces, though one may, indeed, be struck by the anguished intensity of tension it can give rise to. There is, critically, acute awareness of how community and women's issues chafe abrasively against each other, particularly in the wake of heightened communal consciousness and targeted violence. It is considerably illuminating to note that activists often cite 'Mumbai 1992–93' and 'Gujarat 2002' as moments that fundamentally altered the very ways in which gender issues could or could not be addressed. Hamida, a Muslim woman activist allied with an organization working both in Mumbai and Gujarat with Muslim women voiced the concern of how issues had been redefined in the wake of such cataclysmic violence. She has been deeply involved in relief work as well as in continuing social support extending particularly to Muslim women survivors of the 2002 violence.

> The impact of Gujarat or the Mumbai riots on Muslim women is tremendous. There is a sense of oppression from two sides: from within by conservative and fundamentalist forces and from outside by Hindu communalist forces.... Muslim women get marginalized. In an atmosphere of communalism, women's questions do not get centralized; this needs to be done. How do we look at women? In the kind of atmosphere in Gujarat, should we raise the women's question at all? Or only that of the identity of Muslims as a community, a minority?

In what she says, the sense of being pulled every which way by contradictory affiliations emerges acutely.

> In education and so on Muslim women are very poor. And there is so much pressure on the community, and violence. As it increases, the community is further ghettoized and minority politics increases. Our *samaj* [society] is backward, there is so much violence—is there place for us? Where do we go?

Another woman activist working principally with Muslim women, who has been assisting in the follow-up of several cases of death and injury in the Gujarat violence, reflected:

> What is it to be Muslim today? Civil society has failed in Gujarat. After 55 years, the question 'What is your name?' becomes important. We are seen as different; we begin to see ourselves as different. An 'Othering' takes place. We are not just activist, or woman, but Muslim.

The lament, that issues concerned with the misuse of provisions for divorce under Muslim Personal Law to the detriment of women or the question of maintenance in the event of divorce are all forced to recede into the background in the face of targeted attacks against the community, is real.[6] Muslim religious leaders rage against the foregrounding of such issues when, as they argue, the whole community is under attack. Women activists are castigated for even bringing up such issues and for, as it were, letting down the community. Further discomfort centres around the fact that Muslim Personal Law has become the battleground for both Hindu and Muslim fundamentalists, while a concern such as domestic violence against Muslim women is one that Muslim religious leaders certainly would rather was not addressed. Again, as activists assert, communal violence always has negative impacts on women: in its wake the community male elders seek to regulate women's mobility, their dress, their behaviour and the like. In Gujarat, for instance, in some cases, men remain reluctant to admit incidents of rape and are known to have applied pressure on women in their family to prevent them from reporting or following these up. There are activists who believe that the stance of religious leaders is detrimental to what they consider to be the 'wider' battle: that of the gender struggle or of human rights issues. Regardless of the climate of communalization, Muslim women's concerns within the larger concern of the rights of women in general should not be marginalized. One should continue to raise voices on all such subjects, allowing none to be removed from review.

The issues acquire further layers of intricacy once it is recognized that Muslim women may be projected as a single category only at the risk of a great degree of generalization. Among women activists are those who find it disconcerting that relevant 'women's issues' are thought to include only aspects such as maintenance, divorce inheritance. These affect only married or once-married women, while there are a small but undeniable number of Muslim women who remain unmarried, either voluntarily or due to a host of factors including familial responsibilities, economic conditions and the like. *All* such issues tend to be put on the back burner when the community considers itself under siege; however, while some support may be garnered on the questions of maintenance or *talaq*, there is little acknowledgement of the legal status or requirements of, for instance, single women within the community who have to fight a separate internal battle for their own space. The elucidation here of some of these fraught themes reminds us of the complexity of the struggles being waged and does not permit us the ease of simplification.

Working with overtly religious leaders or caste elders is also an issue that several activists find contentious. Sajjid, for instance, as we earlier recorded, refuses to link himself with any sectarian and religious groups. The association for youth, funded through small local contributions, that he is linked with in Jogeshwari, at first called itself the Muslim Youth Association. However, to de-link it from any connection purely with religion, and to stress its 'progressive' character, they soon started referring to it as the Modern Youth Association. Sajjid and the other young men associated with the group worked with several non-governmental associations in relief and rehabilitation work in the months and years after the violence of 1992–93. This interaction exposed them, as Sajjid said, to a range of ideas concerned with social issues, secularism, justice, globalization and the like. From this emerged the idea of forming the association. Among other activities, it has held several public protests, for instance against the system of donations in colleges and alcohol addiction, and also runs a small book bank lending school books to poor children in the neighbourhood. The association renders constant support and maintains regular contact with survivors' families; it also works to build communal amity through arranging collective neighbourhood celebrations involving Hindus and Muslims, mediating local tensions and encouraging interaction between all groups on a range of shared concerns such as sewage collection, road maintenance and the like.

Ashraf keeps aloof from religious *jamaats*. While he relies on some support from individuals and non-denominational non-governmental organizations, he remains largely an independent worker. Concerned with issues of communal amity, he is also particularly interested in education and works with his wife to tutor underprivileged young boys and girls, both Hindu and Muslim, to help them through school. His attention focuses on individual youth in the slums, and he involves himself in encouraging students as far as their abilities will take them, even assisting them with information regarding possible employment opportunities. When he moved to Jogeshwari, after a while Ashraf started going to the local mosque. However, this was not for the purpose of participation in the prayers. He aimed to know how people thought, what the *maulvis* taught and preached in order to be able perhaps to contest these ideas in the course of his interaction with Muslim neighbours. He expressed considerable contempt of the kind of Muslim who focuses only on religious matters without addressing the problems of poverty and educational backwardness that confront the community.

There are others who would like to underline their distance from the *maulanas*. Several women activists in Gujarat and Mumbai, for instance, including some who confine their work largely within the Muslim community, talk of tense engagements with religious leaders who insisted on men and women saying *namaaz* in the relief camps in order to be entitled to assistance and who were openly derisive of violence-hit Muslims who had opted to stay in ethnically-mixed areas, implying that they had only got what was coming to them. Jannat, a young woman activist from Baroda, who has worked with the PUCL among the survivors of the Gujarat carnage, was extremely outspoken in her critique and disagreement with religious diktat:

Especially after communal violence, the pressure on women, even young girls, to don the *burqa* increases.... The Quran says so many things: One has to ask a woman's consent prior to the *nikah*, for instance. These things are not kept. But *purdah* is wanted. There are more women on whom it is forced than those who actually want it. At some level, our right is being snatched away. We should openly state that there are things in the Quran we don't give regard to.

Again, she asserted:

Women's issues—divorce or *nikahnama*—should not be side-lined. Some fundamentalist organizations are gaining head-way. They tell the people that all this happened because they have lost the faith, have given women too much freedom, discarded the *burqa* etc...

Critically, such activists wish to underline not their or their community's 'minority' or 'Muslim' identity, but to align their struggles as democratic citizens with other deprived or oppressed groups including, for instance, women, Dalits, tribals and the econ-omically disadvantaged. This alignment is by no means auto-matically achieved. There is rueful acknowledgement of the fact that it often appears far easier to get Muslim clergy, in particular, to protest against any perceived move to contain personal laws or to demonstrate against a proposed visit by the Israeli President to India than to forge common ground on issues not viewed as directly concerned with the community.

In the previous chapter, we had negotiated a tangle of contest-ations over community identity, particularly with relation to sectarian associations. These contests as well as those we witness here implicate inevitably at some level divisions of other kinds, such as class and social position. From the preceding pages, what is clear is the extent of such disputes and the fact that they are multi-layered and complex. Those who are unable to ascribe un-ambiguously to a fixed definition of the community in terms of religious identity also disagree among themselves on a range of critical issues. As a result, boundaries are again drawn in or pressed out according to a range of varying factors. While Muslim activists who work, on their own or as part of one or another association, primarily with the Muslim community often feel more con-siderably the pressure to remain silent on questions of women's rights or justice in the wake of targeted attacks from outside, it is not, as we may have perceived, always the case that they acquiesce or find themselves in agreement with the views and strategies of religious leaders. On the other hand, some Muslim activists who work regardless of the religious question on issues of social justice and rights are also sometimes reluctant to push too far.[7] As one stressed:

> There is just so much pressure on Muslims right now. Ever since the Shah Bano case, Mumbai violence and now Gujarat they are so much the target.... Yes, divorce, abandonment of women without proper maintenance, all these are issues of concern, but right now the community is hurting terribly. It would not be fair.... It would be a further violence to take up these things right now.

How far should the issue of justice be pushed? In a previous chapter we had acknowledged with Das and Kleinman (2001) that in the life of a community, 'justice is neither everything nor nothing'. Not all Muslim activists would agree. Shakeel Ahmed leads Nirbhay Bano Andolan, a group based entirely on voluntary effort, which works essentially to educate the poor and marginalized with regard to rights and justice in order to empower them to battle with the authorities on issues of concern. Shakeel identifies leaders in different areas; each takes the responsibility of finding more volunteers, particularly among the youth, as well as of sensitization of people in his or her local quarter. Shakeel's efforts have taken root in a number of Mumbai slum areas including Nagpada, Wadala, Koliwada, Sion, Goregaon, Bandra and Antop Hill. The volunteers are themselves largely slum dwellers, ordinary people, many of them fairly young.

Though he came from a poor family, Shakeel left a fairly well-paid job in Mumbai, appalled at the treatment meted out to the labourers by his employer, and eventually found his way to Latur, where he took up relief work for the earthquake victims. The *jhatka* [shock] of the violence of Mumbai in 1992–93 was in a way central to the realignment in his work. Several persons came together in the wake of the violence to form an association to fight the fear and suspicion that was creating havoc among Hindus and Muslims in the city. The association finally evolved into the Nirbhay Bano

Andolan. Shakeel completed a formal degree in law, an educational acquisition that has enabled him to empower the local groups he works alongside with careful information about legal and official procedures, modes of follow-up for cases and the rights of common citizens. It is not surprising that *nyaya* [justice] forms the pivot of Shakeel's social thought. Indeed, Shakeel's work with the victims and survivors of the violence was critical in shaping for him an ethic of peace that centred fundamentally around the notion of justice. He has been at the forefront of the campaign to ensure that those indicted by the Srikrishna Commission Report, particularly police officers, be brought to book and has also been engaging with victims' families in their struggles for compensation and justice. As he argues:

> *Nyaya* is not a question only about Muslims, it is an issue for the whole *samaj* (society).... Every problem is seen as being one of a community, either Muslims or Dalits or whatever.... Justice is an issue for the society as a whole. People question why we must pursue this? Why reopen old wounds? [*zhakham hare karne ki zaroorat kya hai?*] However, without *nyaya*, from where will peace come in society? If people see that the government is not giving justice, they will take the law into their own hands.... The *mohalla* committees do not talk of justice. They advocate that we embrace [*gale mil jayen*] with the same police who did wrong. The police has committed gross injustices with common people. We cannot raise this issue in the *mohalla* committee....

The sense of discontent with the *mohalla* committees is not expressed by Shakeel alone. Waqar Khan in Dharavi has his reservations for different reasons, though by no means is he dismissive of the extent of the work they have achieved in different areas of the city. Rather, he expresses unhappiness that the *mohalla* committees are no longer quite as tightly-knit and active as they were a few years ago for he is convinced that the 'danger' of communal tension is in no way a thing of the past.

Waqar's own work in peace and conflict resolution has received considerable support from the Mohalla Committee Trust. Waqar's tryst with social activism, particularly in the area of communal harmony, has its own self-conscious evolution. A migrant to the city, Waqar came to Dharavi in Mumbai as a young boy to earn a living along with his family. His story encapsulates the dream of so many of Mumbai's migrant population. From selling bananas off a cart, he slowly progressed to tailoring and selling garments made out of used clothes. This move in turn led the way to a gradual entry into the ready-made garments business; the second-hand material gave way to the use of new textiles. In 1984, Indira Gandhi was assassinated. Waqar was travelling back to Mumbai from a business visit to Baroda. In front of him in his compartment sat a Sikh family. Some people started harassing them, abusing the wife, even pulling off the turban of the Sikh gentleman. Waqar and his companions managed to make them finally back off; and they soon alighted from the train. But, as Waqar put it, the Sikh family was so broken and cowed down [*sahmi si*] that he escorted them to their home.

As with Pyar Ali, Waqar's engagement with the question of communal accord emerged not from any formal learning but from deep reflection on the contradictions and paradoxes of daily living within his own small world. The violence of 1992–93 plunged Waqar in at the deep end. Struggling with relief activities and efforts to restrain conflict in his own neighbourhood, Waqar was convinced that something had to be done at the local level by local people.

> Neighbours who had lived side-by-side for decades were turning against each other. People had built businesses, homes, spent their whole lifetime in doing so—these were destroyed in minutes in front of their eyes. I thought I should go mad. What is this that was happening?

Waqar's answer was the creation of a message, a simple, direct message that he felt would appeal to the people he wanted to reach. The search was not for an erudite message; not a 'white dove' as he put it, that has abstract symbolism and that people have to think about before they can understand, but one that appealed to the 'heart' not the head'. It was his photograph of four children (all Muslim incidentally, with the Hindu child being his own son) dressed in the religious garb of the Hindu, the Muslim, the Christian and the Sikh that became, when disseminated across the city, through the efforts of the Mohalla Committee Movement, the face of Mumbai's resolve to put the violence behind. Subsequently,

Waqar worked on the creation of a small documentary film, with actors and studio facilities from Dharavi itself, again inscribed with the message of peace. With the assistance of members of the trust, the film was sent to Prasar Bharati (National Broadcasting Corporation) which televised it as violence broke out in Gujarat.

Waqar engages with social activists, non-governmental organizations and researchers from across the city, yet the nucleus of his activities and the centre of his attention always remains Dharavi:

> I can't stop violence everywhere, but if something happens or if trouble is sought to be created in my little neighbourhood, I can speak out. I must speak out.... Why should Christians alone stand up for Christians? Muslims like me should do it. Even the Congress does that: It will stand up a Muslim candidate for Muslim issues. The wrong message goes out.

To return to an earlier point, for Waqar and his associates, the work of building peace initiatives at the local level cannot be halted because the systems of authority somehow contrive to deny legal remedy or justice to victims. While justice must always be worth striving for, for ordinary people the resumption of life in the everyday demands compromise and negotiations of a far more complex and nuanced kind. In Dharavi, neighbours had to learn to talk with each other and share in common problems. Muslim shopkeepers needed to understand that they should re-employ their Hindu helpers for these were familiar with the work and were not among the attackers. Why should they be penalized [*Unke pet pe lat kyon mare?*] for the acts of others?

This section has sought to underline the fragile and tentative character of the labours of a variety of individuals (and groups) to trace novel paths through uncharted terrain. While these efforts are seemingly unified in their reluctance to adopt wholeheartedly a Muslim 'habit,' as it were, there are differences in the extent or intensity of disagreements with religious leaders. The work of re-imagining and remaking the world cannot moreover be without some internal contradictions on what the issues of import are for the Muslims; these dissensions depend in part certainly on the particular contexts of work and clientele being addressed. On the other hand, *all* the individuals aforementioned carry a vision which places Muslim concerns alongside those of other deprived sections of society *or* reworks them in the more abstract language of the rights of citizens or human rights.

'we-awareness' *versus* 'generalizability'

This chapter and the previous one have manifested that there is evidently a considerable tussle between the elements allied with religion per se and those who call themselves 'secular' among the Muslims I have been working with. Here, I will try and work through Heller's (1984) critique of integrations founded on religion or morality before trying to view these, alongside material from the field, in slightly different light. Now, earlier it had been argued that Heller proposes higher-order objectivations including religion as paths towards a more developed individuality. At some point though she begins to argue that religion and/or morality, for instance, create a 'we-awareness', which has specific implications. What is this 'we-awareness' and what are its implications?

While religion inhibits the tendency towards particularity in everyday life, it does so by fostering what Heller calls 'we-awareness'. There are certain unpalatable corollaries that, according to her, attend we-awareness, not merely adventitiously, but invariably. When a person becomes part of an integration or collectivity, a collectivity of community, religious group or nation, the integration is seen as an extension of the person himself or herself. As a consequence, the association is less one of ideas based on critical reflection, and more one of spontaneous, instinctive, rather 'earthly' bonding. The person is thus capable of making great sacrifice in the name of the integration or community, but is also *incapable* of acknowledging any inadequacies or rifts in content or values of the collectivity. In other words, for Muslims who bind themselves to rigid understandings of the faith, the possibility of critical consideration of the dilemmas this may entail closes.

But this is not all. In turning to another section in Heller's complex argument in the classic work *Everyday Life* (1984), it becomes possible to unravel that a more significant difficulty with we-awareness may be the fact that it fails to seriously address the question as to whether the life it advocates is truly possible— to the same extent—for everyone or only for oneself or one's particular group or community. In other words, it is fundamentally 'aristocratic', rather than 'democratic' in principle. The guiding norm for a collectivity based on democratic rather than aristocratic principles would be 'always generalizability, extensibility of the meaningful life to others: in the long run, to the whole of humanity' (Heller 1984: 268). Certainly, as we have seen, several of the Muslim activists here considered the exclusively religious worldview to be 'fundamentalist' in character and questioned what benefit it could ever hold, particularly, though not only, for women within the community. In fact, this view is often so strong that it leads these activists to spurn any sort of association with religious leaders, and to lump them all together, regardless of hue or inclination.

While this posture might gel, if unintentionally, with Heller's evocations, it nevertheless has awkward implications, with its unfortunate inability to cope with the pull of faith. Though her preference is apparent enough, Heller's argument remains in the nature of a statement, with no clarification in relation to the question of action. Our activists, at least some of them, on the other hand, appear to have worked out their own answers through practical experimentation in the field. Thus, not all of them reject out of hand the need for or the possibility of working with religious leaders, even those of rigid posture, towards broader under- standings of Muslim faith and future. As several activists would acknowledge, faith is integral to the daily life of most Muslims; leaving religious elders out of the loop would diminish their own credibility with their community. They would end up talking with a much smaller audience. While some would like to work only with those leaders who are willing to contemplate *ijtihad* or the possibility of reinterpretation of religious doctrine in the light of the requirements of contemporary life, there are others who believe that even the 'fundamentalists' must be accorded a degree of attention. It is acknowledged that organizations such as the Jamaat- e-Islami or the Jamaat-e-Ulema-e-Hind among others play a crucial role in post-violence situations. Muslim religious organizations are among the first offerers of assistance to victims and survivors. But the thinking proceeds further. As Sophia, among others, argued:

In the camps it was often the religious organizations working.... People ask why we work with the *maulvis* in Gujarat? They after all worked with the injured and traumatized to the extent they could. They are also learning new ways of thinking from the experience.... We did not usually talk with religious leaders... but now I find myself being the bridge between these and the social, women's sector or groups.... They may want us to oppose the UCC [Uniform Civil Code] and propose the idea of Shariat courts; that is not going to happen. But now they are willing to listen and I can talk to them openly about our differences; make them understand.... They have started taking a more liberal approach with regard to women.... I am invited to *madrasas*. They have seen that the women and young girls did a lot of work in the camps... girls with 9th and 10th standard education. Women's groups also worked with them, trained them. They [religious leaders] know now that things cannot go back to being just the same as before... some changes will have to come.

It may be possible to avoid interaction with particular persons, but are the questions so easily dismissible. A few activists at least certainly do not think so. As another Muslim woman activist from Gujarat offered:

We should not leave the opportunity to engage with the *maulvis*. We need to involve them, so that they do not stonewall all our efforts. Further, we cannot decide whom to work with on the basis of personalities; we have to address the questions they are raising. We find it possible to talk with the Tablighi Jamaat leader [in our area]. He raises the question of values: submission to God's will, setting a good example for others.... Can we ignore these? Even if we disagree on some points, we have to dialogue, slowly build more areas of agreement.

Even Shakeel would possibly admit the practicality if not the piety of strategic, but selective, interaction with religious ideologues:

We think we should work only with secular people; but we realized that we need to engage with other people of different ideologies also. We should make an entry and talk to others as well, or we are talking only to ourselves. We can't make them untouchable.... Though we keep our distance from communal, political or religious organizations, in local level issues decisions have to be taken. In our areas, there are issues—displacement, corruption etc. [At such time] we have to work together, whatever the ideology....

There are thus differing approaches and modes of communication: one, which admits common ground only on non-religious issues of public or local level interest; another, which sees conversation on spiritual matters as a way of encouraging religious leaders to participate more in civil concerns or to at least not oppose these; and, a third, even more proactive, which actually tries to converse seriously with religious leaders for the reframing of Muslim religio-legal and social practice. Sophia, Hamida and some others are engaged intently in this third form of interaction. From the perspective of Heller's argument, the three have differing implications. The first two approaches involve selective, if varying, cooperation with those for whom religion is a form of 'we-awareness', without any attempt at alteration of that vision.

But the last approach involves something more. And it is signal of the possibility of the transformation, under certain conditions, of 'we-awareness' into greater critical awareness through careful reworking and dialogue. Here this is done through conversations related to provisions within Muslim Personal Law. Certain specific areas have been selected for redress, because an immediate onslaught on the whole may only provoke hostility. A common *nikahnama* [marriage contract], clearly specifying the terms of matrimony and the amount of *mehr* [dower] is being framed through ground-level interaction with Muslim women in different parts of the country to be put before religious leaders on the Muslim Personal Law Board. The misuse of the procedure of triple *talaq* [divorce] by men is also an issue being slowly addressed, through an attempt to frame standard procedures for divorce, which do not partake of complete arbitrariness. At their own level and in their own limited regions, activists continue to raise with religious leaders questions about Muslim men's violence against women and about Muslim women's need for and access to education, emphasizing that these cannot be sidelined because of communal attacks; indeed the attacks must spur *more* not less initiative.

These are efforts at repair from within, but they do not, significantly, cease there. For one, the highlight on the concerns of Muslim women demonstrates that a broader concern with women's issues including, for instance, education is slowly seeping into the Muslim guiding imagination. Further, these labours are combined with attempts, however gradual and intermittent, to persuade Muslim leaders to let their voices be heard on issues that concern them as citizens *as well as* as a community or a 'minority', be it the oppression of dalits, attacks against Christians, terrorist violence and the like. The potential, if fragile and still in the process of being worked out, for the release of the religious imagination (the 'we-awareness') towards less restricted leanings may allow us to proceed beyond the 'orthodox/secular' or even 'fundamentalist/liberal' divide to the visualization of at least one (and maybe not the only) possible mediating alternative.

notes

1. I here understand the concept of empowerment to denote the gaining of voice and establishing a presence and thence the feeling of being able to make a difference in one's own life and in the lives of others in one's social world, however small. This often, in particular, implies the negotiation—with a degree of success—of systems of power, authority and bureaucracy.

2. While there surely are religious leaders or views of all kinds, from the more inclusive to the more exclusive, for the most part these activists tend to fuse (or confuse) them and often, though not invariably, incline to the view that there should be no truck with religious leadership. For the bulk of this chapter therefore, unlike the previous one, I too make no distinction between various sects or forms of religious inclination. Towards the end of the chapter, though, there is a more nuanced discussion, and some threads are separated out.

3. Heller (1984: 261) has to say:

   A world-view is neither a scientific nor a philosophical synthesis, it is not a political ideology: it is rather the manifested form taken by an amalgam, a fusion of the resultants of these factors (or of some of them), and it is their internalization for service in the everyday life of the individual.

4. If we are continuing to follow Heller, it must be mentioned that she had a deep suspicion of social and grassroots movements that sought 'natural allies' among political parties, because parties tend towards pragmatism and

searching for possibilities unlike movements which express the 'Ought'. However, such alliance is not impossible, she would admit, under the right circumstances. The parties would have to remain active and relentless opponents of political conservatism (see Heller 1985b).

5. Among the groups, some international and some very localized, with which some of the activists we speak with here are associated are Awaaz-e-Niswaan, Youth for Voluntary Action (YUVA), Vikas Adhyayan Kendra, Action Aid India, Rahat Welfare Trust, Nirbhay Bano Andolan, Muslim Youth for India, Modern Youth Association, People's Union for Civil Liberties (PUCL), some zonal divisions of the Mumbai Mohalla Committee Trust, Tulsiwadi Project, Bombay Aman Committee, Sahiyar and so on.

6. Ever since the controversy over the Shah Bano case in the 1980s, the question of Muslim Personal Law has remained a deeply troubled one, despite the passing of the Muslim Women (Protection of Rights on Divorce) Act 1986. Subject to constant politicization, the issue continues to be one on which the Muslim clergy by and large refuses to negotiate, while the Hindu Right uses it as a weapon to beat the opposition with.

7. Though this is not a subject that can be pursued here, as may be surmised, non-Muslim individuals and groups working with the Muslim community must also face serious queries and doubts. They sometimes lament the fact that Muslims will not trust them, particularly in a post-violence situation, such as in Gujarat. Women occasionally find themselves even wondering if it is their saris or their *bindi* that marks them as 'Other' and makes Muslims wary of them. They also hesitate to raise issues concerned with *triple talaq* or maintenance, which they feel may alienate Muslims who do not want to discuss these questions with 'outsiders'.

chapter seven

through a dark tunnel: the face of the future

It is when we think of the world the aesthetic of indifference
might bring into being that we recognize the urgency
of remembering the stories we have not written
Amitav Ghosh (2002: 62)

I will tell you one experience. In Malegaon, there was a mother and son. The son was barely 18 years old. He had just taken his examinations and come home. Some boys came; he was beaten up at home. They took him to hospital. When the boy was eight years old, his father had died. His mother had washed dishes for other people and tried to bring him up. She just sat by his bed, with folded hands, praying and looking at her son. The officer sitting at the hospital said: 'He is at fault'. I shouted at him: 'He is dying. He was 18 years old. His mother is grieving here for her child. How can you say such a thing?' Later, when I went back, the mother phoned me. She said: *'Mera bachcha ab nahi raha. Aap meri aulad ab de sakenge?'* [My child is no more. Can you return him to me?] We are in a dark tunnel. *Hum ghum rahen hain andhere mein* [We are wandering around in the darkness]. I was so excited that justice could be done, but I had no answer for her. 'He will get *insaaf* (justice) up there', I told the mother.[1] 'Where there is no education... no jobs for those educated, no protection of life and property, no dignity of life... how can you talk of law and order?.... We are not defending those who do wrong. Catch them. Give them whatever punishment you decide.... But do not harass all Muslims, everyone.'

muslims, the police and the state

Just a few days before in mid June 2004, when I sat down to start writing this, four persons, three men and one woman, were shot dead in an 'encounter' with the Ahmedabad police on suspicion that they were terrorists linked with the Lashkar-e-Toiba involved in a plot to kill Gujarat Chief Minister Narendra Modi. Hardly a day later, doubt was raised about the claim that the woman, Ishrat Raza, a resident of Mumbra and student at Mumbai's Khalsa College was a 'terrorist'. The Ahmedabad police was reported to have defended its action on the grounds that the fact that the woman was in the car with three suspected terrorists was reason enough for her to be treated as a suspect.

Several questions have been raised by the media and human rights organizations, though, interestingly, rarely by academics, about 'encounters' and custodial deaths.[2] The rules governing arrest by the police and the question of proof—the hard work involved in law and justice—have been, at various points of time, addressed.[3] Rarely does one hear of police injuries or deaths in these kinds of encounters—are they really resorting to violence only as a last option? Why does this violence always involve death? Is it not enough to use violence to disarm or minimize threat rather than kill? Where are the deadly weapons these terrorists would have to carry to be such an immense threat to the police? We barely hear anything of these, particularly with respect to more recent episodes. To what extent can a society tolerate the lazy (in)justice of the rule of 'encounters' in which suspicion is equivalent to proof and is considered sufficient grounds for instant death without the trouble of trial or judgement?

In an article titled 'In Lawless Maharashtra' published in 1998, P. Sainath reported that Maharashtra showed the worst figures in the country in terms of custodial deaths. Such deaths were on the whole increasing and the increase was by far the greatest in the four states then ruled by the BJP—Maharashtra (where there was a BJP–Shiv Sena government), Uttar Pradesh, Rajasthan and Gujarat. As he pointed out, from the analysis: 'Your chances of dying in custody increase exponentially if you are poor. There is an added risk in being a *Dalit or belonging to some other minority segment.*

However, if you are a powerful ganglord, you tend to do well in Maharashtra's jails.' [Emphasis added].[4] By 2001-2, however, Maharashtra was followed in custodial deaths by West Bengal and Andhra Pradesh. Bihar is another state with dismal figures. In Gujarat, a newspaper article on 'encounter' deaths of Muslims in recent years brings out the dubious nature of the allegations on the basis of which the suspects were killed.[5] The Prevention of Terrorism Act (POTA) which was passed in 2001 provided the authorities with sweeping powers of arrest and detention and made even simpler perhaps the justification for 'encounter' killings of alleged 'terrorists'. Of the 240-odd persons in Gujarat detained under POTA by September 2003, *all* were Muslim.[6] The use of confessions made in police custody as evidence under POTA would also allow more easily for the employment of methods of torture to extract such declarations of guilt. In a recent article writer Arundhati Roy asserts that:

In Tamil Nadu... [POTA] has been used to stifle criticism of the state government. In Jharkhand 3,200 people, mostly poor adivasis accused of being Maoists have been named in FIRs under POTA. In eastern UP the Act is used to clamp down on those who dare to protest about the alienation of their land and livelihood rights. In Gujarat and Mumbai it is used almost exclusively against Muslims.[7]

Amnesty International's report on illegal detentions in Gujarat states that all those charged with conspiracy under POTA are Muslims. The report expressed concern that there was a 'breakdown of the rule of law in relation to the Muslim minority in the state' and used data to show that police

routinely resorted to arbitrary and illegal and incommunicado detention, denied access of detainees to lawyers and relatives, denied access to medical attention and used torture or illtreatment to induce confession. Provisions of POTA which were claimed as 'safeguards' for detainees by the Government of India when the statute was passed, appear to have been routinely ignored, along with legal safeguards contained in the ordinary criminal law and Supreme Court guidelines for arrest and detention.[8]

In Maharashtra, there have been several allegations regarding the misuse of POTA, particularly against Muslims. The case of Khwaja Yunus, under investigation now, is one of the most controversial.[9] In the aftermath of the 1993 serial bomb blasts, TADA (Terrorists and Disruptive Activities Act) was used extensively to detain Muslims in large numbers.[10] In 1997, following a large number of complaints regarding 'fake encounters', the National Human Rights Commission had passed directions to the states regarding the procedures to be followed in the cases of deaths in police encounters. The Commission made it clear that:

Under our laws, the police have not been conferred any right to take away the life of another person. If, by his act, the policeman kills a person, he commits the offence of culpable homicide whether amounting to the offence of murder or not, unless it is proved that such killing was not an offence under the law. Under the scheme of criminal law prevailing in India, it would not be an offence if death is caused in the exercise of the right of private defence... [or] the police... use force, extending upto the causing of death as may be necessary to arrest the person accused of an offence punishable with death or imprisonment for life.

Despite these strictures passed by the National Human Rights Commission (NHRC), however, little has changed with respect to encounter killings or custodial deaths. There is not much evidence of the independent investigations demanded by the NHRC being taken seriously by state authorities.[11] The NHRC has also been investigating cases of the abuse of POTA and in recent times the Act has come up for review, given the widespread concern over its misuse.[12] Enough has been said to bring out the point that for Muslims in the areas under study, therefore, the dread of arbitrary arrest, detention and even torture remain pervasive. The experience, charted through the course of this book, of horrific and, sometimes, continual violence in which the losses to life and property are excruciatingly high conjoins with the not unjustified fear of the forces whose task is protection and maintenance of peace to fulfil the fifth, though not the least, of the criteria by which Young (1990) defines an oppressed ethnic, racial, social or religious group violence.

five faces of oppression

In defining a group for the purposes of her argument, Young says (1990: 46):

> Group affinity... has the character... of 'thrownness': one finds oneself as a member of a group, which one experiences as always already having been. For our identities are defined in relation to how others identify us, and they do so in terms of groups which are always already associated with specific attributes, stereotypes, and norms.[13]

Despite all that may be said to the contrary, the reality of groups or of Muslims as a group (or community) in this sense is difficult to deny; our negotiation of the idea of the stigma of Muslim identity in an earlier section only assists to accentuate this. To a far greater extent than others, and similar to Dalits and increasingly tribals, Muslims must also live, as Young's argument would proceed, with the knowledge that they must fear systematic and often periodic violence on their persons or property which seeks to damage, humiliate and destroy (1990: 61). The violence, moreover, tends to be tolerated. The extent to which such group violence is appallingly successful in its ends, the way in which it is handled by the state as well as the legitimacy it tends to receive mark it off sharply from any offensive or retaliatory act that may be carried out by the other side.[14]

There are four other criteria set forth by Young, apart from violence: these are exploitation, marginalization, powerlessness and cultural imperialism. Young sometimes appears to write a little loosely for she is pitching at a high level of generalization: her categories are not always defined precisely and there is obviously overlap between them. Despite this, however, it may be possible (and worthwhile) on the basis of the discussions in previous chapters, to examine the extent to which her criteria apply to the Muslims. The criterion of exploitation is perhaps the most difficult to negotiate, for various reasons. Young argues that the crux of exploitation is the steady process of the transfer of the results of the labour of one group to the profit of another. Three categories are demarcated on the basis of this definition: capitalist exploitation, gender exploitation and racial exploitation. While it is possible to demonstrate the exploitation of the working class through the labour theory of value and the oppression of women through their exclusion from privileged activities resulting in wealth or status and their confinement in activities whose benefits accrue to men, such as nurturance and domestic labour, the racially *specific* forms of exploitation are more difficult to identify. With respect to the African-Americans and Hispanics of the US that Young speaks of, she distinguishes menial labour as a category that exemplifies a racially specific form of exploitation. There is an assumption that oppressed racial groups ought to be in a position of servitude to racially superior groups, that the jobs they do transfer benefits to the privileged group and further enhance its status, and that the services of these groups are available not just to a 'capitalist class' but to a much larger public.

While considerable material has been evaluated in an earlier chapter that evidences the backwardness and deprivation of Muslims in general, such data is by itself unable to confirm or deny a thesis of exploitation. In any case, exploitation is not necessary to (or even sufficient for) the overall argument regarding oppression and the line of reasoning will not be pressed further here. The evidence is on the other hand sufficient to demonstrate the *marginalization* of Muslims in the overall economy and in terms of particular parameters of asset possession, enjoyment of amenities and well-being. Marginalization constitutes a situation in which a whole category of people is excluded from full or useful participation in social and economic life. The concentration of Muslims at the lower end of the occupational structure, their relative absence in positions of economic strength and their predominance in the unorganized category and that of self-employment—hardly of the wealth producing sort—all adduce to the fact that they remain in a position of considerable economic vulnerability.

In elaborating on what she refers to as powerlessness, Young largely speaks of the oppressed group as being denied the skills, prestige, authority and autonomy of the professional classes, though she also mentions the power of political leaders and state bureaucracies. Our analysis in chapter three has manifested the relative isolation of Muslims from decision-making positions at all levels of the political structure, the bureaucracy and administrative hierarchies as well as the domain of the modern professions.

Nevertheless, there is need to enquire a little further into this issue and to consider in particular the various reasons put forward from time to time to account for the educational backwardness of Muslims and their invisibility at the highest levels of the professions and of government service. In positing her thesis, Young nowhere queries the internal dynamics or divisions within a group that may contribute in part towards perpetuating an already compromised situation and affecting further its outcomes.

It has been argued (Rajgopal 1987: 62) that there is not much point in being disappointed by the low figures of Muslims in the professions since their representation at secondary and higher levels of education itself is barely 25 per cent that of other communities. We therefore need to address the question of why Muslims have for so long remained on the margins of formal, mainstream education. Ahmad (1994) looks closely at different explanations: Muslims have been slow to take up mainstream education because of their leaning towards spiritual learning or because of a minority complex that has kept them from integration or, Muslims have been discriminated against and thence have not entered the area of modern education and employment. He finds both explanations partial and in themselves problematic. In brief, his argument, substantiated by a range of data, is as follows: secular education for Muslims as for other communities was always the domain of only those sections of society for which it was a norm and for which entry into the professions and government service was something actively sought after. This section—the upper and middle classes—were also the ones to whom religious education was restricted. Contrary to popular understanding, religious education has never been the pursuit of the lower castes and classes; rather it has been the reserve of the upper social strata.

In other words, it has largely been Muslims of a particular social and economic background that have pursued modern education; *this is a fact that also holds for other religious communities*. It is not true that Muslims have always been slow to take up formal and non-religious education. Data for the colonial period reveals that in the North West Provinces and Oudh, Muslims were over-represented in comparison with Hindus in schools and colleges. They were also ahead of Hindus in literacy figures; in fact, Muslim males were ahead of Hindus in terms of literacy in English throughout the period from 1891 to 1931 (Ahmad 1994: 182). While it would be easy then to argue that it must be the large-scale migration of the Muslim middle classes after Partition that has contributed to the decline of the community's fortunes in the post-Independence period, this is again an explanation that is incomplete. The fact is that the size of the middle class among Muslims has always been small and its spread in different areas, thin. Thus, the low representation of Muslims in education is more because of the low proportion of those classes and castes within the community that would normally go in for education. Migration played some role in further lowering the strength of the middle class; however, divisions among Muslims have always been sharp and its middle class was in any case small in relation to that among Hindus (Ahmad 1994: 181–83).

Why did the size of the middle class not increase after Independence? Here Ahmed returns to the issue of discrimination, but he also contends that the lower middle classes, which could have through education and upward mobility swelled the ranks of the middle class, did not have that opportunity until recent decades. Their economic position declined after Independence and while recent shifts have brought about greater prosperity the change is slow. And, again, when faced with the option of educating their children this newly prosperous class may well choose—*in the first instance at least*—religious over modern education. This is because the occupations that their children will pursue—the family craft or business—do not require the input of modern education. The latter would not be rejected, but would be relegated to second choice or the option chosen for one rather than all children. Its selection would be directly dependent on the perception of its possible advantage or relevance to the occupation and aims being pursued.

When Muslims actually come into education, other problems emerge. Razzack and Gumber (2002) point out that interestingly Muslims do not seem to spend less on education than other communities, even Hindus. They also incline more towards private education rather than government schooling, one of the reasons perhaps for their spending more on school fees than Hindus. However, the discontinuation rate for Muslims is higher everywhere, even while less of them have ever enrolled at school. The reasons for discontinuation are worth elaborating. Most students, boys as well as girls, cite failure and loss of interest in studies as the main reason, followed by financial constraints. These reasons are similar to those alluded to most frequently by Hindus. While social reasons (including religious reasons) are cited by more Muslim girls (17.53 per cent) than Hindu girls (for whom domestic chores seem a more significant factor), the total percentage citing such reasons is less than those mentioning failure, loss of interest in studies (27.18 per cent) and financial constraints (25.07 per cent).

There is also regional variation. While the Muslim literacy rate is lower than that of Hindus everywhere except in Karnataka, it is generally higher in the south than in the north. There are also more Muslim-managed schools in the south; this makes education more accessible to Muslims and improves their enrolment and attendance rates somewhat. Muslims in the south, in general, particularly in Karnataka and Kerala, also spend more on education than those in the north. If Muslims are willing to spend on education but more in the private than the government sphere, it is certain that in general they do not lack an interest in pursuing schooling. However, there may be reasons why they prefer to keep away from government schools. These may include the inadequate number of schools in the Urdu medium and of textbooks and teachers for such schools. Also included is the fact that curricula may be alienating for Muslims: we have yet to create reading materials that fully engage India's pluralistic and diverse history and cultures. It does seem therefore, in sum, that there is a gap between potential demand and possible supply which needs to be bridged by the careful management of educational resources towards addressing the specific requirements of Muslims.

Since this discussion will surface again when we consider the implications for policy formulation of what has been recounted so far, I will proceed at this point to an examination of the last of Young's criteria—cultural imperialism. In fact, some of what has been said in the preceding paragraph directly leads us to this issue. Though the term may sound more than a little daunting, what Young means by cultural imperialism essentially is: a group's experience of 'how the dominant meanings of a society render [its own] particular perspective...invisible at the same time as they stereotype one's group and mark it out as the Other' (1990: 58–59). The worldview and experience of the dominant group get projected as the norm; its values and goals—even its history and culture— are the most widely disseminated in society. Hence, the perspectives of other groups tend to be marked by deficiency or negation rather than being valued in themselves; these groups are viewed as lacking or falling short of dominant ideals and ethos. Such groups find themselves positioned outside the pale of dominant meanings and structures of experience, inferior and stereotyped images of themselves prevail and no effort is made to include them in the dominant vision of the world.

One acknowledges, if somewhat ruefully, that the concept appears to capture with piercing effectiveness the experiences of our Muslims. While we have seen that Hindu communal ideologies labour with damning success to demonize the Muslims, there are also the more insidious workings of a culture and its socialization and educational processes that take the superiority of Hindus and the 'stranger' status of Muslims for granted. These intersect with material and social structures and practices to isolate Muslims in ghettos which may then be carefully avoided even as they are without compunction assailed. The surprising ease with which this may happen emerges again from the reminiscences of the playwright, Vijay Tendulkar,[15] who records a familiar expression used casually by adults during his younger years: '*Manoos ahes ka Musalman?*' (Are you a human being or a Muslim?) Apart from the fact that what he recalls tells us how effortlessly Muslims may be 'othered', it also reminds us how far back such processes go; while anti-Muslim sentiment is in the ascension today, it is not by itself a product of recent times. Tendulkar also mentions the way in which Muslims were (and still are) portrayed in historical plays, such as those dealing with Shivaji and Aurangzeb. These plays, viewed without critical input, by growing boys and girls became the lens through which they perceived Muslims, a pattern of socialization insinuating and effective.

The first such play I saw had Shivaji's son and the Maratha emperor after him, Sambhaji, as the hero. According to the history of that period, he was a passionate womaniser and an alcoholic and a generally irresponsible young man who preferred a martyr's death in Mughal emperor Aurangzeb's prison to conversion to Islam. [Aurangzeb]... was painted in loud colours, a religious fanatic, a ruthless tyrant, an obnoxious figure with a long white beard on a crooked face, wearing garish costumes and shouting swearwords supposedly in Urdu and Farsi (I did not understand them but felt very piqued by them) at Shivaji's son and the ruling Maratha emperor Sambhaji and his men. In short, he was like the villain in any commercial Hindi *masala* film of today, alternately comic and repulsive. The rest of the Mughal characters in the play were drunkards, lechers, capable of any dastardly act and big-mouthed cowards who always lost in a fight with Sambhaji's brave little men. The Maratha[s]... stood in sharp contrast to these Mughal ruffians and buffoons. All the applause-winning dialogues were given to Sambhaji and his men by the playwright; the 'enemy camp' only spouted hatred.... Apart from this, our school text-books carried excerpts from Marathi historical plays which shaped our ideas of our past and also the present to a large extent.

As Tendulkar recalls:

A Muslim meant someone with a beard. The word also conjured up an unclean appearance, uncouth behaviour, lack of education and culture.... In their routine existence, most Hindus had very little to do in Muslim localities... except passing through them in a tram or a bus. For them, it was an alien part of the city, seg- regated in their psyche like the prostitutes area.

In another place he recalls the inevitable association by Hindus of Muslims with violence and behaviour that verged on the berserk. The reverberation of these images with those familiar to us from our own time, and depicted briefly in chapter two, is sinister and infinitely saddening. Even the spatial segregation of Muslims ap- pears to be a process with an uncomfortably longer history than one might like to imagine. Muslims are the classic 'outsiders', taunt- ingly advised to 'go to Pakistan' and constantly questioned regard- ing their loyalty to the India.

From denial of appeasement to admission of suppression, indeed of oppression: the path traversed by this book has been painfully inexorable and may prove, perhaps, immensely unpopular. How- ever, neither scholarship nor policy will benefit by acceding all too easily to the demands of a reactionary politics. We may not shirk from acknowledging that the overall policies of Independent India have failed its Muslims, just as it has failed Dalits and tribals.

It is indeed through a dark tunnel that the history of Indian Muslims is currently passing. Militancy, the rise of extreme ideologies and the politics of terror are usually intimately linked with social, cultural and economic structures which marginalize, and with the non-inclusion in participation and decision-making of whole groups or categories of people. A pluralistic and democratic polity can ill afford the disaffection of such large numbers; indeed, it may not be content with avoiding discontent but must actively seek to encourage fulfilment.[16] Towards this end, there is a great deal to be done. Drawing from the lessons of my own ethnography and from a host of other writers, the last section attempts to put together some of the crucial concerns and questions that have emerged in the course of this work and that may have critical implications for those engaged with the making of policies.

data collection and policy-making: framing questions and concerns

Of the most critical urgency is the requirement for data, as this book itself has shown, and it appears that some steps may soon be taken to remedy this situation, through a Central Government decision.[17] It has been both disquieting and enfeebling that the only data readily and periodically available for a long time, through the censuses of India (and the National Family Health Survey), was that related to population, sex ratio and fertility rates with respect to religious groupings. Such data when interpreted partially is able to feed all too easily into discourses condemning apparently 'unacceptably high Muslim growth rates' (Basu 1996: 136). On the other hand, the collection of economic data by religion and of other kinds of development statistics was evidently deemed contrary to secular aims and there has been a great deal of diffidence about it. Such data has only begun to be available on an all-India basis slightly more systematically through the efforts of autonomous or semi-autonomous bodies such as the National Sample Survey Organization or the National Centre for Applied Economic Research and international organizations, as the UNDP.[18]

As Razzack and Gumber maintain (2002: 44) it is counter-productive to maintain a secrecy about statistics for it only allows policy makers and people at decision-making levels to be influenced by fallacious arguments concerning the apparent 'appeasement' of Muslims and permits stereotypes to flourish. Indeed, according to them, it would be constructive to have the reports of the Minority Commission tabled in Parliament on an annual basis. It is only when more accurate data is available that we will be able to address the specific problems of different groups. Shariff (1995: 2953) also points to the need for the cross-tabulation of data on literacy by religion and of distribution of workers by religion and industry. He asserts that the census is well-placed to generate such data. John and Mutatkar (2005), who show in their careful state-wise analysis of available statistical material, the high degree of poverty among both urban and rural Muslims, assert the value of such data and analysis in providing an empirical basis for the making of public policy. As they argue (2005: 1337):

Of late, there have been debates in the public sphere regarding affirmative action policies for certain religious minority groups for their socio-economic advancement.... These debates have been prompted by political deliberations in this regard by certain state governments in India. To examine whether religious diversity in our country has economic dimensions and to provide an empirical basis to such debates, it is imperative to examine the relative economic status of religious groups in India.... [This] has very important implications for public policy....

Back in 1987, Kuldip Nayar expressed his reservations about another kind of reticence: that exercised by newspapers regarding the role of different communities in conflict situations.[19] As he said, the absence of information may only serve to fuel rumour and incite over-reaction: 'Newspapers have a convention not to mention the name of communities in a communal riot, but it has not lessened rioting. Of course, it is advisable not to spill everything out, but sometimes vagueness can be dangerous.'

An argument is not going to be made here for changing media practice. It is nevertheless the case that when I attempted to find out if there were any consolidated statistics available regarding injuries and the loss of lives and property, community-wise, due to ethnic conflict in post-Independence India, I drew a virtual blank.[20] It was not even possible to put figures with any accuracy for the areas covered in the course of fieldwork. One of the ways this could be a handicap emerged when more than one Gujarati Hindu, working in the area of communal harmony, expressed to me the firm conviction that Hindus had suffered more than Muslims—in terms of loss of life and property—in *every* riot, except the one in 2002. Of course, one could refer to fact-finding reports on particular riots to dispute such a claim, but there is definitely need for some consolidation at a more general level. In the same vein, there is a requirement for the age, class and ethnic breakdown of those killed in police firing, 'encounters' and custodial deaths.[21]

Moving from the question of data, we may turn to the crucial issue of improving the educational profile of Muslims. In writing about this subject Ahmad (1994) argues that the community needs to organize its own schools, which can cover both requirements of secular and religious education. Despite the fact of the backwardness of Muslims on the whole, there are certain sections of the community that have adequate material and educational resources to initiate and support such efforts. Like other scholars (for instance, Razzack and Gumber 2002), Ahmad sets aside reservation as a possible measure for the educational upliftment of Muslims. The reasons include the need to avoid community-based allocations which may contravene the spirit of a secular Constitution, the possibility of provoking hostility in a communalized atmosphere and the fact that reservations most often benefit only the upper layers of a social group, leaving the most deprived untouched.

These arguments need not necessarily be seen as definitive. There is probably no convincing legal reason why Muslims of the most backward classes or Muslims of Dalit origin should be denied reservations. Some states do include Muslims among Other Backward Classes. Indeed, while a community-based reservation policy would be both unconstitutional and unjustifiable, it may be considered equally discriminatory for Muslim and Christian Dalits to be denied reservations, which are extended to Buddhists, Sikhs and Hindus.[22] As mentioned earlier, some states have made a case for affirmative action for Muslims. Andhra Pradesh, after the Assembly elections in 2004, decided to extend 5 per cent reservations in jobs and educational institutions to Muslims. The move was subsequently stayed by the High Court, as it heard arguments for and against the issue. While the BJP has come out against the policy, it is also by no means clear how such a policy would be applied or how much Muslims themselves are in favour of it. Some Muslims are opposed to religion-based legislation of this kind, while Dalit Muslims feel that the benefits of such policies would go to the top-most social and economic layers, while leaving out the most deprived. Suffice to say here that the reservation policy is one that needs careful consideration of all its implications, rather than outright dismissal.

While there have been for a long time some educational institutions run by Muslims, more perhaps in the south than in the north, the efforts to increase access to modern learning and the mastery of the English language without neglecting religious instruction have increased in recent times. Against a backdrop of communal hostility and savage violence, Mumbai, for instance, has seen the setting up, over the last few years, of at least four such institutions. There is an English-medium High School run by the Tablighi Jamaat for both boys and girls, another by the Islamic Research Foundation, a third by Dr Shehnaz Shaikh, the Al Mu'minah Girls High School, and a fourth, the Al-Jamia-Tul-Fikriya Islamic School, set up by a businessman Suhail Shaikh.[23] Such schools run by Islamic associations or along their lines may be one answer to the dismal standards of education among Muslims, particularly of the deprived classes. However, the schools do not appear to explicitly aim to work with the most disadvantaged sections of society.[24] Moreover, not all as yet offer education up to the high school level. They are, further, unable to address the requirement of the integration of their students within a plural society, a process that, as Tendulkar's recollections bring out, must be considered crucial.

Whatever the success of such initiatives, they are not the only ones available. Several efforts, if small and struggling, have been started directly in areas of least advantage. These include, for instance, the Shaheen High School and Rahat Welfare Trust started by Irfan Merchant in a Mumbai slum apart from a range of small grassroots movements to improve municipal schools, provide primary-level learning for boys and girls and provide scholarships and textbooks to needy students at higher levels. Such efforts are taking shape in parts of Gujarat as well; in most places they tend to involve NGOs working together with local-level Muslim groups or associations, often composed of relatively young persons. For instance, the Modern Youth Association in Jogeshwari (East) with which Sajjid is connected has worked with some NGOs, to found a small book-bank which lends school texts to students for the year, and to make available some scholarships for college students. The group also tries to spread information about employment opportunities, including in the government services, in the neighbourhood and to help candidates obtain and fill up the application forms for these. In Ahmedabad's Vatva, Altaf and his sister provide poor parents, particularly riot survivors, information about available assistance with school fees and have been working with some organizations to send a large number of orphaned and underprivileged children to a school in Madras, where they would receive free, mainstream education.

While Ahmad (1994) may be right to ask the Muslim community (or those within it who can afford to do so) to enhance its presence in the field of education, it is unlikely that this will be sufficient to redress the imbalances in place both in urban and rural areas. Moreover, schools run by the community require state recognition, which is not always easy to obtain. The state would be well-advised to establish schools and colleges in Muslim-dominated areas and preferably to run separate schools for girls. The employment of female teachers in girls' schools would also be a step enabling greater access for Muslim girls. As has been suggested by others as well, state-run schools should take into account the linguistic requirements of the target population (Razzack and Gumber 2002). School curricula and methods of teaching are in urgent need of revision to make them more participative as well as genuinely pluralistic. The autonomy of boards of education needs to be ensured to screen them, as far as is feasible, from the shifting ideological perspectives of successive governments.

The 1991 Supreme Court judgement in the case of St Stephen's College versus the University of Delhi stipulated that minority institutions shall make available at least 50 per cent of the annual admissions to members of communities other than the minority communities. Razzack and Gumber (2002) are of the opinion that this condition needs to be revised. Minority institutions were permitted under the Constitution in order to protect the linguistic, cultural and religious identity of the groups: the current legal stipulation erodes the spirit of that constitutional provision. It is true that Muslim-run educational institutions have not perhaps as much attraction for those outside of the community as do, for instance, Christian ones, which have been in the field considerably longer and have a wider reach. Even so, studies have shown that Muslim-managed schools and colleges often tend to have a larger percentage of non-Muslim as compared to Muslim students (Rajgopal 1987: 63). A rigid reliance on the stipulation may possibly lead to the denial of state recognition for institutions that while otherwise competent are unable to meet the admission criteria set by it.

Within all this, one must address the question of the places of the traditional centres of religious learning or *madrasas*. *Madrasas* in south Asia have come under scrutiny in recent years, mainly because they (or some of them) have been perceived as possible centres for the training or harbouring of militants. It would indeed be difficult to prove that most *madrasas* have this deadly distinction. However, they suffer from other difficulties and are making certain kinds of adjustments to modern learning; both these aspects require closer understanding. While most *madrasas* do provide only minimal religious learning and fail to equip students with the critical skills and larger conceptual apparatus necessary for modern social and cultural conditions, there are trends of change and alternative interpretations. There are signs that graduates of *madrasas* themselves are beginning to understand the need for expansion of the kinds of education provided by these institutions. Further, in Kerala, for instance, by working together with the *madrasas*, the state government has ensured that their education is streamlined and integrated with wider patterns. In West Bengal, the State Council of Higher Secondary Education has given recognition to the *madrasas*. This, as well as other factors, such as the low cost of education in the *madrasas*, has led to many non-Muslims entering these institutions. In turn the *madrasas* have eased the Arabic language requirement for their new students. From the examples of Kerala and West Bengal and, more recently, Bihar emerges the distinct possibility, if the State shows active and positive involvement, of redefining *madrasas* rather than isolating them, through a process of careful educational integration.

Training for vocation appears to be a measure of singular importance for Muslims, who are shown to be at the bottom of the occupational hierarchy in terms of employment, enjoying to a far lesser extent than other groups the benefits and prestige of regular, salaried work. Setting up technical and vocational training facilities close to Muslim-dominated areas, with special sections for women, may provide something of a remedy (Razzack and Gumber 2002). It would be necessary to ensure that Muslims receive equitable allocation from funds directed towards the setting up of small-scale industries as well as other government benefits and welfare measures. However, this is not sufficient. It may also be essential to redirect Muslims towards the higher end of the occupational structure and to repair—really and visibly—the social image of them as 'hewers of wood' or 'drawers of water' (see Hasan 2001: 288). While improving standards in education will go some way towards this, it is also necessary to provide information regarding rights and opportunities. Perhaps the use of newspapers in languages other than only English or Hindi for advertising by government agencies could be considered.

The improvement of urban civic services in areas occupied mostly by Muslims would go a long way in removing the stereotype of them as 'unclean' and 'uncultured'. These areas often tend to be slums, but services could be bettered by charging the residents. Improving roads, transport facilities and public facilities in such areas would also provide better access and, thus, weaken to some extent at least the image of these areas as frightening and unapproachable 'Pakistans'. No doubt, such measures will not come easily, for there are always political dimensions to these questions. In fact, one might argue that where Muslims are in large numbers perhaps they can ensure that their local leaders are held accountable for taking alleviative measures. This may not always work in practice, but there are clear indications that Muslim youth and neighbourhood groups, such as some of those profiled in chapter six, intend to act and protest on these issues in order to make politicians answerable.

In formulating measures for social and educational development, it would be probably best to target deprived Muslims along with others assessed as specially disadvantaged. Nevertheless, as outlined previously, there is also need to address Muslim-specific issues, and those issues *sometimes perceived from the outside as being*

Muslim-specific, such as relatively higher growth rates. Religious reasons alone must obviously be considered inadequate to account for high Muslim birth rates.[25] For Christians the religious injunction against intrusive birth control measures or abortion is equally if not more severe. Nevertheless, Christian fertility rates are far lower than those of Muslims and in some states than those of Hindus as well. As studies have shown, an improvement in female literacy and education levels is likely to have a depressive effect on fertility rates (see also Shariff 1995). Low income and education levels contribute to higher growth rates among Muslims; another factor, interestingly, is the low infant mortality rate shown by the community, across income levels.[26] As the figures in Table 7.1 demonstrate, education and to a somewhat lesser extent income lowers fertility, regardless of religious affiliation.

Table 7.1

Mean number of live births according to religion, education and income: all India (1988–89)

	Hindu	Muslim	Others	All
All	3.09	3.51	2.83	3.13
Mean live births by levels of education				
Illiterates	3.37	3.72	3.50	3.41
Up to primary	3.16	3.57	3.19	3.22
Secondary and higher	2.33	2.71	2.83	3.35
Mean live births by levels of income (per month)				
Less than Rs 500	3.20	3.47	3.64	3.21
Rs 501–750	3.28	3.74	3.46	3.34
Rs 751–1,000	3.07	3.56	3.11	3.13
Rs 1,001–1,500	3.03	3.53	3.05	3.08
Rs 1,501 or more	2.65	3.21	2.49	2.68

Source: Adapted from Shariff (1995: 2951. He has sourced the data from Operations Research Group 1990: 10–11 and 17).

The links between fertility decline and socio-economic development in general, especially educational development, may be perceived even in data derived from the Indian Census of 1991. B.C. Mehta (2005: 157–160) analyses urban and rural figures to show that the Muslim population has begun to decline and the rate of decline has picked up at a considerable pace. By comparing the completed fertility levels of the oldest age group (65 and above) with the age group of 40–44 years, he shows that over about two decades fertility has declined at each level of education (illiterate, literate, middle, matric and graduate) and across *all* religious groups. Muslims do lag a little behind other communities at each level, but the trend towards a decline emerges quite sharply. While the decline is very low among illiterate or just literate Muslim urban women (4.3 and 7.7 per cent decrease in TFR respectively), it is high among women who have completed matriculation (24.6 per cent) and very high among graduates (45.9 per cent). Figures for rural India show a comparable trend.

While there is certainly need to develop banks, industries and commercial enterprises in areas of Muslim concentration, the crucial question of security underwrites such advancement. Private industry and business, in particular, tends to move out of areas that get defined as 'communally-sensitive' and that suffer the consequences of long closures due to violence and curfews. We are honing in therefore on the most critical of issues: justice and security in the face of communal conflagration. It is imperative that recommendations of commissions of enquiry into communal violence begin to be taken seriously and acted upon, and that justice in the case of great social crimes be made a priority. It may not be desirable to have to depend on the army to provide internal security on an increased scale; nonetheless, the central government must impress on states the need to avoid any delays in using the appropriate measures to stem violence. If it is difficult to penalize communities, it may well be necessary in the short term at least—and to increase the stake of the authorities in the maintenance of peace—to institute punitive economic sanctions against states which have poor records of great social crimes.

There may be ways in which the State could actively promote pluralistic urban living. This is of course not possible without the assurance of security to those living in culturally and ethnically diverse neighbourhoods, which may not be forthcoming in particular if the neutrality of the police force is under some doubt. It does appear to people that it is safer to live with their own kind, and urban housing societies and colonies often make caste, region or religion as a criterion of membership. This practice has very recently been upheld as permissible in a Supreme Court judgement. The conferment of legality on such practice may be contrary to desired public policy and is itself a highly controversial decision, but for it to be changed one would need an amendment of the various Cooperative Societies Acts' incorporating the rule that 'no society shall be formed, or if formed, membership in so society shall be confined to persons of a particular persuasion, religion, belief or region'.[27]

Expecting legislation to be changed in any near future is probably unrealistic, even though one understands well that it is precisely such segregation that encourages the mistrust and fear so obvious in Tendulkar's reminiscences and is, in the long run, socially extremely harmful. One could suggest proceeding otherwise, at least in the short- and medium-term. While religious and ethnic enclaves remain, there could be attempts to *capitalize* on these by promoting neighbourhood festivals of local history, music, craft or cuisine. Muslims are often found in the older and inner parts of cities and they usually have long histories of residence. Such cultural festivals could do much to open up these neighbourhoods in an interesting and unusual way for outsiders, removing fear and promoting understanding through the appreciation of difference. The promotion of intercourse and commerce simultaneously is, in practical terms, the strongest argument for pluralism.

We have already spoken earlier about the necessity of improving the representation of Muslims in the police and armed forces. As analysed, while this is not a sufficient guard against discrimination or injustice, it is certainly a factor that would inspire greater confidence in these authorities and go a considerable distance in the promotion of fairness. It may be desirable for the authorities to institute special moves to encourage Muslims to apply to the forces in areas and in languages that would ensure easy access for them. Assessment of police attitudes towards the minorities is essential; this should be part of larger periodic and planned programmes: training police at various levels in professional ethics, social and cultural issues, gender concerns, human rights and how to deal with and what to expect from different groups and communities. What is currently very essential is taking *mohalla* people and elders into confidence in the fight against terrorism. As of now, the police have tended to adopt a confrontationist attitude towards Muslims;

all Muslims have in effect become suspect. As mentioned earlier, there has been a degree of arbitrariness about adopted methods of surveillance, search and interrogation; this has resulted in alienating the community even further from the police and the State.

There is no point in underlining the fact that nothing is possible without political will. In fact, it may be more pertinent to assert that a great deal probably is. The law courts, for instance, have in recent times become a refuge for those denied impartiality or justice through other means. There may be no attempt, further, to deny the multi-stranded complications within the Muslim community itself. Discord along the lines of class, gender and sectarian tradition has been intimated briefly. Inequalities of educational access add further complexity to the situation. While religious leaders may take certain paths, greater confidence has here been placed on the sustained local-level efforts of individuals and small groups, whose struggles have been explored in an earlier chapter. Feroz Ashraf, Sajjid and others believe that if through education and training it is feasible to inject into the system as many Muslims as possible—in different places and varying levels—it will no longer continue to be viable to ignore them; this may, in turn, act as a lever for intra-community transformations. Like Altaf, these activists would change politics by becoming a part of it, rather than wait for it to alter itself or seek to reform it from without. Individual and local efforts such as these will always have a measure of success.

It is true that analysis and discussions along the lines that have been incorporated in the preceding pages are immediately suspect for the kinds of political and administrative implications that could possibly unfold from them. Bina Agarwal (1995) acknowledged that the call 'Give land to women' threatened for those out to protect the status quo such frightening degrees of structural—economic, social and political—change that it was defeated almost before it began to be made. Academic labour, however, may not fight shy of pursuing difficult problems, even when remedies look frightfully remote. The difficulty of solutions cannot become an excuse for not framing the right questions. Before we summon up the guts to act, we need have the courage to see.

notes

1. Mr Amin Khandwani, former corporator and MLA, currently chairperson of the State Minorities Commission of Maharashtra. The Commission has faced its share of problems in the past. It has the unenviable task of examining cases of minority discrimination and injustice brought to its notice. It also investigates incidents of communal violence or police bias against minorities. Mr Khandwani was speaking of his powerlessness, despite his official position and political stature, to ensure justice in such cases. Most of the time he spoke of his personal experiences garnered during a long career in politics, rather than strictly in his official capacity.

2. See, for example, 'NHRC Seeks Report on "encounter deaths"', *The Hindu Online*, 4 January 2003 accessed at http://www.hinduonnet.com/2003/01/04/stories/2003010404341100.htm on 18 June 2004. Also *India Human Rights Report 2003* prepared by the Department of State, USA accessed at http://www.ncbuy.com/reference/country/humanrights_toc.html?code=in on 18 June 2004.

3. See *Letter to Chief Ministers regarding the procedure to be followed in cases of deaths in police encounters* by National Human Rights Commission at http://www.nhrc.nic.in/sec-2pdf. Accessed on 18 June 2004.

4. P. Sainath, 'In Lawless Maharashtra', *Frontline* 15(14) 1998 accessed at http://www.flonnet.com/fl1514/15141240.htm on 18 June 2004.

5. All the cases analysed in the article were of Muslim deaths and there have been no enquiries into the killings. Leena Misra, There's a Hollow Ring to Encounter Stories in Gujarat, *The Times of India*, 22 October 2002. Accessed online at http://www.timesofindia.indiatimes.com/cms.dll/articleshow?artid=25998097 on 18 June 2004. Mishra also adds: 'Although political regimes have lauded themselves for such encounters as a "step towards curtailment of crime", an Additional Director General of police...[told her that], "killing of a criminal does not amount to controlling of the crime".

6. Leena Misra, Only Minorities Figure in Gujarat's POTA List, *The Times of India*, 15 September 2003, p. 5.

7. Arundhati Roy, 'How Deep Shall we Dig?' *The Hindu*, 25 April 2004 accessed at http://www.countercurrents.org/roy250404.htm on 21 June 2004.

8. Amnesty International Report titled *Abuse of Law in Gujarat: Muslims Detained Illegally in Ahmedabad* accessed at http://web.amnesty.org/library/Index/ENGASA200292003?pen&of=ENG-IND on 21 June 2004.

9. See 'Mother of Blast Accused says Police Killed her Son', *The Times of India*, 14 June 2003, p. 3. While there appears to be evidence of foul play in this custodial death, the case has become very contentious with the Mumbai police coming into conflict with the CID, which is conducting the inquiry. The recent arrest of four senior police officers raised considerable hue and cry, with the Shiv Sena and VHP, in particular, crying foul. There were allegations that the evidence of torture made by a co-accused Dr Abdul Mateen on the basis of

which the case was investigated was false and that he was acting on behalf of 'terrorists'. See, for instance, 'We have Enough Evidence on Yunus Assault: CID', *The Times of India*, 8 March 2005, p. 7; 'The Situation Should have been Dealt with much Earlier', *Bombay Times*, 10 March 2005, p. 1; 'Police may Call on R.R. Patil after "Demoralizing" Arrest of Bhosale', *The Times of India*, 9 March 2005, p. 3; 'Yunus Kin Plan New Plea', *The Times of India*, 9 March 2005, p. 3 and 'Court has Given us Justice: Bhosale', *The Times of India*, 18 March 2005, p. 3.

10. Anil Singh, 'Human Rights Activists Advise Restraint', *The Times of India*, 4 December 2002, p. 3. Indeed, several POTA cases have been subsequently dropped or dismissed for lack of evidence; this usually after the detainees have suffered for varying lengths of time. See, for instance, *The Hindu* report of 27 May 2004 'Maharashtra to Support Repeal of POTA', accessed at http:// www.hindu.com/2004/05/27/stories/2004052702311300.htm end URL on 21 June 2004 or *The Indian Express* (Mumbai Newsline) report of 28 April 2004 'Only 7 left of 18 Accused, Bomb Blast Case Flounders' accessed at http://cities.expressindia.com/fullstory.php?newsid=82963 on 21 June 2004.

11. See Leena Misra, 'There's a Hollow Ring to Encounter Stories in Gujarat', *The Times of India*, 22 October 2002. Accessed online at http://www.timesof india. indiatimes.com/cms.dll/articleshow?artid=25998097 on 21 June 2004. In Maharashtra, a few cases are being investigated. One is the case of Khwaja Yunus, mentioned earlier.

12. 'POTA—The missing link' accessed at http://www.chennaionline.com/ society/CrimeandSociety/10pota.asp on 21 June 2004; Press Trust of India report 'Statutory Powers given to POTA Review Committee', 21 October 2003 accessed at http://www.rediff.com/news/2003/oct/21pota.htm on 21 June 2003.

13. She draws on the concept of 'thrownness' as enunciated by Martin Heidegger (1962) who speaks of 'Being' as thrown into the stream of time, not choosing the world but finding itself already subjected to it, part of an otherness which matters to it and with which it must contend. *Being and Time*, trans. John Macquarrie and Edward Robinson, Oxford: Basil Blackwell.

14. Let us quote what Young has to say about the question of legitimacy:

Group violence approaches legitimacy, moreover, in the sense that it is tolerated.... Even when they are caught, those who perpetrate acts of group-directed violence or harassment often receive light or no punishment. To that extent society renders their acts acceptable (1990: 62).

15. Vijay Tendulkar, 'Muslims and I'.

16. I base this argument on theories of democracy in plural societies elucidated by Rawls (1993) and Taylor (1998), for instance, and elaborated by Bhargava (1998a). Democracy predicates itself on reasonableness and participative discussion. It does so *necessarily*, both as a moral and pragmatic imperative. As Bhargava argues, in his elucidation of the minimum conditions for the survival of democracy (1998a: 10), 'democracy is incompatible with violent

settlements of disputes over power' and the state must be relatively independent of groups and classes in society. He continues (1998a:10), and his
argument goes even further than the one I have made, in that it argues that
democracies based on *pragmatic consensus* are unstable in relation to those
based on consensus as a *moral imperative*:

> Therefore each class and ethnic group must learn to live with the fact
> that its objectives cannot be met in entirety. This happens in two ways,
> because of the presence of two kinds of situations. It happens when a
> perfect balance of forces exists or else when each class or ethnic group
> happens to have just about as much power as every other one. People
> may then realize the necessity of a consensus for which no compelling
> reason exists from within. A democracy produced in such tremulous
> situations is a modus vivendi. *Quite another situation arises when out of
> enlightened self interest, or for a broader moral vision of granting one another
> respect, people are prepared from within their own set of internal reasons to
> forsake in part their objectives to arrive at a principled compromise. This is a
> necessary condition for stable democracies* [emphasis added].

17. Recently, the Prime Minister set up a high-powered committee to study the
    social, economic and educational status of the Muslim community. The com-
    mittee is to submit its report in 15 months. It is to be headed by former Delhi
    High Court chief justice Rajinder Sachar and has several academics as mem-
    bers, including Professor T.K. Oommen of Jawaharlal Nehru University,
    former Jamia Hamdard University Vice Chancellor Saiyid Hamid and
    Abusaleh Shariff of the National Council for Applied Economic Research.
18. After much of this book was already written, the Census data for 2001 relating
    to religious groups was released. For the first time, there has been an attempt
    to correlate data on religion with that on certain socio-economic indicators
    such as education and occupation. Much furore was raised by the fact that at
    first unadjusted data was publicly referred to, which apparently showed very
    high Muslim growth rates. As a result of the controversy, there was a call
    from some sections against this kind of data collection and analysis. However,
    it must be asserted, that despite what misuse the data might be sometimes
    put to, it is vital for us to have it in order to analyse in a comparative perspec-
    tive and for policy purposes the 'well-being' of different communities or
    sections of them.
19. Kuldip Nayar, 'Meerut's Roll of Heroes', *The Telegraph*, 24 October 1987, p. 11.
20. The National Police Commission Report (Government of India 1981) had
    figures, though these were not broken down by caste or community. Home
    Ministry Reports sometimes afford some data, and there is an appendix in
    Engineer (1995a) which professes to chart casualties of Hindus, Muslims,
    the police and others in communal riots in India from 1950 to 1994. The data
    claims several sources, but it is by no means complete or accurate. For in-
    stance, for 1993, three incidents of communal violence are recorded and a
    total of only 315 persons are said to have died. Finally, State Crime Reports
    offer some facts but again casualties are not categorized according to any
    parameters.

21. The NHRC gives figures for each state, but these are not broken down into any categories. Civil liberties groups and NGOs in different places no doubt have some data relating to cases in their areas, but there are no consolidated figures.

22. Indeed, the Supreme Court is currently hearing a petition on this matter and has asked the Central Government for its response on the subject.

23. There is no attempt to claim that communal violence *per se* led to the setting up of these schools, but it no doubt has its place in each one's complex history. Each school appears to have a somewhat different trajectory, though there are interconnections. To give an example, the Al Mu'minah Girls High School was started by Dr Shehnaz Shaikh partly out of what she describes as a personal spiritual transformation which led her to becoming a Muslim 'by choice' rather than 'by default', by the accident of birth. She realized her daughter received negative images of Muslims in the elite school she attended and decided to start her own school imparting a modern but Islamic education. Dr Shaikh's religious transformation was wrought interestingly by the lectures of Zakir Naik, who is head of the Islamic Research Foundation, which runs one of the schools described here. 1993 was indeed a watershed moment for her. It changed a good deal of her assumptions about Muslim security and made her realize the extent of people's hostility towards Muslims. Though it probably churned up intense questions of identity, it was not then but several years later, under the influence of Naik, that she chose to properly follow the 'tenets of Islam'. While she would describe her decision as purely personal, it has had profound implications for her social relationships, occupational arrangements and political beliefs.

24. This assessment is based on my reading of the introductory literature provided by them. I do not mean that the schools reject candidates from poorer households; however, they do not seem to go out and seek them. In fact, the language in which they couch their initiatives is that of offering or increasing schooling 'choices' for parents. This would tend to omit those who begin with almost no options. There are, though, the efforts of philanthropists such as Rehana Undre whose school in rural Maharashtra has become the refuge for and provides free education to children who suffered or were rendered orphans due to violence in Mumbai and Gujarat. The schools offers Urdu as a second language to students and maintains certain Islamic customs— including the use of a head-scarf for girls—but otherwise offers education in line with the Indian Council for Secondary Education (ICSE).

25. It may be mentioned that targeting growth rates through family planning has become an issue of some concern even for Muslim leaders in the recent past. Under the initiative of Maulana Kalbe Sadiq, vice-president of the All-India Muslim Personal Law Board, the board is likely to take up the issue in the near future. Maulana Sadiq presents a viewpoint on family planning that interprets it as permissible in the context of Islam and, further, points to the employment of population stabilization programmes in several Muslim countries. Some of these countries are Indonesia, Iran, Tunisia, Morocco, Turkey, Egypt and even Bangladesh (see Rahul Singh, 'Green signal: Muslim Countries Show the Way in Birth Control', *The Times of India*, 9 April 2005, p. 14).

26. This last may be due, in part, to the close kinship networks and marital circles of Muslims, contributing somewhat to the physical security of the children. For Muslim women who marry in more tight-knit circles and more often among kin, the support of the natal family in childcare and in the care of the new mother may be of some importance in adding to the life-chances of the child, particularly the first child and the girl child. This is corroborated by the fact that Muslims show, according to more recent data from the 2001 Census, higher sex ratio than Hindus across most Indian states (Basu 2004: 4295).

27. Times News Network, 'SC Okays Same-Community Housing Societies', *The Times of India*, 20 April 2005, p. 1. The decision of the Supreme Court has become the focus of considerable debate and disagreement. There is a strong sense that the verdict stems from a concentration on the letter rather than the spirit of the law. There is fear, moreover, that in Gujarat further ghettoization could set in place following on this decision. On the other hand, several societies that seek to limit membership on particular ethnic grounds have expressed their happiness with the judgement. See 'SC Upholds Discrimination in Group Housing Societies', *The Times of India*, 21 April 2005, p. 16; Times News Network, 'Mumbai Bonds: To Each His Own', *The Times of India*, 21 April 2005, p. 5; Times News Network, 'SC Nod Could Create More Ghettos in Gujarat', *The Times of India*, 22 April 2005, p. 8.

BIBLIOGRAPHY

Agarwal, Bina. 1995. *A field of one's own: Gender and land rights in south Asia.*
Cambridge: Cambridge University Press.
Ahmad, Imtiaz. 1973. *Caste and social stratification among the Muslims.* Delhi:
Manohar Book Service.
———. 1994. 'Muslim educational backwardness'. *In* Amrik Singh and
G.D. Sharma, eds, *Higher education in India: The social context*, pp. 171–93. Delhi:
Konark Publishers.
Ahmad, Mumtaz. 1991. 'Islamic fundamentalism in South Asia: The Jamaat-i-
Islami and the Tablighi Jamaat of South Asia'. *In* Martin E. Marty and
R. Scott Appleby, eds, 1991a. *Fundamentalisms observed*, pp. 457–530. Chicago:
University of Chicago Press.
Ali, Tariq. 2002. *The clash of fundamentalisms: Crusades, jihads and modernity.* London:
Verso.
Antoun, Richard. 2001. *Understanding fundamentalism: Christian, Islamic and Jewish
movements.* Altamira Press: Walnut Creek, C.A.
Antze, Paul and Michael Lambek, eds, 1996. *Tense past: Cultural essays in trauma
and memory.* New York: Routledge.
Appadurai, Arjun. 1997. *Modernity at large: Cultural dimensions of globalization.*
Delhi: Oxford University Press.
———. 1998. Dead certainty: Ethnic violence in the era of globalization. *Develop-
ment and Change* 29(4): 905–25.
Barve, Sushobha. 2003. *Healing streams: Bringing back hope in the aftermath of
violence.* New Delhi: Penguin Books.
Basu, Alaka M. 1996. 'The demographics of religious fundamentalism'. *In* Kaushik
Basu and Sanjay Subrahmanyam, eds, *Unravelling the nation: Sectarian conflict
and India's secular identity*, pp. 129–56. New Delhi: Penguin Books.
———. 2004. The squabble that never ends: Religion and fertility. *Economic and
political weekly* 39(39): 4294–96.
Beinin, Joel and Joe Stork. 1997. *Political Islam: Essays from Middle East Report.*
London: I B Tauris Publishers.
Bhargava, Rajeev. 1998a. 'Introduction'. *In* Rajeev Bhargava, ed., *Secularism and
its critics*, pp. 1–28. Delhi: Oxford University Press.
———. ed. 1998b. *Secularism and its critics.* Delhi: Oxford University Press.
Bharucha, Rustom. 2003. Muslims and others: Anecdotes, fragments and uncertainties of evidence. *Economic and political weekly* (October 4): 4238–50.

Bloch, Maurice. 1986. *From Blessing to violence: History and ideology in the circumcision ritual of the Merina*. Cambridge: Cambridge University Press.

Bose, Ashish. 1997. *Population profile of religion in India*. Delhi: B R Publishing Corporation.

Burgat, François. 2004. Divergent agendas in United Yemen: The politics of Islah and Da'wah Salafiyya. Paper presented at Oxford Centre for Islamic Studies, 25 February.

Burton, Frank. 1978. *The politics of legitimacy: Struggles in a Belfast community*. London: Routledge and Kegan Paul.

———. 1979. Ideological social relations in Northern Ireland. *British Journal of Sociology* 30: 61–80.

Caplan, Lionel. 1990. 'Introduction'. *In* Lionel Caplan, ed., *Studies in religious fundamentalism*, pp. 1–24. London: Macmillan.

Chandavarkar, Rajnarayan. 1998. *Imperial Power and Popular Politics: Class, Resistance and the State in India, c.1850–1950*. Cambridge: Cambridge University Press.

Chandra, Bipan. 1984. *Communalism in modern India*. New Delhi: Vikas Publishing House.

Chipasula, Stella and Frank, eds, 1995. *The Heinemann Book of African Women's Poetry*. Oxford: Heinemann Educational Publishers.

Choueri, M. Youssef. 1997. *Islamic fundamentalism*. London: Pinter.

———. 2004. Impact of Mawdudi and Qutb on modern Islamic thought. Paper presented at Oxford Centre for Islamic Studies, 4 February.

Concerned Citizen's Tribunal-Gujarat 2002. 2002. *Crime Against Humanity: An Inquiry into the Carnage in Gujarat, Findings and Recommendations*, Vol. 1 & 2 Mumbai: Citizens for Peace and Justice.

Dale, Stephen. 2003. 'Trade, conversion and the growth of the Islamic community in Kerala'. *In* Rowena Robinson and Sathianathan Clarke, eds, *Religious conversion in India: Modes, motivations and meanings*, pp. 54–74. Delhi: Oxford University Press.

Das, Veena. 1986. 'The work of mourning: Death in a Punjabi family'. *In* M.I. White and S. Pollak, eds, *The cultural transition: Human experience and social transformation in the Third World and Japan*, pp. 179–210. London: Routledge and Kegan Paul.

———. 1990. 'Our work to cry: Your work to listen'. *In* Veena Das, ed., *Mirrors of violence: Communities, riots and survivors in south Asia*. pp. 345–98. Delhi: Oxford University Press.

Das, Veena and Arthur Kleinman. 2001. 'Introduction'. *In* Veena Das, Arthur Kleinman, Margaret Lock, Mamphela Ramphele and Pamela Reynolds, eds, *Violence, social suffering and recovery*, pp. 1–30. Berkeley: University of California Press.

Das, Veena and Ashis Nandy. 1986. 'Violence, victimhood and the language of silence'. *In* Veena Das, ed., *The word and the world: Fantasy, symbol and record*. New Delhi: Sage Publications.

Das, Veena, Arthur Kleinman, Mamphela Ramphele and Pamela Reynolds. 2000. *Violence and subjectivity*. Berkeley: University of California Press.

Das, Veena, Arthur Kleinman, Margaret Lock, Mamphela Ramphele and Pamela Reynolds. 2001. *Remaking a world: Violence, social suffering and recovery*. Berkeley: University of California Press.

Dayal, John, ed. 2002. *Gujarat 2002: Untold and re-told stories of the Hindutva lab*. New Delhi: Media House.

Desai, A.R. 1984. 'Caste and communal violence in post-partition Indian Union'. *In* Asghar Ali Engineer, ed., *Communal riots in post-Independence India*, pp. 10–32. Hyderabad: Sangam Books.

Durkheim, Emile. 1965 [1912]. *The elementary forms of the religious life*. New York: Free Press.

Dworkin, Ronald. 1993. *Life's dominion: An argument about abortion, euthanasia, and individual freedom*. New York: Knopf.

Eaton, Richard. 1997. *The rise of Islam and the Bengal Frontier 1204–1760*. Delhi: Oxford University Press.

Eck, Diana. 1993. *Encountering God: A spiritual journey from Bozeman to Banaras*. Boston: Beacon Press.

Engineer, Asghar Ali, ed. 1984. *Communal riots in post-Independence India*. Hyderabad: Sangam Books.

Engineer, Asghar Ali. 1989. *The Muslim community of Gujarat: An exploratory study of Bohras, Khojas and Memons*. Delhi: Ajanta Publications.

———. 1995a. *Communalism in India: A historical and empirical study*. New Delhi: Vikas Publishing House.

———. 1995b. *Lifting the veil: Communal violence and communal harmony in contemporary India*. Hyderabad: Sangam Books.

———. 1998. 'Indian Muslims: Their backwardness and its causes'. In Shernaz Cama and Sudhir Chandra Mathur, eds, *The muse and the minorities: Social concerns and creative cohesion*, pp. 176–85. New Delhi: Steering Committee of The Muse and the Minorities.

Ernst, Carl. 1992. *Eternal garden: Mysticism, history and politics at a south Asian sufi center*. New York: State University of New York Press.

Esposito, John L. 1998. *Islam and politics*. New York: Syracuse University Press.

Feldman, Allen. 1991. *Formations of violence: The narrative of the body and political terror in Northern Ireland*. Chicago: University of Chicago Press.

———. 2000. 'Violence and vision: The prosthetics and aesthetics of terror'. *In* Veena Das, Arthur Kleinman, Mamphela Ramphele and Pamela Reynolds, eds, *Violence and subjectivity*, pp. 46–78. Berkeley: University of California Press.

Frank, Arthur. 1995. *The wounded storyteller: Body, illness and ethics*. Chicago: University of Chicago Press.

Fridman, Lea Wernick. 2000. *Words and witness: Narrative and aesthetic strategies in the representation of the holocaust*. Albany: State University of New York Press.

Fuller, C.J. and John Harriss. 2000. 'For an anthropology of the modern Indian state'. *In* C.J. Fuller and Véronique Bénéï, eds, *The everyday state and society in modern India*, pp. 1–30. New Delhi: Social Science Press.

Ghosh, Amitav. 2002. 'The ghosts of Mrs. Gandhi'. *In the Imam and the Indian: Prose pieces*, pp. 46–62. New Delhi: Ravi Dayal and Permanent Black.

Girard, René. 1977. *Violence and the sacred*. Baltimore: John Hopkins University Press.

Goffman, Erving. 1973. *Stigma: Notes on the management of spoiled identity.* Harmondsworth: Penguin Books.

Government of India. 1981. *Sixth report of the National Police Commission.* New Delhi: Government of India.

Gupta, N.L., ed. 2000. *Communal riots in India.* Delhi: Gyan Publishing House.

H.R.H. Prince of Wales. *Islam and the West:* a lecture given in the Sheldonian Theatre, Oxford on 27 October 1993. Oxford: Oxford Centre for Islamic Studies.

Hallencreutz, Carl F. and David Westerlund. 2002. 'Anti-secularist policies of religion'. *In* David Westerland, ed., *Questioning the secular state: The worldwide resurgence of religion in politics,* pp. 1–23. London: Hurst and company.

Hansen, Thomas Blom. 2003. 'Bridging the gulf: Global horizons, mobility and loval identity among Muslims in Mumbai'. *In* Crispin Bates, ed., *Community, empire and migration: South Asians in diaspora,* pp. 261–85. Hyderabad: Orient Longman.

Haq, Anwarul Haq. 1972. *The faith movement of Mawlana Muhammad Ilyas.* London: George Allen and Unwin.

Hasan, Mushirul. 2001. *Legacy of a divided nation: India's Muslims since Independence.* Delhi: Oxford University Press.

Hasan, Zoya and Ritu Menon. 2004. *Unequal citizens: A study of Muslim women in India.* New Delhi: Oxford University Press.

Hasan, Zoya. 2004. Social inequalities, secularism and minorities in India's democracy. *In* Mushirul Hasan, ed., *Will secular India survive?,* pp. 239–62. Gurgaon, Haryana: imprintOne.

Heidegger, Martin. 1962. *Being and Time.* Translated by John Macquarrie and Edward Robinson. Oxford: Basil Blackwell.

Heller, Agnes. 1984. *Everyday life.* London: Routledge and Kegan Paul.

———. 1985a. *The power of shame: A rational perspective.* London: Routledge and Kegan Paul.

———. 1985b. A socialist in exile. *New Socialist* 29: 10–13 and 38–39.

———. 1990. *Can modernity survive?* Cambridge: Polity Press.

Herman, Judith Lewis. 1994. *Trauma and recovery: From domestic violence to political terror.* London: Rivers Oram Press.

Hodgkin, K. and S. Radstone, eds, 2003. *Contested Pasts.* London: Routledge.

Human Rights Watch. 2002. *We have no orders to save you: State participation and complicity in communal violence in Gujarat* 14(3): 1–68.

———. 2003. *Compounding injustice: The government's failure to redress massacres in Gujarat* 15(3): 1–72.

Janet, Pierre. 1925. *Psychological Healing,* Vols 1–2. New York: Macmillan.

Jeffery, Patricia, Roger Jeffery and Craig Jeffrey. 2004. Islamization, Gentrification and Domestication: 'A Girls' Islamic Course' and Rural Muslims in Western Uttar Pradesh. *Modern Asian Studies* 38(1): 1–53.

John, Rijo M. and Rohit Mutatkar. 2005. Statewise estimates of poverty among religious groups in India. *Economic and political weekly* XL(13): 1337–45.

Kakar, Sudhir. 1995. *The colours of violence.* Delhi: Viking Penguin India.

Kanapathipillai, Valli. 1990. July 1983: 'The survivor's experience'. *In* Veena Das, ed., *Mirrors of violence: Communities, riots and survivors in south Asia,* pp. 321–44. Delhi: Oxford University Press.

Karawan, Ibrahim A. 1997. *The Islamist impasse*. New York: Oxford University Press.

Kettani, M. Ali. 1986. *Muslim minorities in the world today*. London and New York: Mansell Publishing Limited.

Khalidi, Omar. 1995. *Indian Muslims since independence*. New Delhi: Vikas Publishing House.

———. 2001–2. Ethnic group recruitment in the Indian army: The contrasting cases of Sikhs, Muslims, Gurkhas and others. *Pacific Affairs* 74(4): 529–52.

———. 2003. *Khaki and the ethnic violence in India*. New Delhi: Three Essays Collective.

Khan, Dominique-Sila. 2003. 'Diverting the Ganges: The Nizari Ismaili model of conversion in South Asia'. *In* Rowena Robinson and Sathianathan Clarke, eds, *Religious conversion in India: Modes, motivations and meanings*, pp. 29–53. Delhi: Oxford University Press.

Khanna, Rajeev. 2002. Hate tracts being distributed in Gujarat towns. *The Asian Age*. 26 April, p. 9.

Khilnani, Sunil. 1998. *The idea of India*. Harmondsworth: Penguin Press.

Kleinman, Arthur. 1997. *Social suffering*. Berkeley: University of California Press.

Koselleck, Reinhart. 1985. *Futures past: On the semantics of historical time*. Translated Keith Tribe. Cambridge, Massachusetts: MIT Press.

Langer, Lawrence. 1991. *Holocaust testimonies: The ruins of memory*. New Haven and London: Yale University Press.

Lifton, Robert J. 1967. *Death in life: Survivors of Hiroshima*. New York: Random House.

Linde, C. 1993. *Life stories: The creation of coherence*. Oxford: Oxford University Press.

Malkki, Liisa H. 1995. *Purity and exile: Violence, memory, and national cosmology among Hutu refugees in Tanzania*. Chicago: University of Chicago Press.

Manz, Beatriz. 1995. 'Reflections on an antropología comprometida'. *In* Carolyn Nordstrom and Antonius C.G.M Robben, eds, *Fieldwork under fire: Contemporary studies of violence and survival*, pp. 261–74. Berkeley: University of California Press.

Marty, Martin E. and R. Scott Appleby, eds, 1991a. *Fundamentalisms observed*. Chicago: University of Chicago Press.

———. 1991b. 'Conclusion: An interim report on a hypothetical family'. *In* Martin E. Marty and R. Scott Appleby, eds, 1991. *Fundamentalisms observed*, pp. 814–42. Chicago: University of Chicago Press.

———. eds, 1993a. *Fundamentalisms and society: Reclaiming the sciences, the family, and education*. Chicago: University of Chicago Press.

———. 1993b. 'Introduction: A sacred cosmos, scandalous code, defiant society'. *In* Martin E. Marty and R. Scott Appleby, eds, *Fundamentalisms and society: Reclaiming the sciences, the family, and education*, pp. 1–19. Chicago: University of Chicago Press.

———. eds, 1993c. *Fundamentalisms and the state: Remaking polities, economies and militance*. Chicago: University of Chicago Press.

Marty, Martin E. and R. Scott Appleby. 1993d. 'Introduction'. *In* Martin E. Marty and R. Scott Appleby, eds, *Fundamentalisms and the state: Remaking polities, economies and militance,* pp. 1–9. Chicago: University of Chicago Press.

———. eds, 1994. *Accounting for fundamentalisms: The dynamic character of movements.* Chicago: University of Chicago Press.

———. eds, 1995. *Fundamentalisms comprehended.* Chicago: University of Chicago Press.

Mattingly, Cheryl. 1998. *Healing dramas and clinical plots: The narrative structure of experience.* Cambridge: Cambridge University Press.

Mayaram, Shail. 1997. *Resisting regimes: Myth, memory and the shaping of a Muslim identity.* Delhi: Oxford University Press.

———. 2004. Hindu and Islamic transnational religious movements. *Economic and political weekly* 39(1): 80–88.

Mehta, B.C. 2005. Religion and fertility: Buttressing the case. *Economic and political weekly* XL(2): 157–60.

Mehta, Deepak. 1997. *Work, ritual, biography: A Muslim community in north India.* Delhi: Oxford University Press.

———. 2000. 'Circumcision, body, masculinity: The ritual wound and collective violence'. *In* Veena Das, Arthur Kleinman, Mamphela Ramphele and Pamela Reynolds. eds. *Violence and subjectivity,* pp. 79–101. Berkeley: University of California Press.

Mehta, Deepak and Roma Chatterji. 2001. 'Boundaries, names, alterities: A case study of a 'communal riot' in Dharavi, Bombay'. *In* Veena Das, Arthur Kleinman, Margaret Lock, Mamphela Ramphele and Pamela Reynolds, eds, *Remaking a world: Violence, social suffering and recovery,* pp. 201–49. Berkeley: University of California Press.

Mishra, Naveen and Sudhir Kumar Singh. 2002. *Status of minorities in south Asia.* Delhi: Authors Press.

Mistry, Malika B. 1998. *Fact sheet on the levels of education and exposure to media among Muslim women in India.* Mumbai: Centre for Study of Society and Secularism.

Munson, Henry. 1993. *Religion and power in Morocco.* Connecticut, New Haven: Yale University.

Muslim India. 1985. Representation of Muslims in police force. p. 300.

NSSO 438, 468 reports. Government of India.

Pandey, Gyanendra. 1990. *The construction of communalism in colonial north India.* Delhi: Oxford University Press.

People's Union for Democratic Rights. 2002. 'No relief, no rehabilitation' in Siddharth Varadarajan, ed., *Gujarat: The Making of a Tragedy.* New Delhi: Penguin.

Pfaff-Czarnecka, Joanna, Darini Rajasingham-Senanayake, Ashis Nandy and Edmund Terence Gomez. 1999. *Ethnic futures: The state and identity politics in Asia.* New Delhi: Sage.

Punwani, Jyoti. 1991. Without any stakes in the riot. *The Independent.* 6 January, p. 5.

Radstone, Susannah and Katherine Hodgkin, eds, 2003. *Regimes of memory.* London: Routledge.

Rajgopal, P.R. 1987. *Communal violence in India*. New Delhi: Uppal Publishing House.

Rawls, John. 1993. *Political liberalism*. New York: Columbia University Press.

Razzack, Azra and Anil Gumber. 2002. *Differentials in human development: A case for empowerment of Muslims in India*. New Delhi: NCAER.

Robinson, Rowena. 2001. Religion on the net: An analysis of the global reach of Hindu fundamentalism and its implications for India, *Sociological Bulletin* 50(2), 236–51.

———. 2003. *Christians of India*. New Delhi: Sage Publications.

Ross, Fiona. 2001. 'Speech and silence: Women's testimony in the first five weeks of the public hearings of the South African Truth and Reconciliation Commission'. *In* Veena Das, Arthur Kleinman, Margaret Lock, Mamphele Ramphele and Pamela Reynolds, eds, *Remaking a world: Violence, social suffering and recovery*, pp. 250–80. Berkeley: University of California Press.

Rothberg, Michael. 2000. *Traumatic Realism: The Demands of Holocaust Representation*. Minneapolis: University of Minnesota Press.

Saberwal, Satish and Mushirul Hasan. 1984. 'Moradabad riots, 1980: Causes and meanings'. *In* Asghar Ali Engineer, ed., *Communal riots in post-Independence India*, pp. 209–27. Hyderabad: Sangam Books.

Sarkar, Tanika. 2002. Semiotics of terror: Muslim women and children in Hindu Rashtra. *Economic and political weekly* 37(28): 2872–76.

Saxena, N.C. 1983. Public employment and educational backwardness among Muslims in India. *Political science review* 22(2).

Scarry, Elaine. 1985. *The body in pain*. New York: Oxford University Press.

Scheper-Hughes, Nancy. 1992. *Death without weeping*. Berkeley: University of California Press.

Shariff, Abusaleh. 1995. Socio-economic and demographic differentials between Hindus and Muslims in India. *Economic and Political Weekly* 30(46): 2947–53.

———. 1999. *India Human Development Report: A profile of Indian states in the 1990s*. Delhi: Oxford University Press.

———. 2000. Relative economic and social deprivation in India. Paper presented in an international seminar on 'Alternative conceptualizations of poverty', International Development Research Centre, Oxford University, 27–28 October.

Siddiqui, M.K.A., ed., 1998. *Muslims in free India: Their social profile and problems*. New Delhi: Institute of Objective Studies, p. 39.

Sikand, Yoginder. 2002. *The origins and development of the Tablighi Jamaat (1920–2000): A cross-country comparative study*. New Delhi: Orient Longman.

Spivak, Gayatri C. 1990. *The Postcolonial Critic: Interviews, Strategies, Dialogues*. Edited by Sarah Harasym. New York: Routledge.

———. 1992. *Thinking academic freedom in gendered post-coloniality: T B Davie Academic Freedom Lecture*. Capetown: University of Capetown.

Sreenivas, Janyala. 2002. Communal harmony is drama: VHP pamphlet. *Indian Express*, 12 April, pp. 1–2.

Srikrishna, B.N. n.d. *Report of the Justice B N Srikrishna Commission appointed for inquiring into the riots at Mumbai during December 1992–January 1993 and the March 12, 1993 bomb blasts*, pp. 1–228. *In* Sabrang Communications Compilation, *Damning Verdict*. Mumbai: Sabrang Communications and Publishing.

Srinivasan, Amrit. 1990. 'The survivor in the study of violence'. *In* Veena Das, ed., *Mirrors of violence: Communities, riots and survivors in south Asia*, pp. 305–20. Delhi: Oxford University Press.

Tambiah, Stanley. 1997. *Leveling crowds: Ethnonationalist conflicts and collective violence in south Asia*. New Delhi: Vistaar Publications.

Taylor, Charles. 1998. 'Modes of secularism'. *In* Rajeev Bhargava, ed., *Secularism and its critics*, pp. 31–53. Delhi: Oxford University Press.

Tibi, Bassam. 1998. *The challenge of fundamentalism: political Islam and the new world disorder*. University of California Press, Los Angeles.

Van der Kolk, B.A. and O. Van der Hart. 1991. The intrusive past: The flexibility of memory and the engraving of trauma. *American Imago* 48(4): 425–54.

Van der Kolk, B.A. and Rita Fisler. 1995. Dissociation and the fragmentary nature of traumatic memory: Overview and exploratory study. *Journal of traumatic stress* 8(4): 505–25

Varadarajan, Siddharth, ed., 2002. *Gujarat: The making of a tragedy*. New Delhi: Penguin.

Varshney, Ashutosh. 2002. *Ethnic conflict and civic life: Hindus and Muslims in India*. New Haven: Yale University Press.

Westerlund, David. 2002. *Questioning the secular state: The worldwide resurgence of religion in politics*. London: Hurst and Co.

Wiedmer, Caroline. 1999. *The claims of memory: Representations of the holocaust in contemporary Germany and France*. Ithaca and London: Cornell University Press.

Wilkinson, Steven I. 2002. Putting Gujarat in perspective. *Economic and Political Weekly* 38(17): 1579–83.

Young, Allen. 2000. 'Suffering and the origins of traumatic memory', *In* Arthur Kleinman, Veena Das and Margaret Lock, eds, *Social Suffering*, pp. 245–60. New Delhi: OUP.

Young, Iris M. 1990. *Justice and the politics of difference*. Princeton, New Jersey: Princeton University Press.

Young, James E. 2000. *At memory's edge: After-images of the holocaust in contemporary art and architecture*. New Haven and London: Yale University Press.

Youth for Unity and Voluntary Action. 1996. *Planned segregation: Riots, evictions and dispossession in Jogeshwari East*. Mumbai: YUVA.

Zaidi, Z.H. 1989. Conversion to Islam in south Asia: Problems in analysis. *American journal of Islamic social sciences* 6(1): 93–117.

INDEX

ABOUT THE AUTHOR

Rowena Robinson is Associate Professor in Sociology, Department of Humanities and Social Sciences, IIT Bombay. She has earlier taught at the University of Delhi. She is author of *Conversion, Continuity and Change: Lived Christianity in Southern Goa* (Sage, 1998) and *Christians of India* (Sage, 2003), and editor of *Religious Conversion in India: Modes, Motivations and Meanings* (Oxford, 2003) and *Sociology of Religion in India* (Sage, 2004).